D0202915

THE DECLINE AND ABOLITION OF NEGRO SLAVERY IN VENEZUELA
1820–1854

Contributions in Afro-American
and African Studies

The Decline and Abolition of Negro Slavery in Venezuela

1820-1854

JOHN V. LOMBARDI

Contributions in Afro-American
and African Studies, Number 7

A Negro Universities Press Publication

GREENWOOD PUBLISHING CORPORATION
WESTPORT, CONNECTICUT

Library of Congress Catalog Card Number: 74–105976
SBN: 8371–3303–3

A Negro Universities Press Publication
Greenwood Publishing Corporation
51 Riverside Avenue, Westport, Connecticut 06880

Printed in the United States of America
Designed by Selma Ordewer

For
Cathryn Lee Lombardi

Contents

Preface

ALTHOUGH the story of the abolition of Negro slavery in Venezuela could begin long before the wars for independence and the founding of the Venezuelan republic, I chose to concentrate on the period from 1820 to 1854 for a number of reasons. In 1820 the patriot Congress of Angostura passed the first legislation governing the future of the servile institution in republican Venezuela. This event symbolizes a transition from the chaotic slave policies followed by the contestants in the independence movement to a consistent national policy. Moreover, the 1820s are also a transitional period economically, marking the beginning of a radical shift in the Venezuelan economy from cacao production to coffee production; and as I will show, this change had a significant effect on the nature of slavery and on the process of abolition in Venezuela. Moreover, 1820 is a better starting date than 1810, for example, because it allows an evaluation of the effects of the independence movement without becoming involved in the fascinating but marginal controversies of independence historiography.

This monograph was undertaken to provide a case study of the operation and demise of slavery in a country not dominated by the institution. The literature abounds with analyses of slavery in countries where the existence of the institution exercised a preponderant influence and where abolition came only after violent controversy. But little attention has been paid to areas such as Venezuela where slavery exercised a smaller influence and where it was abolished relatively quietly.

The study is organized into two main parts preceded by an introduction and followed by appendices and a bibliography. The Introduction provides an overview of Venezuelan history from 1810 to 1855, serving as a background for the chapters that follow.

Part I begins with a chapter on the origins of Venezuelan slave policy during the wars for independence and, in Chapter 3, continues with an analysis of the organization and operation of the manumission system. Part I concludes with an examination of the fate of the children born free to slave mothers as a result of the various republican free birth laws and explores the program of apprenticeship established for them.

Once the legal theory and administrative practice of the slave system is thoroughly explained, Part II begins the discussion of the causes and progress of abolition. Since one of the accomplishments of this monograph is to show the economic foundations of abolition, Chapter 5 explores the development of the Venezuelan economy and its effect on slavery. Closely related to the slave's place in the economy, and in a large measure directly dependent on it, is the role of the slave in society. Chapter 6 discusses the shifting position of the enslaved Negro in Venezuela. The seventh and final chapter, building on the preceding sections, explains how and why the abolition of Negro slavery became law in 1854.

The text is supplemented by two appendices. One contains numerical information on slavery, manumission, and abolition while the other contains a series of export tables to support the discussion in Chapter 5. A bibliographical essay with a selected list of works consulted ends this monograph.

Bloomington, Indiana
May 1970

Acknowledgments

THIS project was planned and completed under the very able direction of Professor Lewis Hanke. Throughout the study his comments, criticisms, suggestions, and advice were invariably helpful. I am eternally in his debt for his assistance in all phases of this effort.

In the course of my research I have been fortunate to receive assistance from many institutions and individuals. Without their help and guidance this project could not have been completed. It is, therefore, a pleasure to acknowledge their help.

A very special place in these acknowledgments is reserved for Don Pedro Grases. Throughout my stay in Caracas, Pedro Grases was an inexhaustible and invaluable source of encouragement and advice. He put not only his unique and extensive library at my disposal but also his wide knowledge of Venezuelan history and historians. A first class bibliographer as well as historian, Pedro Grases was always willing and able to help locate misplaced or unavailable items. Through his efforts I was saved countless hours of fruitless searching. His friendship and profound knowledge helped make my research trip extraordinarily pleasant.

Financial assistance for the study was provided first by a Fulbright-Hayes Fellowship, administered by the Office of Education, United States Department of Health, Education, and

Welfare. This grant allowed me nine months research in Venezuela during 1966. At the end of this period when it appeared that the research on the project would have to be terminated, I was rescued by a generous grant from the Fundación Creole in Caracas. I am grateful to Dr. Alfredo Anzola, president of the Fundación, for his receptivity to my proposal. Moreover, my good friend Mr. George Hall, executive director of the Fundación, was a constant source of encouragement and assistance during my Caracas visit. To fill out the remaining time in Caracas, I am grateful to the Universidad Central de Venezuela, Escuela de Historia for giving me a part-time position as Profesor Contratado during the spring of 1967. The Director of the Escuela de Historia, Professor Germán Carrera Damas, was kind enough to offer me not only his friendship and hospitality but also the benefit of his extensive and critical knowledge of Venezuelan history and historiography. Many concepts in this monograph have been refined and some completely changed as a result of our conversations.

In addition to the institutions and individuals mentioned above, other Venezuelans offered numerous and indispensable services. The Fundación John Boulton, a unique and invaluable historical institution, provided me with assistance for a number of specific tasks, in particular the microfilming of important documents. My friend and the able director of the Fundación Boulton, Professor Manuel Pérez Vila, was a constant source of information and advice.

The Academia Nacional de la Historia under the distinguished direction of Don Cristóbal Mendoza allowed me many privileges. This corporation is the guardian of one of the finest libraries and archives in Venezuela, and its newspaper collection is one of the two main collections in the country. Without the full cooperation of the staff at the Academia, my task would have been much less pleasant.

Venezuela's Archivo General de la Nación, under the extraordinarily able direction of Dr. Mario Briceño Perozo, contains the finest collection of documents on Venezuelan history in the country. Dr. Briceño's fine staff provided me with many extra services for which I am very grateful.

In the Biblioteca Nacional, my searches for newspapers and rare pamphlets was greatly aided by Sr. Jesús María Sánchez, circulation chief. The Biblioteca, under the watchful eye of Dr. Luís Barrios Cruz, is among the most important repositories of Venezuelan imprints. Its newspaper collection ranks as one of the two best in the country.

At the Archivo Arquidiocesano de Caracas and the Registro Principal of Caracas, I received the same exemplary service and assistance encountered elsewhere in Venezuela.

In addition to the aid of these institutions, a number of individuals gave me helpful suggestions and criticisms at various stages of this project. Professors Stanley J. Stein and Magnus Mörner made valuable comments on my original research proposal, and Professors E. Bradford Burns and Bailey W. Diffie contributed many helpful comments on the final draft of the monograph. I have benefited greatly from the advice and assistance of Dr. James A. Hanson. In Venezuela I want to thank Dr. Pedro Manuel Arcaya for obtaining permission to inspect his father's fine library, now donated by the Arcaya family to the nation. Teniente Coronel Pérez Tenreiro graciously allowed me to inspect documents from his excellent personal collection. At the Casa Natal del Libertador the curator Don Manuel Pinto C. generously helped me find information in the Revenga family papers. In addition, I would also like to remember here the late Dr. Vicente Amézaga Aresti, not only for his friendship and advice, but also for a very fine translation of part of Chapter 2 which appeared in the *Boletín Histórico* of the Fundación John Boulton.

At Indiana University Professor Martin Ridge generously aided me in the final phases of preparing this book for publication. Professors Robert E. Quirk and David M. Pletcher suggested many important changes in Chapters 2, 3, and 4, parts of which appeared in an article in the *Hispanic American Historical Review* under their capable editorship.

My wife Cathryn Lee Lombardi deserves a special note of thanks for her help and patience. Without her support and assistance this book would never have been completed.

Since the limits of space preclude listing all those other individuals who have in one way or another contributed to the completion of this monograph, I wish to express here my thanks to all of them.

Without the help of the individuals and institutions mentioned here, this book would never have acquired its present form. Although many omissions and errors have been caught and eliminated through the efforts of these people, I alone am responsible for those that remain.

Parts of this book have appeared in various journals. I wish to acknowledge here the help of the editors of these journals in polishing, criticizing, and publishing some of this material. In Caracas, *Cultura Universitaria*, the organ of the Universidad Central de Venezuela, published my article "Los esclavos negros en las guerras venezolanas de la independencia," in their number XCIII (October–December 1966) on pages 153–168. The Fundación John Boulton, an energetic supporter of historical studies, published my article "Los esclavos en la legislación republicana de Venezuela," in its *Boletín Histórico*, number XIII (January 1967) on pages 43–67. Finally, the official guardian of Venezuelan historical tradition, the Academia Nacional de la Historia, published my article "Sociedad y esclavos en Venezuela. La era republicana. 1821–1854," in their *Boletín* number LII (July–September 1969) on pages 515–527. In the United States the publisher of the *Hispanic American Historical Review*, Duke University Press, graciously permitted the use of material from my article "Manumission, *Manumisos*, and *Aprendizaje* in Republican Venezuela," which appeared in number XLXI (November 1969) on pages 656–678. Also parts of Chapter 5 appeared in a joint article with Professor James A. Harison, in *Agricultural History* (November 1970), titled "The First Venezuelan Coffee Cycle."

The two maps illustrating this book were prepared by Cathryn

Lee Lombardi, based on maps included in José Gil Fortoul, *Historia constitutional de Venezuela*, 3 volumes published in Caracas by the Ministerio de Educación, 1954.

Abbreviations

AGN,	Archivo General de la Nación (Caracas)
Gran Col.–Int. de Ven.	Gran Colombia–Intendencia de Venezuela
Int. y Just.	Interior y Justicia.
Caracas, 1833, Memoria	Caracas. *Memoria que presenta el Gobernador de la Provincia de Caracas a la honorable Diputación de la misma reunida en sus sesiones ordinarias de 1833.* Caracas: Damirón y Dupuy, 1833. [Province, title, publisher, and date vary.]
Caracas, 1834, Ordenanzas	Caracas. *Ordenanzas, resoluciones y acuerdos de la Diputación Provincial de Caracas: que se hallan vigentes el dia 10 de diciembre de 1834, impreso por acuerdo especial de la Diputación.* Caracas: A. Damirón, 1834. [Province, title, publisher, and date vary.]
Hacienda, 1836, Memoria	Venezuela. *Exposición que dirige al Congreso de Venezuela en 1836 el secretario de Hacienda.* Caracas: Valentín Espinal, 1836. [Title, publisher, and date vary.]
HAHR	*Hispanic American Historical Review.*

Int. y Just., 1836,
Memoria

Venezuela. *Exposición que dirige al Congreso de Venezuela en 1836 el secretario del Interior y Justicia.* Caracas: A. Damirón, 1836. [Title, publisher, and date vary.]

PRO, FO 80/1

Great Britain. Public Record Office (London). Foreign Office 80 (Venezuela), Vol. I.

U.S. Dept. State, Consular, No. 84, IV

United States. Department of State. Consular Despatches. File Microcopies of Records in the National Archives, No. 84, Vol. 4.

U.S. Dept. State, Diplomatic, Venezuela, No. 79, I

United States. Department of State. Diplomatic Despatches. Venezuela. File Microcopies of Records in the National Archives, No. 79, Vol. I.

THE DECLINE AND ABOLITION OF NEGRO SLAVERY IN VENEZUELA
1820–1854

CHAPTER 1

Introduction

VENEZUELA, "*Tierra de Gracia*" as Columbus called it, has a history of such variety and complexity it almost defies description. Few other areas of the world have passed through so many stages of historical development with such rapidity. From a poverty-stricken outpost of Spain's empire in the sixteenth century, known primarily as a source of Indian slaves and pearls, Venezuela grew to become the most profitable nonmining economy in Spanish America during the eighteenth century. This late flowering of the colony—a result of the energetic commercial operations of the Compañía Guipuzcoana, or Caracas Company—was based on the cultivation and export of the valuable cacao seed. A climate and soil specially suited to cacao combined with a protected and growing market ably exploited by some of Spain's most capable businessmen proved an irresistible formula of prosperity for the backward colony.[1]

Yet this increased activity, much of which was funneled through the growing city of Caracas, could not and did not take place without causing serious structural changes in the society and economy of this province. As the Caracas Company encouraged increased production of cacao and reaped comfortable profits from its trade, the creole landlords grew rich on the income from their expanded acreage.

In order to capture the full benefit of the cacao boom, the

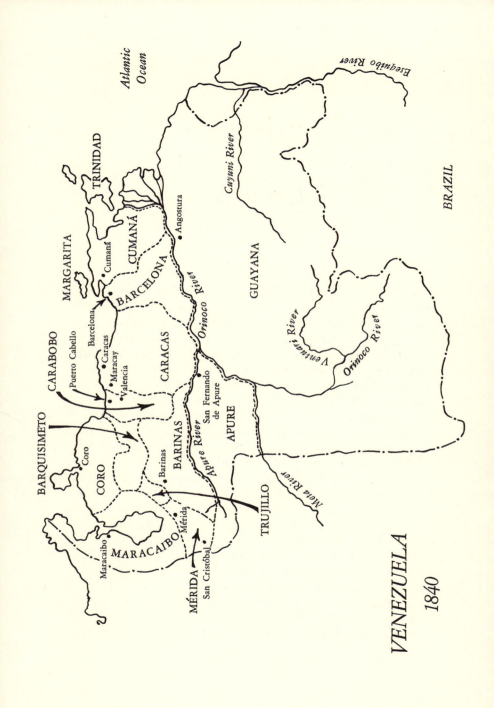

VENEZUELA
1840

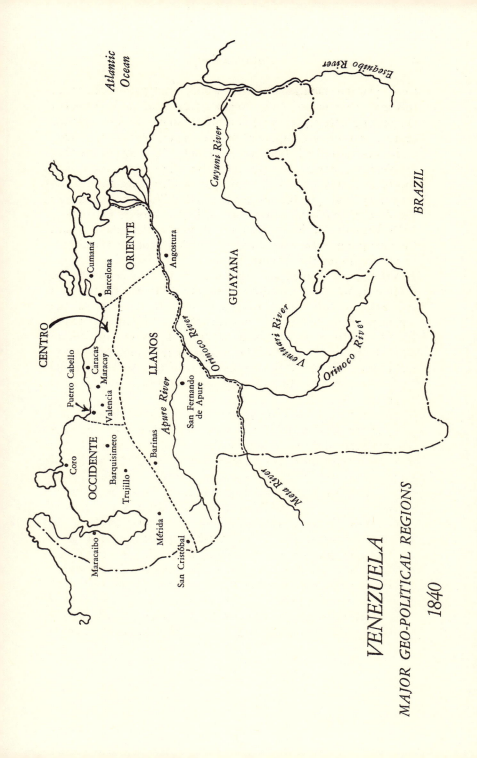

VENEZUELA

MAJOR GEO-POLITICAL REGIONS

1840

creole planters soon realized they would need more workers; in this case, that meant more Negro slaves. And so Venezuela's languishing slave trade, carried on fitfully since the late sixteenth century as a minor component of the general Spanish American trade, was revitalized. Between 1730 and 1780 a record number of Negroes entered the province. But the cacao boom was short-lived, lasting no more than forty or fifty years. And as the return on cacao plantations declined after 1780, the volume of the slave trade fell off as well. So far did the process go that, by 1810, with the declining fortunes of Venezuelan planters and the disruption of the slave trade by the Napoleonic wars, almost no slaves entered the province.[2]

Although the slave trade was ended in 1810 by action of the Caracas Junta, the institution of slavery itself still existed in a reasonably healthy state. In the ensuing forty years, in the region we know today as Venezuela, the controlling oligarchies endeavored to find a way of eliminating the odious institution from their land. In spite of the almost total unanimity of opinion against the servile institution from about 1824 on, these leaders were unable to work out a method of abolition until 1854.

The purpose of this monograph is to provide a detailed case study of the decline and abolition of Negro slavery in a country where slavery did not dominate the economy or society. It is clear from the controversy generated by comparative studies of slavery in the Americas that more information is needed before any definite conclusions can be formulated about the common characteristics of the servile institution in Latin America. Ever since Frank Tannenbaum's influential comparison of slavery in Latin America and the United States appeared, scholars have been unable to agree on the underlying similarities and differences of the Anglo-American and Latin American slave systems. Indicative of this is the steady stream of monographs and interpretive essays attempting to clarify the situation. Yet, in spite of the suggestive insights in such works as Stanley Elkins's *Slavery* or Marvin Harris's *Patterns of Race in the Americas*, there is still no agreement on just exactly how slavery in Latin America differed from slavery in the United States, if in fact any significant differences existed. Part of the difficulty arises from the concentration of scholarship on Brazil and Cuba, the two most important slave areas in Latin America. Another obstacle lies in the temptation to generalize for all of Latin America from the Brazilian or Cuban experiences.[3]

Before the comparative analysis of slavery in the Americas can be advanced beyond its present state, careful and detailed investigations of slavery in less prominent regions of Latin America need to be made. Such case studies will help us discover whether it does in fact make sense to speak of Latin American slavery as a definable system.

Venezuela is a particularly good place to begin a series of case studies of this type. While slavery was an important part of the Venezuelan economic structure, particularly during the eighteenth century, it never came to dominate the country. Moreover, the decline and abolition of slavery in Venezuela appears to have been strikingly different from the Brazilian, Cuban, or United States experience. This study is not designed to explore the comparative aspects of Venezuelan slavery in relation to other American slave systems; rather it is designed to provide one of the case studies so necessary if a successful comparative history of slavery in the Americas is to be attempted.

This monograph, then, concentrates on the decline and eventual abolition of Negro slavery in Venezuela from 1820 until 1854. But in order to place this account in proper perspective, it is necessary to have a clear view of the major outlines of Venezuelan history during the first half century of its independence.

AN OVERVIEW

Venezuelan history from 1810 to 1854 is best divided into three major sections. The independence era rather neatly fills the time from 1810 to 1830. Although a good case can be made for breaking the independence section at 1823, when the last remnants of Spanish forces were driven from their stronghold in Puerto Cabello, such a division ignores the fact that Venezuela, as a separate political and administrative unit, did not really emerge until General José Antonio Páez took that region out of the Bolivarian confederation of Gran Colombia. From 1830 to 1848 Venezuela was ruled by General Páez and his friends who assured the fledgling republic a modicum of stability. This era of the Conservative Oligarchy saw the capture of Venezuela by a commercial-financial elite which reorganized the republic in its own interest. This era is particularly interesting because it witnessed the transformation of Venezuelan agriculture from a cacao-oriented economy to a coffee-oriented economy. Yet the tensions generated during the reign of the Conservatives by rapid economic growth, followed by falling coffee prices, provided the stimulus for the organization of a systematic opposition that, for lack of a better term, called itself Liberal.

By 1848 General Páez had lost much of his charisma and found himself out-maneuvered by his chosen successor, General José Tadeo Monagas. Monagas, to create his own dictatorship, adopted the disaffected Liberals and temporarily became their standard-bearer. The rule of the Liberal Oligarchy lasted, albeit frequently challenged, until 1858 when a new full-scale civil war broke out in Venezuela.

In this Introduction I do not propose to resolve the myriad historical controversies surrounding these three major periods. This is not the place to explore the social content of the wars for independence, nor can I become involved in a detailed discussion of the origin and development of Venezuelan political parties during the first half of the nineteenth century. Rather, the purpose of this Introduction is to present a short synthesis of the major outlines of republican Venezuela's history in accordance with the current state of Venezuelan historiography. It is well to point out that most of the interpretations presented

here should be regarded as purely tentative, since the monographic spadework necessary for an adequate synthesis is still
lacking. By and large, the best general history of Venezuela is
still the fifteen-volume work of Francisco González Guinán
written at the turn of the century.[4] Since then Venezuelanists
have spent most of their time and effort in two areas. First,
studying the political and military aspects of the independence
epic; and second, compiling and publishing documentary series
on the nineteenth century. Only in recent years have Venezuelan historians and their foreign counterparts begun to reexamine
the historical truths handed down by past generations of
scholars and to delve deeper into the rich archival materials
available in Venezuela. Yet, so new is this urge to reexamine
and research the past that the most exciting work done so far
has been in the genre of the historical essay, which on the basis
of a minimum of new material tries to reevaluate accepted interpretations and point out more productive avenues of investiga-
tion.[5] Therefore, it is much too soon to attempt an authoritative
synthesis of early nineteenth-century Venezuelan history.

THE INDEPENDENCE

Although all students of Latin America are familiar with the
general outlines of the epic of South American independence,
little attention is usually given to the local characteristics of the
process. Argentines learn about the heroic deeds of their idol,
San Martín; Venezuelans contemplate the majesty of their
favorite son, Simón Bolívar, in his grandiose but futile effort to
create an American empire. Yet, if we look closer at the revolutionary process begun in 1810, it becomes clear that the most
important events—in terms of the future development of the
various regions—occurred at the local provincial level rather
than in the continental theaters of Bolívar or San Martín. Nowhere, perhaps, is this better seen than in Venezuela.

In 1810, the leaders of the native Caracas aristocracy, that
proud and wealthy group known as the *mantuanos*, resolved in

a *cabildo abierto* to take control of the government of the province of Caracas and hold it in trust for their beloved monarch, Ferdinand VII. The mantuanos explained that since Napoleon Bonaparte had captured their sovereign, invaded Spain, and placed a usurper on the throne, they, as loyal subjects, were forced to assume authority in Ferdinand's dominion of Caracas and preserve it for their legitimate king. Should the unwary ask what was wrong with the king's officials already governing the province, the mantuanos would reply that those officials' titles to office were only valid when the king remained in Spain and on the throne. With the king, alas, in captivity, the governing authority reverted to its original source: the people.

And so the creole elite of Caracas asserted its right to govern the land it already owned. Once asserted, however, this right proved a bit more difficult to maintain than the mantuanos had expected. In order to make their bid for power succeed, the Caracas authorities had to acquire the support of the other provinces in the Captaincy-General of Venezuela; in each provincial capital the local oligarchies had followed the example of Caracas and claimed the right to govern their region. Caraqueño diplomacy succeeded everywhere in Venezuela except in Coro, Maracaibo, and Guayana. These provinces not only refused their allegiance; they reaffirmed loyalty to Spain and Spanish officialdom.[6]

From this point on until 1823, when the Spaniards were permanently expelled from Venezuelan territory, the creole revolutionaries were occupied with the enormous task of winning control of their land while at the same time establishing a viable and stable government. The independence movement has long been divided into phases corresponding to the military fortunes of the patriot forces. In spite of its limitations, this kind of organization has a certain convenience for the purposes of this discussion.

The first phase of the revolution, called the First Republic or *Patria Boba*, extends in traditional historiography from 1810 to 1812, when the patriot forces under Francisco Miranda capitulated to the Spanish captain Domingo Monteverde. During the Patria Boba, so named for the somewhat infantile and idealistic proceedings of the mantuanos, the first constitutional government of the republic was established. But the history of the First Republic is a sad account of lost opportunities, frustrated dreams, and petty jealousies. At almost no time during those painful months was Venezuelan leadership united or effective.

During the weeks following the creation of the Caracas Junta, the creoles found it increasingly difficult to create a governmental structure that could withstand the intense pressures from the various competing segments of Venezuelan society. The constituent Congress of 1811 had created an intricate paper government with an elaborate but almost powerless plural executive, but it was a feeble structure and could not contain the stresses of a political movement which carried overtones of a social revolution. Moreover, the easy military victory many creoles apparently expected was not forthcoming. In fact, during this interlude, the Caracas government was never able to control Coro or Maracaibo.[7]

While it is not the purpose of this Introduction to explore in depth the social content of the independence movement, it is well to point out that the would-be revolutionaries of Caracas came to realize that their revolt to acquire political and economic freedom had also unleashed another, and perhaps more significant, revolt. The *pardos*, that underclass of nonwhites identified by their resemblance to a pure Negro stereotype, clearly saw in the turmoil created by the creole push for dominance a chance to improve their own station in life.[8] They joined the armies and bandit raiding parties of both sides in the civil war, and some of them did manage to change their status. The Negro slaves, too, evidently saw their creole masters' bid for political liberty as their chance to acquire personal liberty. In any case, these three drives for liberty during the early years of the First Republic were to a large extent contradictory, and in this contradiction can be found much of the reason for the patriots' defeat by the Royalists.[9]

This, however, is not to ignore some of the other elements of the defeat. Certainly the government of the First Republic was a weak and vacillating instrument of war; certainly the existence of a strong pro-Spanish fifth column in most of Venezuela contributed to the defeat; yet the most striking characteristic of this early period was the inability of patriot commanders to rally the masses to their standard. It was the Royalists who in these years brought together the hordes of Venezuelans. It was the Royalist banner which apparently drew in those pardos and slaves hoping to turn the upheaval into a means of achieving equality and liberty. And it was due primarily to this Royalist success that the Venezuelan patriots found themselves defeated, dispersed, jailed, or exiled by the end of 1812.[10]

Although to most observers the patriot cause appeared dead at the end of 1812, the Royalist victory was not as complete as Domingo Monteverde might have liked, and 1813 proved to be a year of transition. While Royalists tried to rebuild the king's government in Caracas, patriot guerrillas successfully challenged Royalist control of the Oriente region of Venezuela, and the island of Margarita was taken for the patriot cause. Moreover, from a base in New Granada, Bolívar began what has come to be called *La Campaña Admirable.* In a spectacular march from the Venezuelan-Colombian border he swept all before him and took Caracas in August of 1813. Two months later he had the local government so well in hand that it conferred on him the title *Libertador* and named him Captain-General of the Venezuelan forces.[11]

These patriot successes, although impressive, were not destined to last. Near the end of 1813 a new Royalist force was created in the Venezuelan flatlands, the *llanos*, by José Tomás Boves. A Spaniard raised in Venezuela, Boves was one of the finest *caudillos* to appear during the independence. Gifted with the necessary charisma to attract and hold the wild nomads of the llanos, Boves almost single-handedly threw the patriots out of Venezuela in 1814. However, Boves himself was killed in one of the last encounters with patriot forces in that year.[12]

By the end of 1814 the military situation looked good for the

Royalist cause. There were no main-force patriot units left in Venezuela, and resistance had been reduced to isolated guerrilla bands wandering the Oriente. Moreover, 1815 saw the arrival in Venezuela of a Spanish expeditionary force under General Pablo Morillo, ordered there to pacify the dissidents. Thus, in 1815 the patriot war effort reached its lowest point.

From the beginning of 1816, the Venezuelan War for Independence took on a new character. Bolívar, with the assistance of President Alexandre Petión of Haiti, staged two expeditions to the coast of Venezuela. Although neither of these efforts was entirely successful, they did officially commit Bolívar to a policy of freeing the slaves.[13] From the time of the Haitian expeditions until 1819—when Bolívar left Venezuela to conquer Colombia by crossing the Andes—the patriot cause acquired a certain unity of command and purpose. Up to 1819 rival Venezuelan caudillos had carried on their operations almost independently. Each one, whether Bolívar in Haiti or Santiago Mariño and José Tadeo Monagas in the Oriente, seemed to operate only in accordance with his own personal ambitions. During the three years after the Haitian expeditions Bolívar managed to impose a loose organization on these local caudillos and at the same time gained a grudging acceptance of his leadership. This was no mean accomplishment, given the strength of the men who were forced into submission. But although it took much diplomacy, many threats, and a political execution, by 1819 Bolívar was strong enough to allow a convention to meet to legitimize his position.[14]

Equally important for the future of Venezuela was the emergence of a new patriot warrior, José Antonio Páez. Energetic, forceful, and ambitious, Páez reconstructed the llanero armies of Boves, only this time they were turned against the Spaniard. By 1819 Páez had established himself as one of the most important patriot generals accepting, for the time being, the leadership of Bolívar.[15]

The Second Venezuelan Congress met in Angostura in 1819 and proceeded to the task of confirming Bolívar's authority by electing him president of Venezuela and producing the second constitution of Venezuela. Backed now by a semblance of government and a secure military base in the Oriente, Bolívar set out across the Andes to conquer Colombia and from there, hopefully, the rest of Venezuela. His plan worked; in the same year Colombia was liberated at the battle of Boyacá, and Bolívar entered Bogota triumphant. Unfortunately, this victory was soured by a small uprising among his own caudillos in Venezuela. Santiago Mariño led a movement, near the end of 1819, to depose Bolívar and establish himself as supreme commander. But the return of the Libertador and his victorious army ended that experiment, and the pliant Congress of Angostura ratified Bolívar's plan to create a Colombian confederation out of Venezuela, Cundinamarca (now Colombia), and Quito (now Ecuador), and named him provisional president of Gran Colombia.[16]

Now firmly established, Bolívar began the reconquest of Venezuela from Colombia through the Occidente region. The campaign was successful, and at the battle of Carabobo, 24 June 1821, the major Spanish force was defeated and the definitive liberation of Venezuela was assured.

The nine years from the battle of Carabobo until the liquidation of Gran Colombia in 1830 form one of the more interesting periods of Venezuelan history. Although much of Venezuelan historiography centers on the military campaigns of Bolívar, equally interesting events took place in Venezuela proper. During the first five years of Gran Colombia an extraordinarily significant shift occurred in the balance of personal power within Venezuela. While recognizing the titular authority of Bolívar, rival caudillos maneuvered for supreme command. The most successful was José Antonio Páez, who managed during this time to replace Bolívar as the first caudillo of Venezuela.[17]

While this local power struggle worked itself out, the Colombian confederation became a reality. The Congress of Cúcuta in May of 1821 prepared a constitution for Gran Colombia and organized the confederation. By 1823 Bolívar's campaigns to the south were well along, and in Venezuela the last Royalist strong-hold at Puerto Cabello was destroyed by Páez.

The period from 1823 to 1826 was replete with military prep-arations to help support Bolívar's armies in Peru and with numerous efforts by the Bogota government to organize and administer the vast area of Gran Colombia. In Venezuela, Páez quietly consolidated his forces and waited for the right moment. Dissatisfaction with Bogota grew rife in these years as Venezue-lans came to feel that their interests were neglected in the capital.[18]

Finally, in 1826, Páez got his opportunity. The incident itself was a rather minor one involving excesses by troops under Páez's command in recruiting soldiers for Bolívar's armies. Since the incident took place in Caracas, the Caracas cabildo protested, and the Congress in Bogotá called for Páez to appear to answer charges. Páez's supporters staged a turbulent meeting of the Valencia cabildo which begged him to assume command and protect them against the imagined threat of a Spanish recon-quest of Venezuela. Naturally, the general accepted this call to duty, and from then on José Antonio Páez was the de facto chief executive of Venezuela, even though he professed alle-giance to Bogota and Bolívar. In any case, the Páez coup d'état carried serious separatist overtones, especially when the Caracas cabildo reversed itself and joined Valencia in supporting Páez. In order to preserve the apparent unity of Gran Colombia, Bolívar was forced to return from his victorious military cam-paigns to reassert his authority, challenged not only in Caracas but in Bogota as well. He arrived in Venezuela in 1827 and was received with all the outward signs of enthusiastic welcome. Yet, for all the honors accorded Bolívar and all the reforms he enacted during this short stay, there was never any doubt that the effective leader of Venezuela was José Antonio Páez. Bolívar evidently saw this, since he confirmed the llanero general in all his offices and backed him against all comers.

Unfortunately for the grandiose Bolivarian plan, Gran Colom-bia was fast on the road to disintegration, and Bolívar, the only impediment to the centrifugal forces of separatism, was failing physically as well as politically. Late in 1829, after numerous attempts to shore up the confederation had failed, Páez took Venezuela out of Gran Columbia. In 1830 Bolívar resigned the presidency of Colombia and took the road to exile, only to die before leaving the shores of America.[19]

THE CONSERVATIVE OLIGARCHY

Traditionally in Venezuelan historiography, the period stretching from 1830 and the establishment of Venezuela until the presidency of José Tadeo Monagas in 1848 has carried the name the Conservative Oligarchy. More properly this era should be called the dictatorship of José Antonio Páez, but because the general did not personally exercise the reins of power throughout the period, perhaps the traditional designation is as good as any.[20] More useful for the purpose of this Introduction is an attempt to define the characteristics of the Conservative Oligarchy.

Perhaps the most significant aspect of this era was the central role played by General Páez. We have seen how he created for himself the position of the most powerful caudillo in Venezuela and how he was capable of challenging even the great hero Bolívar. The culmination of this process, of course, was the separation of Venezuela from Gran Colombia and the repudiation of the Bolivarian dream of a united America. During the first years of Venezuelan autonomy, Páez worked to create a nation that would prove, in the end, to be the greatest monument to his glory. And in this task he inadvertently, or perhaps consciously, created a party that, backed by his military prowess and charismatic personality, would govern the country until a new caudillo emerged in response to changing economic and political conditions.

The outlines of the Páez faction, the Conservative Oligarchy, became clear during the first years of the 1830s. One of its characteristics was a strong anti-Bolivarian tendency. This characteristic is not surprising, since few *Paecistas* during the thirties were related to Bolívar or owed their fame and fortune to him. Also, both Páez's revolt of 1826 and the final separation of 1830 were in essence revolts against the personal power and ambition of Simón Bolívar. For Páez to have accepted ardent Bolivarians in his camp would have been suicidal, and any Bolivarian who wished to follow Páez would certainly have been considered a traitor.[21] A second, and perhaps more significant, characteristic of the Páez group was the overwhelmingly civilian makeup of the leading cadres. Páez, evidently committed to the goal of building an enduring and prosperous state, gathered about him the rich and the well-born, the merchants and the bankers, men of substance and education. These individuals were entrusted with the extraordinarily difficult task of creating a nation, and Páez appeared content to follow their lead. It might appear strange that the great warrior should have been so willing to turn over his victory to be administered by civilians rather than by his comrades in arms. But on further reflection it becomes clear that he had little real choice. As of 1830 most of the prominent Venezuelan military leaders were either loyal to Bolívar or looking for a chance to overthrow Páez and establish themselves as the supreme leader. Thus, for Páez to turn over the administration of his new nation to rival warriors would have been disastrous. His solution to this dilemma was the creation of a captive civilian bureaucracy to run his country— the stroke of a master politician.[22]

Of course the Conservative Oligarchy did not appear instantaneously with the separation of Venezuela from Gran Colombia, but rather evolved as a cohesive unit during the first six or seven years of the 1830s. In the beginning it was not perfectly clear just which individuals would belong. During the first few months of 1830 the only clearly perceived political fact was the supremacy of General Páez. But as the constituent Congress deliberated in Valencia throughout 1830, a pro-Páez majority began to emerge. Certainly, few individuals in the Congress were loyal Bolivarians, and clearly the civilian, legalist party had a majority over the military group. But it took the administration of General Páez (1830 to 1834), and the first years of the succeeding administration of Dr. José María Vargas to delineate the shape of the Conservative Oligarchy.

Once the constituent Congress had created a semifederalist constitution providing for the indirect election of a president through very limited suffrage,[23] General Páez was duly elected constitutional president of Venezuela, thus recognizing in law what was obvious in fact. The presidency of Páez was primarily occupied with two tasks. The first, and possibly the most important effort of this administration, was the military stabilization of Venezuela. This is not to say that Venezuela was ever seriously threatened either from Spain or from the remnants of Gran Colombia. Quite the contrary; the major threats to the territorial integrity and public peace of the new nation came from dissident Venezuelans within the country. Some of the threats were serious challenges to Páez's control, such as the ill-fated uprising of General José Tadeo Monagas in the Oriente region of Venezuela. This uprising struck responsive chords among many heroes of the War of Independence who felt cheated out of their due by the civilian Páez government. It also attracted considerable support from the clergy who were disgruntled by the powers accorded the state over the Church in the constitution of 1830. Monagas led the movement ostensibly to reconstitute Gran Colombia or, failing that, to separate the Oriente from Venezuela under a constitution that would protect religion and the rights of the military. In any case, the rebellion was short-lived since Páez rushed to the scene of conflict and negotiated a settlement with the dissidents. But a more interesting threat to internal security came from the irregular bandit forces roaming the hills of central Venezuela. The most significant of these bands was led by Dionisio Cisneros, whose success had made him a folk hero. But Páez, still capable of operating on the same personalist level as a guerrilla leader, maneuvered Cisneros into accepting the authority of the government and becoming a personal dependent of José Antonio Páez.[24]

The second task faced by the Páez administration was the erection of the administrative apparatus of statehood, the organization of an efficient bureaucracy. It was in the accomplishment of this task that the Conservative Oligarchy came into being. In the effort to establish the principal organs of government and to create the legal machinery necessary for the state to function, the civilian elite developed a consciousness of its own identity, an understanding of its own interests, and the power to gain its objectives.

One of the questions that has plagued Venezuelan historians is that of the pre-1830 backgrounds of the Conservative oligarchs. To date we have no adequate analysis of the origins of this elite. It has been conjectured that the oligarchy was composed as ex-Royalists, men who themselves or whose parents had remained more or less loyal to the banners of the king and whose strategic position in commerce or finance enabled them to lead the Páez government. It is certain there was a large number of lukewarm patriots in the Conservative ranks; it is not yet clear exactly how they emerged as the leaders, nor can we say with any degree of certainty what the relationship was between Royalist sympathies and pro-Páez leanings.[25] Nonetheless, what was clearly evident at this point was the dominance of financial and commercial interests within the elite, and in the long run this dominance was more important than the political loyalties of these men during the revolution.

Symbolic of the growing importance of the financial and commercial sectors of Venezuelan society was the enactment, in April 1834, of a stringent creditor law. The law, known throughout Venezuelan history as the *Ley de 10 de abril de 1834*, eliminated all the protections against usury contained in Spanish legal tradition. After 10 April 1834 contracts could be made stipulating any rate of interest under any conditions, and the courts were directed to enforce the terms of these contracts no matter how onerous they might be. Although in later years this law was to become a bone of contention between the Conservatives and their opponents, in 1834 it received almost universal approbation from all levels of society. Most Venezuelans who had any voice in public affairs believed such an exaltation of financial and commercial rights absolutely essential for the rebuilding of the war-torn republic. Moreover, planters and merchants alike saw the guarantees implicit in the 10 de abril law as an encouragement to prospective investors whose capital was so badly needed. Certainly the law had the effect expected of it; during the thirties Venezuelan planters rebuilding their ruined plantations and expanding their acreage in order to take advantage of the coffee boom never lacked the necessary investment capital. To be sure, the rates of interest and the terms of loans were not always the most lenient, but given the high profitability of coffee and the planters' unbounded optimism, capitalists were always able to find willing borrowers.[26]

So, by the end of the first Páez administration, the accomplishments of the Conservative Oligarchy, backed by the military prowess of General Páez, were indeed impressive. Venezuela in 1834 was an independent autonomous republic enjoying a semblance of internal peace. The new republic, organized along liberal civilian lines, basked in the warmth of a booming agricultural export economy based on the cultivation of coffee. The planter class appeared content to busy itself with the job of converting old cacao plantations to coffee or of opening up new land for more coffee. These individuals, originally the lords and masters of Venezuela, watched unconcerned as commercial and financial leaders took control of the government and economy of their country.

So strong was the civilian tendency within the Páez government that, in the elections of 1834, Dr. José María Vargas was imposed on Páez as his successor. Vargas was the epitome of the Conservative oligarch. A man suspected justly of Royalist leanings, Vargas had not participated in the War of Independence. But he was a learned man, a compassionate doctor of medicine, and a prominent member of the elite. In spite of these virtues, or perhaps because of them, Vargas was an unwilling candidate and a very mediocre politician. Elected to the presidency against his will, Vargas's administration was an unmitigated disaster. It was one thing for the administrative apparatus to be controlled by civilians, but it was quite another matter to have a civilian chief executive at the center of power.[27]

The Vargas administration proved from the very beginning to be vacillating and weak. Vargas himself lacked the forcefulness and ruthless ambition necessary to maintain presidential power. Naturally, the effort to run a government of laws and not of men was doomed to failure in a country where the major element of political power, the caudillo, was the essence of personalism. Vargas was soon threatened by a serious military rebellion which, under the banner of constitutional reform, planned to end the civilian domination of Venezuela and restore control of the country to those valiant heroes who had won independence on the battlefield. In the early stages of the rebellion the *reformistas*, under the leadership of the formidable caudillo of the Oriente, General Santiago Mariño, were successful. Vargas was exiled, and the reformistas occupied Caracas. But the greatest caudillo of them all had yet to speak. The reformistas had fond hopes of bringing Páez in on their side— after all, he was one of the military heroes of independence. They had not counted on the llanero chieftain's superlative political craft, however, and shortly after the expulsion of Vargas, Páez thundered forth from the llanos in defense of the constitution and the legitimate government of Venezuela. His lance again proved invincible, and the reformistas were soon dispersed or defeated. Vargas, brought back from exile, received the restored republic from the hands of the supreme protector, José Antonio Páez.

The net result of this short revolt was to entrench Páez even more firmly in power. By choosing to side with the civilians against the military, Páez accomplished two important objectives. In the first place he seriously reduced the effectiveness of the major military caudillos still left in Venezuela. Practically all of them were compromised in the rebellion, and the failure of their plan reduced many of them to political and military impotence for many years. Second, Páez demonstrated his invincibility and indispensability to the Conservative Oligarchy, the civilian commercial and financial elite. It was as if he had explained to these men that they could do what they liked with the economy and administration of Venezuela, but that the locus of political power would remain with José Antonio Páez. And in fact, after Vargas, the Conservatives never again disobeyed the mandates of their prophet.

There was one further result of the reformista revolt and its aftermath. With the rebellion defeated, the Conservative majority in Congress carried out a vindictive campaign of revenge against those involved in the revolt. Many prominent Venezuelans and their families suffered the loss of political liberties, imprisonment, and in some cases exile. This shortsighted policy embittered and alienated a group which would provide the nucleus of an opposition party in later years.[28]

Even with the support of Páez, Vargas found it impossible to remain in the presidency and, in 1836, less than halfway through his term, he resigned his office. In his place General Carlos Soublette, one of the few high-ranking military men completely loyal to Páez, finished out the term. With the exception of a small uprising in the llanos promptly eliminated by Páez, Soublette had a quiet half term as president. The country continued to prosper on income from the coffee boom, and the Conservative Oligarchy consolidated its position and power. In 1838 elections were held among the restricted electorate, and General José Antonio Páez was again elected president.[29]

The second Páez administration was not as happy an affair as the first one. In the four years from 1839 to 1842 the coffee boom died. A decline in the price of coffee, coupled with increasing labor shortages, reduced the planter's margin of profit to almost nothing, and many Venezuelan planters discovered they were overextended and in some cases unable to make interest payments on their debts. The commercial and financial hierarchy responded to the crisis by foreclosing or refusing to renegotiate loans.[30] By 1842 the agricultural interests had come to see themselves as a persecuted and exploited group; they found an outlet for their frustrations in the activities of the newly organized Liberal party.

Formed officially in 1840, the Liberal party was made up of a nucleus of old patriots, reformistas, and disgruntled planters. These individuals had long been disaffected from the ruling elite for a number of reasons. The old patriots, many of whom had family or personal ties with the Bolívar clan, had, as we have seen, been rather systematically excluded from the Conservative Oligarchy. Many of these old patriots were, of course, also large landowning planters whose economic well-being was tied to the price of coffee and the availability of adequate credit. The reformistas obviously had little allegiance to the Conservative government they had tried to overthrow. In any case, these somewhat disparate elements were fused into the Liberal party after 1840, primarily in response to the declining economic situation of the country.[31]

Unfortunately for the planters, in 1843 the Conservative Oligarchy once again won the elections midst charges of fraud and coercion. General Carlos Soublette, Páez's alter ego, again sat in the presidential chair. Soublette's second administration was much less peaceful than his first. The economic crisis grew worse, and by 1846 the planters were so desperate that some of them staged an abortive revolution.[32] Nevertheless, in spite of the very clear indications of serious discontent and unrest among some of the most influential members of society, the Conservative Oligarchy was unable or unwilling to alleviate the plight of the planters. Congress turned down or President Soublette vetoed every measure proposed which might have had a chance of easing the crisis. Gradually the level of rural violence, which was never very low, began to rise. Bandit bands proclaiming Liberal party slogans appeared, and the Liberal press became more strident and inflammatory in its attacks on the government. In self-defense the Oligarchy began to persecute its most voluble opponents and to attempt to silence the periodical press. It was in this atmosphere of economic distress and political bitterness that the elections for president took place in 1847.

The question asked by Liberal and Conservative politicians alike was: Who would Páez support? After much suspense and backstage maneuvering the oracle spoke, designating General José Tadeo Monagas as the Conservative candidate. This selection of the chieftain from the Oriente appears rather strange in light of Páez's consistent efforts to diminish the role of his principal military competitors. To be sure, José Tadeo had never become involved prominently in Liberal politics; yet many remembered his short-lived separatist revolt in the early 1830s as well as his involvement with the reformista movement. But Páez evidently had his reasons. Perhaps he believed Monagas could be neutralized in the presidency and thus be prevented from leading a Liberal coup d'état. Certainly Páez felt confident of being able to control Monagas. Whatever the reasons for his selection, the blessing of Páez was sufficient recommendation for most Conservatives who proceeded to elect José Tadeo Monagas by the usual fraudulent methods.[33]

The gravity of Páez's miscalculation in electing Monagas was not immediately apparent. But the Conservative oligarchs in the Monagas ministry noted with alarm that the new president was none too anxious to continue the prosecution of dissident Liberals begun under his predecessor. The revelation came, however, when Monagas pardoned the chief Liberal propagandist, Antonio Leocadio Guzmán. Worse was yet to come. In January of 1848, at a meeting of the Congress at which one of Monagas's ministers was to present a report, a riot broke out between the pro-Liberal mob outside the building and the troops guarding the pro-Conservative Congress. Monagas acted quickly, dissolving the Congress with federal troops and pacifying the mob. When the Congress reconvened in a few days it had lost much of its Conservative fervor and was easily intimidated into becoming a rubber stamp for the Monagas government.[34]

THE LIBERAL OLIGARCHY

The conversion of Venezuela's government from a Conservative Oligarchy to a Liberal Oligarchy was more than a military coup. In spite of the Conservative rhetoric, it had become quite clear by early 1848 that Monagas had not only refused to be a Páez puppet but also that he was determined to run Venezuela as his personal fief. To achieve this ambition he soon saw the necessity of eliminating the influence of General Páez and the Conservatives. The first step in Monagas's campaign was the substitution of a Liberal Oligarchy for the Conservative Oligarchy that had so long controlled Venezuela. By the end of January 1848 most Conservative officials had been replaced by formerly proscribed Liberals. He captured the Liberal party and used their leaders to further his personal ambition. To be sure, he acceded to most of the Liberal economic program and had the Congress pass debt relief laws to help the planters, but the net result of his actions was to consolidate his own power. The process went so far that, at the end of January 1848, General Páez declared war on the Monagas government and from his stronghold in the llanos launched a crusade to restore the constitution.

Although Monagas apparently was successful in effecting a change in the ruling elites, he still had to contend with the military challenge of General Páez. In a short campaign Monagas proved how low the llanero captain's prestige had fallen. Páez was unable to rally the traditional hordes of llaneros to his banner and was roundly defeated by late 1848.[35]

By the end of 1851 Monagas could view the accomplishments of his term in office with considerable satisfaction. The major Conservative opposition to his personal power was suppressed, and its supreme leader, Páez, had been defeated and expelled from the country. The Congress under his direction had dutifully passed the major legislation in the Liberal program. Nevertheless, all was not well in the republic. For one thing, the Conservatives in exile on islands off the coast of Venezuela or hiding within the country kept up an unending stream of subversive and incendiary propaganda. Moreover, there was considerable evidence that Conservative agents were stirring up trouble among the restless lower classes and slaves. A second problem remained unsolved. The economic depression in the coffee-producing sector hung on in spite of the pro-debtor legislation of the Monagas Congress. Prices remained low and credit was tight. The Liberals began to wonder if, indeed, José Tadeo Monagas was working for them. Monagas even found it necessary to harass prominent Liberals out of the presidential race in order to have his brother, José Gregorio, elected to succeed him in 1852.[36]

The presidency of José Gregorio was a rather unhappy interlude. There was no apparent solution to the economic crisis, and the opponents of the Monagas family's personal rule grew bolder. To add to these problems, many prominent Liberals began to defect to the opposition. In any case, in this four-year interval the only bright spot was the decree abolishing the institution of Negro slavery. Yet, even this magnanimous gesture was tarnished. Abolition, delayed so many years by various legal stratagems, finally came to Venezuela as an act of war. The Conservatives let it be known in the early 1850s that a victorious Páez would make abolition the first order of business, and in consequence the level of slave unrest appeared to rise. The Monagas Abolition Decree of 1854 was designed to neutralize the effectiveness of this propaganda.[37]

In spite of all his efforts, when José Gregorio turned the presidency back to his brother in 1855 Venezuela was still racked by violent internal dissension, and by 1858 a rebellion—backed by a fusion of Liberals and Conservatives—defeated the Monagas government. But, unfortunately for Venezuela, the defeat of Monagas did not mark the end of a violent decade but rather the beginning of a disastrous civil war.

NOTES

1. For a provocative although partially unreliable analysis of Venezuela's colonial past see Federico Brito Figueroa, *La estructura económica de Venezuela colonial* (Caracas: Universidad Central de Venezuela, 1963).

The standard work on the Caracas Company, recently reissued in Spanish, is Roland D. Hussey, *La compañía de Caracas, 1728–1784* (Caracas: Banco Central de Venezuela, 1962).

2. Brito Figueroa's *La estructura económica*, pp. 112–138, has estimates on the slave trade to Venezuela. See also Miguel Acosta Saignes, *La trata de esclavos en Venezuela* (Caracas: Revista de Historia, 1961); and Philip D. Curtin, *The Atlantic Slave Trade: A Census* (Madison: University of Wisconsin Press, 1969).

3. Frank Tannenbaum, *Slave and Citizen, the Negro in the Americas* (New York: Knopf, 1946). Marvin Harris, *Patterns of Race in the Americas* (New York: Walker, 1964). Stanley M. Elkins, *Slavery: A Problem in American Institutional and Intellectual Life* (Chicago: University of Chicago Press, 1959). An outstanding survey of the literature on slavery in the Americas can be found in the notes to David Brion Davis's perceptive study *The Problem of Slavery in Western Culture* (Ithaca, New York: Cornell University Press, 1966). The difficulties of comparative studies in this field can be appreciated by a careful perusal of Herbert S. Klein, *Slavery in the Americas: A Comparative Study of Virginia and Cuba* (Chicago: University of Chicago Press, 1967); and Eugene D. Genovese and Laura Foner, eds., *Slavery in the New World: A Reader in Comparative History* (Englewood Cliffs, N.J.: Prentice-Hall, 1969).

4. Francisco González Guinán, *Historia contemporánea de Venezuela*, 15 vols. (Caracas: Ediciones de la Presidencia de la República, 1954).

5. In the following notes to this Introduction, I will point out some of the advances in Venezuelan historiography on the 1810–1855 period. For an outstanding evaluation of Venezuelan historiography see Germán Carrera Damas's study entitled "Los estudios históricos en Venezuela," *Cuestiones de historiografía venezolana* (Caracas: Universidad Central de Venezuela, 1964).

6. Perhaps the best account of the early years of Venezuelan independence can be found in the extensively documented work of Caracciolo Parra Pérez, *Historia de la Primera República de Venezuela*, 2 vols. (Sesquicentenario de la Independencia, Nos. 19 and 20 [Caracas: Academia Nacional de la Historia, 1959]). A series of fine bibliographical studies on the Independence era is Pedro Grases's *Estudios bibliográficos* (Caracas: Imprenta Nacional, 1961).

7. Parra Pérez, *Primera República*, I, 403–434; II, *passim*.

8. Venezuela's population during the period under consideration here was composed of four symbolic ethnic groups: whites, pardos, Negroes, and slaves. The largest group, the pardos, probably composed about 80 percent of the population. Pure Negroes and Negro slaves may have accounted for 10 percent at the most. Indians as an identifiable ethnic group no longer existed in the settled portion of Venezuela but may have totaled

around 50,000 in the wild areas of the interior. But, in any event, Indians did not participate in Venezuelan life in any but the most marginal way. The most detailed study of Venezuelan race mixtures is still the classic work by Alexander von Humboldt, *Viaje a las regiones equinocciales del nuevo continente hecho en 1799, 1800, 1801, 1802, 1803 y 1804 por . . . y A. Bonpland*, 2d ed., 5 vols. (Caracas: Ediciones del Ministerio de Educación, 1956). Also useful is the geography by Agustín Codazzi, *Resumen de la geografía* in *Obras escogidas* (Caracas: Ediciones del Ministerio de Educación, 1960), I. See also the items listed in note 9, below.

9. There is a considerable bibliography on the subject of the social content of the independence movement in Venezuela. Particularly useful in this respect is Charles C. Griffin's *Los temas sociales y económicos en la época de la independencia* (Caracas: Fundación John Boulton and Fundación Eugenio Mendoza, 1962). Equally helpful is the critique of Griffin's work by Germán Carrera Damas, "Cuestiones económico-sociales de la emancipación," *Crítica contemporánea*, X (March–April 1963), 13–21. The same author's study "Algunos problemas relativos a la organización del Estado en la Segunda República Venezolana," *Tres temas de historia* (Caracas: Universidad Central de Venezuela, 1961), pp. 90–165, is a very perceptive essay on the social and economic aspirations of the participants in the wars for independence.

10. In addition to the account in Parra Pérez, *Primera República*, passim, it is well to consult the standard biography of Miranda by William Spence Robertson, *La Vida de Miranda* (Caracas: Banco Industrial de Venezuela, 1967). I cite this recent edition of the book because the quotations from Miranda's papers, translated into English in the first edition, have been relocated and restored to their original Spanish form. For a more detailed discussion of the bibliography on this phase of the independence movement see the notes to Chapter 2 of this study.

11. Since much of independence historiography has concentrated on the military campaigns, I must point out here the monumental work of Vicente Lecuna. For this study his most useful effort is the *Crónica razonada de las guerras de Bolívar*, 2d ed., 3 vols. (New York: Ediciones de la Fundación Vicente Lecuna, 1960). Also important is Gerhard Masur's biography, *Simón Bolívar* (Albuquerque, New Mexico: University of New Mexico Press, 1948).

12. Although Boves has been vilified in patriot histories, his role has yet to be properly evaluated. One significant step in this direction is the outstanding monograph by Germán Carrera Damas, *Sobre el significado socio-económico de la acción histórica de Boves* (Caracas: Universidad Central de Venezuela, 1964).

13. The relationship between Bolívar and Alexandre Petión has long

remained shrouded in mystery. We still do not know exactly what agreements were made between these two men. Paul Verna's study *Robert Sutherland, un amigo de Bolívar en Haiti* (Caracas: Fundación John Boulton, 1966), is probably the best examination of this question.

14. Extremely helpful in viewing the broad sweep of Venezuelan independence is the first volume of González Guinán's *Historia* and the relevant chapters in the influential general history by José Gil Fortoul, *Historia constitucional de Venezuela*, 4th ed., 3 vols. (Caracas: Ministerio de Educación, 1953–1954).

15. One of the most interesting figures of the revolutionary period, José Antonio Páez, has yet to receive sufficient attention from historians. One way to approach Páez is through his autobiography, *José Antonio Páez, Autobiografía del General . . . ,* 1st ed., 2 vols. (New York: Hallet y Breen, 1867). For a study of the phenomenon of caudillismo in Venezuela see Robert L. Gilmore, *Caudillism and Militarism in Venezuela, 1810– 1910* (Athens, Ohio: Ohio University Press, 1964).

16. See, in addition to the items cited in notes 11, 14, and 15 above, the monumental study of Santiago Mariño by Caracciolo Parra Pérez, *Mariño y la independencia de Venezuela*, 5 vols. (Madrid: Ediciones Cultura Hispánica, 1954–1957).

17. The best source of information on the Colombian confederation is the excellent work by David Bushnell, *The Santander Regime in Gran Colombia* (Newark, Delaware: University of Delaware Press, 1954). Supplementing Bushnell's bibliography is the exceptional article by Pedro Grases and Manuel Pérez Vila, "Gran Colombia: referencias relativas a la bibliografía sobre el período emancipador en los paises gran colombianos (desde 1949)," *Anuario de Estudios Americanos*, XXI (1964), 151–195.

18. In addition to Bushnell's work and the general histories of the independence cited above, the *Cuerpo de leyes de la república de Colombia* (Caracas: Universidad Central de Venezuela, 1961) gives the legislative accomplishments of Gran Colombia.

19. The disintegration of Gran Colombia is best studied in Bushnell, *The Santander Regime*, chaps. 18, 20, and 21. Another way to view Venezuela on the eve of separation is to read José Rafael Revenga, *La hacienda pública de Venezuela en 1828–1830. Misión de . . . como Ministro de Hacienda* (Caracas: Banco Central de Venezuela, 1953).

20. Although the designation *Conservative Oligarchy* originated in the early nineteenth century, it has become consecrated in Venezuelan historiography through the writings of such authors as José Gil Fortoul in his *Historia*. Dissatisfaction with this term, as well as with its complement, the *Liberal Oligarchy*, is widespread. But until a well-documented analysis of the emergence of Venezuelan political parties appears, these traditional names will have to suffice. For a short discussion of this problem see

"Presentación" in *Pensamiento político venezolano del siglo XIX* (Caracas: Publicaciones de la Presidencia de la República, 1961), X, 9–16.

21. One of the more perceptive essays on the origins of Venezuelan political parties is Laureano Vallenilla Lanz, *Cesarismo democrático*, 4th ed. (Caracas: Tipografía Garrido, 1961). In spite of its obvious tendentiousness and political overtones, this essay is full of valuable insights and hypotheses that should be investigated by historians.

22. This interpretation of the origins and growth of the Conservative Oligarchy is based primarily on the information in González Guinán's *Historia*. However, many of the ideas presented in this essay have also been influenced by a considerable amount of reading in the contemporary periodical press. Also very helpful for an understanding of the entire period of 1830 to 1855 is the fine study by Ramón Díaz Sánchez, *Guzmán: Elipse de una ambición de poder* (Caracas: Ediciones del Ministerio de Educación Nacional, 1950). Unfortunately, this study does not contain an adequate complement of notes.

23. For the text of the 1830 constitution of Valencia see José Gil Fortoul, *Historia*, III, 349–390.

24. González Guinán, *Historia*, II, chaps. 11 and 12. Díaz Sánchez, *Guzmán*, pp. 167–178.

25. This theory is most persuasively presented in Vallenilla Lanz, *Cesarismo democrático*, pp. 185–209.

26. For a more complete discussion of the economic development of Venezuela (1830–1854) see Chapter 5 of this study.

27. González Guinán, *Historia*, II, chaps. 18 and 19. Díaz Sánchez, *Guzmán*, pp. 179–188. See also the analyses and comments by John G. A. Williamson, *Caracas Diary, 1835–1840: The Journal of . . . , First Diplomatic Representative of the United States to Venezuela*, ed. Jane Lucas de Grummond (Baton Rouge, La., 1954).

28. In addition to the account in González Guinán, *Historia*, II, chaps. 21 and 26, see the documents on the reformista movement in *Pensamiento político*, XII, 21–211.

29. González Guinán, *Historia*, II, chap. 27; III, chaps. 28–31.

30. A detailed analysis of this economic crisis is in chapter 5.

31. In addition to González Guinán's account of these events in his *Historia*, III, chaps. 36 and 37, see Antonio Leocadio Guzmán's analysis of the origins of the Liberal party published in 1846 and included in *Pensamiento político*, V, 433–446. For extremely perceptive comments on the development of Venezuelan politics throughout the Páez regime see Robert Ker Porter, *Sir Robert Ker Porter's Caracas Diary, 1825–1842: A British Diplomat in a Newborn Nation*, ed. Walter Dupouy (Caracas: Instituto Otto y Magdalena Blohm, 1966).

32. For some interesting comments by Juan Vicente González, a virulent

Liberal-hater, on the 1846 uprising, see the documents for 1846 included in *Pensamiento político*, III, 79–118. Also helpful is the interrogation of Ezequiel Zamora, one of the leaders of the revolt, in ibid., XI, 320–336.

33. González Guinán, *Historia*, IV, chaps. 60 and 61.

34. The separation of Monagas from his original Conservative supporters can be seen clearly in the series of four public letters written by Juan Vicente González to Monagas in the editorial section of *La Prensa* between 31 July and 25 December 1847 included in *Pensamiento político*, III, 171–198. An interesting account of the congressional incident of 24 January 1848 by Lisandro Alvarado, published in 1894, is in ibid., XIII, 313–323. See also Great Britain, Public Record Office (London), Foreign Office 80 (Venezuela), LIV (PRO, FO 80/54) 143–156 (B. H. Wilson, Caracas, 4 February 1848).

35. González Guinán, *Historia*, IV, chaps. 1–11. See also the account of the Liberal Oligarchy and Monagas in Díaz Sánchez, *Guzmán*, pp. 331–355.

36. González Guinán, *Historia*, V, chaps. 16–21. See also chapter 5 of this study for a discussion of the economic crisis and chapter 6 for a discussion of the revolutionary potential of Negro slaves.

37. González Guinán, *Historia*, V, chaps. 22–32. Part II of this study is designed to explain the eventual declaration of abolition by the Monagas regime.

PART I

* * *

The Slave
System

CHAPTER 2

Slavery and the Wars for Independence

UNTIL 19 April 1810, the Venezuelan Negro slave belonged to a well-defined social group whose rights and duties had been established by almost three centuries of Spanish colonial practice and legislation. He knew, for example, that as the child of a slave mother he was destined to remain a slave forever.[1] As he grew up he found that his mission in life was to serve his mother's master in any capacity asked him. He learned that in addition to having an immortal soul, he was also an object of commerce. Unless he were an exceptionally docile and obedient person he soon experienced the master's right to punish— lashes, stocks, imprisonment, and the like. But the slave's lot in Venezuela was not altogether hopeless. By dint of hard work and good behavior over most of his life, he might be able to bring together the legal price for his emancipation before he became too old to enjoy it. Or even better yet, his master could be a pious soul whose deathbed conscience would impel him to the generosity of manumitting some of his faithful workers. The chances for this sort of release improved if a slave's master also happened to be his father.[2] Unfortunately, however, such generosity never freed all the slaves (some 60,000 of them still remained in 1810),[3] and so, many courageous, discouraged, and

usually ill-treated black men took to the hills to live the precarious life of the runaway. Although hunted sporadically, the
cimarrones managed a reasonably productive existence by raising crops and providing various services to the understaffed
smugglers infesting the coasts, rivers, and oceans of colonial
Venezuela.[4]

By the beginning of the nineteenth century, then, a Venezuelan slave owner could view the future with a certain amount
of confidence. To be sure, the Haitian revolution had been
quite a shock to all slave owners, and in its wake Spain's laws
designed to alleviate the lot of captive black men took on new
meaning. For example, the law prohibited beating a slave to
death, and forbade the useful practice of branding slaves like
cattle.[5] But these and other restrictions contemplated by the
Crown were not all the threat they appeared. After all, Spain
was a long way off, and her laws had rarely been effective in the
rural sections of Venezuela. Local officials sympathized with
the planter's problems of slave control, and the Caracas cabildo
had already appealed the enforcement of the latest and most
lenient slave code. Until this question was settled, however,
things would remain much as before.[6]

THE FIRST REPUBLIC

Nor did the coup d'état of 19 April 1810 worry the complacent
slave owners, at least at first. The authors of this first in a long
series of nineteenth-century *golpes* came from the best class;
many owned slaves themselves and could be counted on to
maintain the existing system. Yet somehow, the movement for
independence began to drift to the left in spite of the respecta-
bility of its instigators. The first symptom of this alarming
tendency was the decree ending the slave trade.[7]

But the mantuanos, those haughty caraqueño aristocrats,
really began to worry during a heated debate over the status of
the pardos.[8] This class, in the middle between the slaves and
the whites, had long been organized and controlled through an
elaborate legal system restricting dress, occupation, travel, and

general civil rights.[9] That some radicals wanted to tamper with this finely tuned engine of oppression was bad enough, but that others thought of eliminating the machine altogether was little short of subversive. Fortunately for the nervous mantuanos, the dangerous scheme collapsed and things remained as they were, at least for a while.

And so, with the Venezuelan independence movement in the hands of the First Republic's timid legislators, Negro slaves could hope for little improvement in their condition. But a Royalist reaction supported by a troubled but still vigorous Spain drowned the First Republic in blood, obligating the neophyte Republicans to change sides, go into exile, or learn the meaning of revolution. Ironically enough, it was that prince of revolutionary dilettantes, Francisco de Miranda, who taught reluctant caraqueños their first radical lessons.

By the middle of 1812 the Republican military campaign to throw Spanish arms out of Venezuela had almost collapsed. The Spanish captain, Domingo Monteverde, starting with only a handful of troops, had made amazing progress. In his drive toward the capital he fully exploited the restless castes, free and slave.[10] Miranda, to stall the Royalists, proclaimed the general enlistment of black slaves from his headquarters in Maracay in May of 1812. Any slave who wanted to fight Spaniards was welcome to do so; in fact, by fighting Spaniards for ten years he would become a free man.[11] This timid gesture appalled the caraqueño notables, and Miranda had to meet their delegates at the Conference of Tapatapa to soothe their fears.[12] In spite of the shaky Republican position, Caracas authorities dawdled for a month before promulgating Miranda's Enlistment Decree on 19 June 1812.[13]

Weaker than even Miranda's original proposal, the Caracas Slave Enlistment Decree only provided for a draft of one thousand Negroes, although it reduced the period of service required from ten years to four. Even though the Caracas Decree promised the owners compensation,[14] it proved highly unpopular and ". . . definitively brought down on the regime and especially on Miranda the [wrath] of the planters, who formed the most

powerful class in the country."[15] Some thought the measure
too drastic. They believed it would cause agriculture to decline
and plantation discipline to become impossible as slaves saw
fellow blacks taken into the armies without the slightest attention to age or military aptitude.[16] Others thought the slaves
would use the decree as an excuse to revolt and kill all the
whites.[17] In fear of such an event, some *hacendados* hid the
news of the Enlistment Decree from their slaves.[18]

In spite of this strong opposition, the law had its defenders.
Many patriots hoped the enlistment of Negro slaves would help
contain the rebellious blacks and prevent a general uprising in
favor of the king.[19] One frightened patriot hacendado even
offered to free all his slaves on the condition they join the
patriot armies fighting Royalist-inspired revolts. The provincial
government rejected this noble proposal as impolitic.[20] In all,
Miranda's slave recruitment policy did not even increase the
armies enough to release peons to the needy hacendados as
some had hoped: it can be considered a failure.[21]

Needless to say, the mantuanos received this first lesson in
radicalism with very poor grace. Many began having visions of
Haiti, and when, in August of 1812, rumors spread of a wild,
destructive slave rebellion along the coast of Barlovento and
surrounding areas, most Republicans began to repent their revolutionary ardor.[22] These events, culminating a long series of
political and military disasters, helped bring about the complete
collapse of Miranda's dictatorship and led to peace with Monteverde. Even Miranda lost heart at the thought of a black rebellion.[23] That kind of revolution could change more than just the
leaders of Venezuela, and he thought it better to make peace
with the Spaniards than to turn the country over to the lower
castes.

PATRIOT INDECISION

After the sad disintegration of the first Venezuelan republic,
both Royalists and Republicans settled down to the serious

business of war. The Royalists had the advantage, being in possession of the capital and the support of rebellious Negro slaves. But the patriots fought on. In the bloody war that followed, rival Venezuelan factions—fighting under Republican or Royalist flags—killed, confiscated, and exiled in the name of liberty and republicanism or Spain and king. Perhaps the most striking feature of this turbulent decade was the similarity of patriot and Royalist war measures.

Insofar as the borrowing of private property for the war effort is concerned, there is little doubt of the practically identical procedures followed by all fighting groups throughout the war.[24] Much the same can be said of the slave policies sponsored by revolutionaries and monarchists. Although Miranda began the policy of conscripting Negro slaves, the Spaniards Domingo Monteverde and Pablo Morillo gained the most from this type of property confiscation during the early years of the war.[25] Negroes in revolt against their *criollo* slave masters could hardly be expected to enlist in the armies of the republic to fight for the preservation of their oppressors.[26]

By August of 1813, the patriots again controlled Caracas, but as in 1812, the Royalist forces rallied slaves and pardos to drive out the Republicans. Both José Tomás Boves and Francisco Rosete, for example, attracted considerable numbers of Negro slaves to their armies, particularly from the llanos and the Valles del Tuy. Republicans, writing in the *Gaceta de Caracas*, claimed that the slaves fought for the king only under compulsion and that most of these unwilling soldiers returned to their master's *haciendas* rather than continue fighting patriots.[27] These partisans forgot to explain why they worried so about slaves being dragooned for royal service, since they believed most of them would soon return to their masters. Possibly they thought valuable property would be destroyed, since Royalists had the unpleasant reputation of putting all the blacks in the front line, presumably to save their white troops.[28]

Patriot concern with the slave question, as expressed in the *Gaceta de Caracas*, had its ulterior motive. One indignant hacendado ended his denunciation of slave enlistment with the ingenuous suggestion that this Royalist policy be made known in the British Antilles. Perhaps then, he thought, some help would come to the patriot cause.[29] It is particularly interesting that at this time some patriots thought they could afford to be viewed as conservers of Venezuelan slavery. They evidently overestimated England's readiness to interfere to put down slave rebellions and underestimated their own need for Negro support. Yet, the *independientistas* were so convinced by their own argument that they tried to enlist British arms in their defense under the pretext of suppressing the slaves. A Venezuelan agent in Barbados was instructed to arrange for the shipment of a thousand English troops, complete with supply train, to cooperate in destroying ". . . the bandits, and fugitive slaves who carry pillage, death, and desolation to many of the best settlements and haciendas."[30]

Evidently, this course was unproductive, because a year later Bolívar tried another tack with the British. In a letter to the *Gaceta Real de Jamaica* in Kingston, ignoring the terrible dangers of slave uprisings, he painted an idyllic picture of Venezuelan castes who lived an easy and delightful life. Bolívar explained that, since the wide variety of colored people in Venezuela was scattered throughout such a large area, no one race or color would want to annihilate the others. He viewed the idea of a racial war as absurd. After assuring his readers that Boves and other Royalist caudillos forced slaves to follow them, Bolívar concluded his analysis by describing Venezuelan slaves as being descended ". . . from a savage race, [that is] maintained in rusticity by the profession to which they are applied, and degraded to the sphere of brutes." He protested that the Venezuelan War of Independence was an international conflict between Spain and Venezuela, not a civil war, and that intervention by England on behalf of Venezuela would not lead to another Haiti. All this verbal sleight of hand, designed to convince the public and presumably British officialdom, was probably unconvincing.[31]

In spite of the patriots' apparent obtuseness, Bolívar, at least, had begun to grasp the significance of the defeats of 1812 and 1814. Of course, all thinking men were patriots, but ". . . the general mass was still ignorant of its rights and unaware of its interests."[32] By the time Bolívar returned to the fight from exile in Haiti, he had learned the necessity of showing the masses where their interests lay. The series of decrees proclaiming freedom for the slaves that grew out of Bolívar's commitment to Haitian President Petión was one way of fighting fire with fire, as Miranda's slave enlistment policy had tried to do some years earlier. But this time the mantuanos, what was left of them, had more courage for the job.

PATRIOT POLICY

The patriot experience with slave soldiers, aside from Miranda's frustrated efforts, began officially with Bolívar's famous proclamation to the inhabitants of Rio Caribe, Carúpano, and Cariaco on 2 June 1816.[33] It could be claimed that Bolívar was only fulfilling his part of the promise made to President Petión since, in exchange for financial and political support, the revolutionaries agreed to declare the freedom of all Venezuelan slaves. But the patriots undoubtedly realized that without the slaves, independence might never be won. That the Republicans cared more about recruiting soldiers than about bringing freedom to all men is evident from the context of the proclamations.[34] Although the terms of the freedom decrees differed somewhat, they all contained the guiding principle that any slave wanting freedom should be willing to fight Spaniards to earn it. The first decree, the most stringent of all, provided that any slave who did not enlist condemned his family to continue in servitude.[35] Evidently, this severity drove some of the inhabitants of the Carúpano area not only to resist enlistment but also to join the Royalists;[36] thus, slaves contributed only minimally to the Carúpano expedition.[37] The slaves along the coast of Ocumare evidenced equal indifference. Although

Bolívar went through the same motions here as in Carúpano, the results were disappointing, and desertions were high among those who did bother to enlist.[38]

After the failure of this expedition, Bolívar wrote to his Haitian supporters complaining that Venezuelan slaves had shown themselves to be such an ignorant and stupid lot, made so by years of Spanish oppression, that they refused their chance to fight for freedom. He could claim only about two hundred of these people in his army at Ocumare.[39] If the Negro slaves were ignorant and stupid, the fault certainly lay with the Venezuelan criollo landlords who had enforced the years of Spanish oppression. However, it is a good deal more likely that the slaves resisted enlistment for much the same reasons many freemen resisted enlistment. Why get killed for a cause they did not understand when the reward for joining was hardship and no pay?

In spite of the reluctance of Negro slaves to flock to Venezuela's banners, Bolívar remained firmly committed to the policy of freeing the slaves. Unfortunately, the civilian hacendados and slave owners did not have Bolívar's dire need for soldiers to encourage their humanitarian instincts. All they could see were plantations ruined by the depredations of war and the lack of workers.[40] But they protested in vain, since the government insisted on its right to take slaves when and where it needed them.[41]

ROYALIST POLICY

Nor did the apparent enthusiasm of Negro slaves for the Royalist cause please all the supporters of Ferdinand VII. The Ayuntamiento of Caracas not only felt the enlistment of slaves unwise but also believed it would certainly contribute to the decadence of agriculture. They accused Morillo of encouraging slaves to join his armies to earn their freedom. Such a practice, claimed the loyal notables of Caracas, would only add another insubordinate group to the free population and would certainly be prejudicial to the country in general.[42] Morillo's answer to the *cabildantes* clarified the Royalist position somewhat. He roundly denied any intention of offering freedom to Negroes who would enlist. Freedom, he claimed, was to be accorded only those slaves encountered in arms and fighting for the king. Naturally, he kept these soldiers in the army and agreed to indemnify their owners. The *Consejo de las Indias*, after deliberate consideration between 1815 and 1818, decided that Morillo had acted prudently, but they could not decide about making slaves an integral part of the Spanish war effort. The matter would have to be passed to the *Consejo de Guerra* for more debate.[43]

Meanwhile, the men charged with defending Spain's rights in Caracas kept busy. Generals Morillo and Francisco Tomás Morales, fearing their enemies might prejudice the government against them, sent their *Vicario General*, José Ambrosio Llamozas, to explain the caste system to the king and councils. After painting in bloody colors Boves's efforts in favor of the king, Llamozas demonstrated the necessity of an intelligent and progressive race policy. The whites were dead, he claimed, the pardos were restless, and the slaves were dangerous. To hold Venezuela for the king and his loyal Spaniards, four or five thousand troops must be sent at once to keep the peace.

But Llamozas saw the troops only as a temporary measure, sort of a stopgap to hold back the castes long enough to make necessary permanent reforms. The first of these long-term reforms, he recommended, should be a modification of the color balance. The slave trade must be ended, or all slaves newly brought into the province must be freed at twenty years of age without compensation to their owners. Evidently, Llamozas wanted to eliminate the danger of slavery as soon as possible, because he recommended a 2 percent tax on all fruits and products to pay for the freedom of well-behaved blacks selected by lot.

Although this system would alleviate the pressure from the slaves, the rest of the colored population still remained with its dangerous egalitarian pretensions. To leaven this loaf, the Vicario recommended white immigration composed of Canarians, Balearians, and Spaniards. Such people could be attracted by offering title to some of Venezuela's unused land.

Since the freedom of slaves would increase the already dangerously large colored population, Llamozas concluded, some individuals should be passed into the white caste. Any pardo legitimately descended from free and legally married parents and grandparents should be registered as white. In this provision, Llamozas's courage deserted him. Such a law would have passed only a minimal number of pardos every year, and those passed would probably have been the least dangerous. Concluding his memorial, Morillo's emissary called for a general administrative overhaul that would allow good men to carefully administer good laws.[44]

With this Royalist picture of the Venezuelan caste situation in mind, it is easier to understand the seriousness of Morillo's 1817 proposition to draft two thousand slaves from haciendas along the Rio Tuy. Before embarking on such a controversial measure, however, Morillo decided to consult local opinion. One of his volunteer advisors, Ignacio Xavier Vzelay, turned in an exceptionally coherent, passionless, and impartial evaluation.

The slaves, Vzelay began, were just like any other war commodity; they could be taken by either side. Since Negroes would do anything to get their freedom, they were an asset to the first army to impress them. Moreover, because of their unique position in Venezuelan society, black slaves made ideal soldiers. They understood discipline, fought with courage and honor to be free, adjusted to varying climates, and endured hard work. Since slaves received such bad treatment on the haciendas, he reasoned, they could be taken over long distances because they would have no desire to return to the area of their servitude. Furthermore, the existence of a group of well-paid and -treated Negro soldiers might help keep the rest of the slaves quiet.

This line of thought must have been rather convincing, given the success of the Royalists in capturing slave support. But in the most interesting part of Vzelay's report he refuted those who stressed the dangers of a slave conscription policy. The specter of French Santo Domingo, he felt, was only a specter. Since the black soldiers were to be used away from home, they would have little chance to stir up trouble. Some, he thought, might object that the formation of a battalion would encourage slaves to believe freedom near, but, Vzelay observed, the damage had already been done by Boves and others who had used the promise of freedom to gather troops. Better to have a legitimate outlet for slave hopes than to close the lid and wait for an explosion. Another pointless criticism was that the measure would take men from the fields. If the battalion were necessary, it would be made up of men from the fields in any case; the question was whether they should be free or slave. If the men taken were slaves, Vzelay explained, the burden of supporting the war would hit the rich who could best bear it. In conclusion, the *consejero* opted for a happy medium. Instead of the two battalions of Negroes he had requested, Morillo should only get one. Furthermore, the levy of slaves should never exceed 6 to 8 percent of any one plantation's labor force. Compensation, naturally, was obligatory.[45]

While Morillo sent out his questionnaires on slave policy and waited for answers, some rule had to be followed by the armies in the field. The effective, if not too honorable, solution was to take all able-bodied slaves encountered and tie them to the Royal cause with ". . . the vain hope of liberty."[46] Had the Royalists won the war, one imagines they would have had a bit of trouble reenslaving their valiant soldiers.

The slaves drafted by the Royalists and Republicans entered the armies in a variety of ways. Sometimes they would join after a commander had promulgated a decree. Other times runaway slaves joined an army to escape capture and punishment. Patriot bands often picked up slaves from plantations as they passed by.[47] This process of slowly draining slave labor from the countryside continued throughout the war until its end in 1823. It is impossible to tell how many slaves in all joined the War of Independence; they generally joined the armies in small groups, rarely in mass, and they deserted frequently.[48] But most importantly, slavery survived independence.

Nevertheless, there is no denying that Bolívar at least tried to eliminate slavery through the agent of the wars of independence. It is unimportant whether he tried because he needed men for his armies, because he feared the advent of a *pardocracía* should the whites be killed and not the blacks, or because he realized the absurdity of a revolution for freedom that maintained slavery and feared another Haiti were the Negroes kept enslaved.[49]

But the effect of the war on slavery is more difficult to define. By and large, the years of devastation contributed mostly confusion and disorganization. These two enemies of oppression hastened the eventual dissolution of Venezuelan slavery. Because the army, during the war, remained the ultimate refuge for runaway slaves, plantation discipline collapsed and the recovery of runaways became next to impossible. Furthermore, Negro slaves discovered a sense of power during these years as the contending armies wooed their support. The war impressed upon their masters the terror of a massive slave revolt. Although the reaction would come, its severity was tempered by fear.

THE LEGISLATIVE REACTION: COLOMBIA

As the threat of a Spanish reconquest of Venezuela grew remote, civilian slave holders became less tolerant of the military policy of slave conscription. In extreme emergencies slave owners had consented to the confiscation of their workers, but once the danger had passed they would countenance no meddling with the sacred right of property. During the height of the wars for independence, military chieftains of all ranks on both sides did what they pleased with slave property. Bolívar, in dire need of soldiers, proclaimed the abolition of Negro slavery through military service. Unfortunately, this short-term libertarianism ended in 1819 when the Congress of Angostura started the reconstruction of slavery in Venezuela.

Indicative of the general dissatisfaction, the Congress of Angostura rejected Bolívar's plea for ratification of his abolition policy.[50] All the delegates agreed slavery was a nasty business and by right slaves should be free. But on the other hand, blacks subjected to slavery were an exceedingly nasty group whose inclusion in society was hardly advisable. Such backward people needed years of careful education before they would be fit for freedom. Therefore, the Angostura delegates proposed to improve the moral state of the enslaved black man through carefully planned laws which would gradually prepare him for liberty.[51]

To certify their liberalism and humanitarianism, the Congress declared that no man might own another, and proclaimed to the world that Venezuela would abolish slavery within a fixed term. Freedom, they said, resembled ". . . the light of the soul, [and] should be given to them [the slaves] by degrees. . . ." It naturally followed that, after the first step in civilizing the Negroes—during which they would learn such useful moral traits as ". . . love of work . . ." as well as the rudiments of reading and writing—freedom would be made dependent on the slaves' own efforts. Of course, those slaves already free would remain so, and those called to serve in the armed forces would also acquire their freedom. The ban on slave imports remained in force. Typically, the Angostura delegates reaffirmed the right of hacendados to payment for any slave property confiscated.[52]

Although the Angostura Law established a number of principles that reappeared in subsequent slave laws, it did not accurately reflect Venezuelan slave philosophy primarily because the law had no legal force. The high-minded declaration of freedom, for example, was perfectly harmless, since the law left the means to the next Congress. The only accomplishment of the law, other than assuring Negroes freedom sometime in the future and denying runaway slaves from neighboring countries the right of asylum, was to place a fine of one thousand pesos for every Negro slave brought into the country.[53] In fact, the Angostura debates merely provided a dress rehearsal for the main event at Cúcuta a year later.

The 1821 Cúcuta Slave Law was the first and most important piece of legislation in the Republican reconstruction of Negro slavery. Since all subsequent slave laws were either modifications of the 1821 Law or based on it, this statement of slave philosophy deserves an extended analysis.[54]

The heart of the law was the provision for free birth of all slave children.[55] In fact, this short article is the only reason the 1821 Law can even be considered an abolition decree. Slavery, in theory at least, was doomed, and any curious mathematician could easily figure out when the end would come. But such a grim outlook for slave owners was tempered somewhat by other sections of the ingenious law.

Since a slave master had to raise and feed the freeborn children of his human chattel, the slave child must pay for his maintenance by serving his mother's master for eighteen years. During these years of service the patron supposedly educated the child so he would be prepared to take on the responsibilities of a Venezuelan citizen.[56]

But the wisdom of the Cúcuta legislators went even farther. At the age of eighteen the freeborn child, now legally quit of any obligation to his patron and ready to enter the world of the free, would be presented to a local board with an account of his conduct. The gentlemen of the board, after careful consideration, would see to the future occupation of the new citizen.[57]

The legislators did not restrict such philanthropy to the freeborn, but included the perpetually enslaved as well. The gradual end of slavery in Venezuela was the purpose of this law, and thus some system of manumission must be devised.[58] But how to reconcile the sacred right of all men to liberty with the equally sacred right of private property? This was, indeed, a dilemma for men firmly steeped in the theories of liberalism so in vogue at the time.

Their solution took the form of a clever manumission system, designed primarily to pay for all slaves freed by the state. A local fund, composed of a variety of taxes on inheritances, would be used for the noble purpose of freeing deserving slaves.[59] A local committee chose those eligible for this grace. Called the *Junta de Manumisión*, this group—formed by the first judge, the parish priest, two citizens, and a responsible treasurer—was appointed by the governor. It collected the tax, chose the most honorable and industrious slaves for manumission, and paid the masters for the slaves freed. Once a year, midst appropriate ceremony, the elect slaves received their certificates of freedom. Unfortunately, however, the local Juntas had no effective powers of coercion to collect taxes, even if they were so inclined.[60]

To round out this legislation, the congressional delegates forbade the selling of nonpubescent children to a different province from their parents. They ratified the 1811 Decree ending the slave trade and guaranteed the liberty of any slaves who had acquired their freedom under the various Republican governments.[61]

Such, then, was the nature of the new Venezuelan slave system. It is well to note that the law need have no practical effect on slave holders for at least eighteen years. Given the unstable political and military conditions of the time, this reactionary law retreated from Bolívar's abolition policy as far as possible. To have reestablished the slave system as it existed prior to 1810 would have been resented by the newly freed slaves as well as by those still enslaved. No doubt some legislators could remember the catastrophic rebellion of 1812. Furthermore, Bolívar, retreating from his abolitionist stand of 1819, backed a free-birth law.[62] Nor should it be forgotten that the war was still being fought and that armies continued to recruit slave soldiers. Could they be expected to fight for a government whose gratitude consisted of a reestablishment of colonial slavery? By and large, the 1821 Manumission Law proved an artful compromise so satisfactory and flexible that it remained the basis for all subsequent slave legislation.

Although this 1821 Law provided the machinery of slave policy, it was quite another thing to make it work. From the day of publication until slavery ended officially in 1854, myriad questions of interpretation and administration streamed into the Department of the Interior from local officials.[63] The difficulties of administration became so great that practically nothing envisioned by the law became effective, with the exception of the free birth of slave children. The manumission program failed by and large, and the collection of inheritance taxes was almost impossible.[64] All this chaos resulted in various reorganizations of the administration of the new system, beginning with Bolívar's detailed decree of 1827.

Although the structure of manumission procedures remained unchanged, Bolívar's decree reflected extreme solicitousness for the right of property.[65] Since the 1821 Law had proved ineffective as an instrument of gradual abolition, and since slaves must be paid for before they could be freed, the obvious solution was to tighten tax collection and administration. Evidently, resourceful heirs successfully complicated tax collection, because the new decree tried to provide quick and efficient collection procedures by centralizing financial administration under the departmental intendants.[66] Bolívar set up a new national office of manumission to coordinate the program.

Lest anyone suspect the government of more interest in taxes than slaves, the Liberator also included various admonitions to slave owners. For example, twenty-nine lashes were more than enough correction for slaves. Slaves must be allowed to change masters at will, and slave owners must feed, clothe, and house their property.[67]

All this solicitude for slaves and the taxes to buy their freedom was counterbalanced by the now explicit criteria for selecting the lucky slaves for manumission. First in preference came those belonging to an estate paying a tax, the oldest first. Second were the most honorable and industrious slaves, the oldest first.[68] This provision made manumission as painless as possible for the owners by removing the old and useless slaves first.

This intricate system, with its involved financial organization, also failed; after the dissolution of Gran Colombia the Venezuelan Congress of Valencia revised it once again.[69]

THE LEGISLATIVE REACTION: VENEZUELA

One of the first Colombian laws reviewed by the Congress of Valencia was the 1821 Manumission Law. While following the Cúcuta formula very closely, the legislators devised a new law in 1830 that made two major changes.[70] First, if born after 1830, the freeborn children of slaves would have to serve their mother's master until the age of twenty-one. The second change provided a government subvention of the manumission program to assure the annual freedom of at least twenty slaves. This humanitarian proposal could not hurt the slave holders very much, since the minimal twenty slaves could easily be made up out of the oldest and least useful. Other than these changes, the 1830 Slave Law incorporated a number of Bolívar's financial reforms designed to eliminate the frauds and complications of tax collection.[71]

It is clear, then, that the legal mechanisms of slave policy were fully established between 1821 and 1830. The curious part of this system is the complete lack of substantial modifications over the years. In 1848 a new slave law passed which, with a couple of minor variations, followed the 1830 Law word for word.[72] Strangest of all, the law proved completely unsatisfactory from almost every point of view. Complaints from slave owners abounded, sometimes about the tax, other times about the sacred rights of property, and still other times about social dangers inherent in manumission.[73] Laws completely changing the system, introduced more than once, always failed passage.[74] Worst of all, the law did not even function. Few slaves were freed, little money was collected, and the yearly government supplement was not forthcoming.[75]

The only exception to this official inertia and indecision came in 1839, when the government bestirred itself to regulate the lives of those freeborn children of slaves who would reach the age of legal freedom in that year. Since article six of the 1830 Slave Law gave the government power to look after the freed men once they were quit of their obligation to serve their mother's master, General Páez issued a decree controlling their conduct.[76]

The purpose of the law is obvious. Rather than allow these freeborn Venezuelans to do as they pleased, work where they liked, or lived where they wanted, the government felt it necessary to tie them to the same kind of job in the same place as they had grown up in. Every manumiso who came of age received a contract with his mother's master until he was twenty-five years old. If there were reasons why the manumiso should not be so contracted, then he must find another person willing to buy his services. If the manumiso had free and legitimate ascendants he could be released to their care, but due to the necessity of legitimacy this was a rather unlikely eventuality.[77] Should the manumiso break his contract, local police had the power to return him to the patron.

These regulations, designed to create a semiservile labor class tied to the land, were reinforced by elaborate police codes evolved by the various provinces of Venezuela.[78] Police measures appeared to many Venezuelans as a panacea for all labor problems.[79] A careful reading of the various Reglamentos de Policía reveals an amazing uniformity in the labor sections of each province's code, and a comparison of the sections governing peons and jornaleros with the terms of apprentice contracts for manumisos clearly demonstrates the careful transition expected from slavery to peonage.

VENEZUELAN FREE-SLAVES

Thus, when born, the legally free slave child could look forward to eighteen or twenty-one years serving his mother's master as a slave. During this time he would acquire the skills of his master's slaves. Treated and educated with slaves, the freeborn manumiso had little opportunity to become more than a peon. Once his eighteen or twenty-one years of education in labor were over, he was recommitted to seven or four more years of the same sort of tutelage under the apprenticeship contracts administered by the local Juntas de Manumisión. Held to this forced labor by the police, the free-slave had no opportunity to learn skills foreign to the interests of his patron. At twenty-five he became a man no longer subject to the odious slave system, only to fall under the jurisdiction of a severe police code whose purpose was to keep the agricultural peon or jornalero on the land under supervision. And so, after twenty-five years of preparation, the freeborn slave child became a peon to work as he always had for the remaining years of his useful life.

NOTES

1. Richard Konetzke, *Colección de documentos para la historia de la formación social de Hispanoamérica, 1493–1810* (Madrid: Consejo Superior de Investigaciones Científicas, 1953), I, 81–82 (Real Provisión, 11 May 1526).

2. Rolando Mellafe, *La esclavitud en Hispanoamérica* (Buenos Aires: Eudeba, 1964), p. 91 and passim. Brito Figueroa, *La estructura económica*, pp. 373–376. For the most complete study of Negro slavery in colonial Venezuela see Miguel Acosta Saignes, *Vida de los esclavos negros en Venezuela* (Caracas: Hesperides, 1967).

3. There is still no accurate computation of population figures for this period. I have chosen 60,000 somewhat arbitrarily as a reasonable estimate based on Humboldt, *Viaje*, II, 234; and Brito Figueroa, *La estructura económica*, pp. 384–385.

4. Konetzke, *Colección*, I, 489–490 (Real Cédula, 23 May 1575). Miguel Acosta Saignes, "Los negros cimarrones de Venezuela," in *El movimiento emancipador de Hispanoamérica. Actas y ponencias, Mesa redonda de la Comisión de Historia del Instituto Panamericano de Geografía e Historia* (Caracas: Academia Nacional de la Historia, 1961), III, 353–398. Brito Figueroa, *La estructura económica*, pp. 353–356.

5. Konetzke, *Colección*, II, 754 (Real Cédula, 12 October 1683); III, 113–114 (Real Cédula, 19 April 1710). At one time Royal theorists be-

lieved a tightening up of the slave system would be useful. See Konetzke, *Colección*, III, 553–573 (Extracto del código Negro Carolino, 23 September 1783). Some years later, however, the royal conscience became considerably liberalized. Konetzke, *Colección*, III, 643–652 (Real Instrucción sobre los esclavos, 31 May 1789); and III, 543–544 (Real Orden aboliendo la práctica de marcar a los negros esclavos, 4 November 1784).

6. Konetzke, *Colección*, III, 726–732 (Consulta del Consejo de las Indias sobre el Reglamento expedido en 31 mayo de 1789 de los negros esclavos de América, 17 March 1794). Humboldt, *Viaje*, II, 105–106.

7. *Materiales para el estudio de la cuestión agraria en Venezuela (1800–1830)* (Caracas: Universidad Central de Venezuela, 1964), I, 40–41 (sobre prohibición de la introducción de esclavos negros, 14 August 1810). This decree was hardly controversial, since the slave trade to Venezuela by 1810 was practically nonexistent. See Brito Figueroa, *La estructura económica*, pp. 112–138.

8. *Libro de actas del supremo Congreso de Venezuela, 1811–1812* (Sesquicentenario de la Independencia, Nos. 3 and 4 [Caracas: Academia Nacional de la Historia, 1959]), I, 254–262 (Session of 31 July 1811).

9. This complicated and sometimes contradictory class legislation is collected in the three volumes of Konetzke, *Colección*.

10. Narciso Coll y Prat, *Memoriales sobre la independencia de Venezuela* (Sesquicentenario de la Independencia, No. 23 [Caracas: Academia Nacional de la Historia, 1960]), pp. 237–239.

11. The text of this decree has evidently been lost, and many authors confuse the Slave Enlistment Decree with the more famous Ley Marcial, which never mentions slaves. See Feliciano Montenegro y Colón, *Historia de Venezuela* (Sesquicentenario de la Independencia, Nos. 26 and 27 [Caracas: Academia Nacional de la Historia, 1960]), I, 224; José de Austria, *Bosquejo de la historia militar de Venezuela* (Sesquicentenario de la Independencia, Nos. 29 and 30 [Caracas: Academia Nacional de la Historia, 1960]), I, 318; and Héctor Parra Márquez, *Presidentes de Venezuela. El Dr. Francisco Espejo: ensayo biográfico* (Caracas: Editorial Cecilio Acosta, 1944), pp. 159–161.

12. For some interesting comment on slave enlistment decrees see the following letters to Miranda in the *Archivo del General Miranda* (Havana: Editorial Lex, 1950), XXIV, 55–56 (M. J. Sanz, 4 July 1812); 199 (J. Cortés de Madariaga, 5 July 1812); 288 (J. Paz del Castillo, 5 July 1812); 211 (F. Paúl, reservadísima, 7 July 1812); and 212 (F. Paúl, 7 July 1812). Also Parra Pérez, *Primera República*, II, 308–309. On the Conference of Tapatapa see Parra Pérez, *Primera República*, II, 299 and Francisco Javier Yanes, *Relación documentada de los principales sucesos ocurridos en Venezuela desde que se declaró estado independiente hasta el año de 1821* (Caracas: Academia Nacional de la Historia, 1943), I, 41. The Acta de la

Trinidad, which solemnized the Conference of Tapatapa and, curiously enough, avoids the slave question, is included in Yanes, *Relación*, II, 132–133.

13. *Archivo Miranda*, XXIV, 413 (Acto sobre la conscripción de los esclavos, 19 June 1812).

14. The Ley Marcial and the Slave Conscription Decree, as promulgated in Caracas on 19 June 1812, can be found in a number of places. See for example *Archivo Miranda*, XXIV, 405–413; and Vicente Dávila, *Investigaciones históricas* (Quito: Colegio "Don Bosco," 1955), pp. 13–17.

15. Parra Pérez, *Primera República*, II, 308–309.

16. *Archivo Miranda*, XXIV, 211 (F. Paúl to Miranda, 7 July 1812).

17. *Causas de infidencia* (Sesquicentenario de la Independencia, Nos. 31 and 32 [Caracas: Academia Nacional de la Historia, 1960]), II, 92 (against Espejo, 1813).

18. *Archivo Miranda*, XXIV, 288 (J. Paz del Castillo to Miranda, 5 July 1812).

19. *Archivo Miranda*, XXIV, 288 (J. Paz del Castillo to Miranda, 5 July 1812); and pp. 55–56 (M. J. Sanz to Miranda, 4 July 1812). *Testimonios de la época emancipadora* (Sesquicentenario de la Independencia, No. 37 [Caracas: Academia Nacional de la Historia, 1961]), pp. 157–158 (Extracto de una noticia de la revolución, 31 December 1812).

20. *Archivo Miranda*, XXIV, 324–325 (N. Ascanio to Miranda, 2 July 1812).

21. *Archivo Miranda*, XXIV, 55–56 (M. J. Sanz to Miranda, 4 July 1812).

22. Austria, *Bosquejo*, II, 103 (Exposición sucinta de los hechos de Monteverde). Coll y Prat, *Memoriales*, pp. 237–238.

23. Parra Pérez, *Primera República*, II, 415–417. Francisco Miranda, *Textos sobre la independencia* (Sesquicentenario de la Independencia, No. 13 [Caracas: Academia Nacional de la Historia, 1959]), pp. 164–165 (Memorial a la Audiencia de Caracas, 8 March 1813).

24. For an outstanding case study of this practice see Germán Carerra Damas, *Sobre Boves*.

25. *Materiales para*, I, 134–135 (Recuperación de la agricultura y estado de las esclavitudes, 10 April 1814); I, 136–137 (sublevaciones de esclavos, 23 May 1814); I, 164–170 (memorial de Llamozas, 31 July 1815); I, 171–178 (El Ayuntamiento de Caracas contra Morillo sobre esclavos, 25 September 1815). Austria, *Bosquejo*, II, 210.

26. As Juan Vicente González so aptly put it, Negro slaves "prefirieron las mismas promesas hechas por los caudillos de la opresión. Y no es que no amasen su libertad, sino que la creían una red ofrecida por los que habían sido sus señores y la preferían recibida del isleño popular, que se rozaba con ellos, vivía entre ellos y con ellos trabajaba la tierra. . . ." Juan

Vicente Gonzáles, "Biografía de José Felix Ribas," *Pensamiento político*, II, 203.

27. *Materiales para*, I, 136–137 (Sublevaciones de esclavos, 23 May 1814) and Austria, *Bosquejo*, II, 210.

28. *Materiales para*, I, 134–135 (Recuperación de la agricultura y estado de las esclavitudes, 10 April 1814).

29. *Materiales para*, I, 136–137 (Sublevaciones de esclavos, 23 May 1814).

30. *Cartas del Libertador*, 2d ed. (Caracas: Fundación Vicente Lecuna, Banco de Venezuela, 1964), I, 139–140 (Instrucciones para el comisionado de Venezuela, 19 June 1814).

31. *Cartas del Libertador*, I, 240–244 (to the editor of the *Gaceta Real de Jamaica*, September, 1815).

32. *Cartas del Libertador*, I, 182 (to Maxwell Hyslop, 19 May 1815).

33. *Decretos del Libertador* (Caracas: Publicaciones de la Sociedad Bolivariana de Venezuela, 1961), I, 55–56 (Carúpano, 2 June 1816). For an excellent survey of the major steps in republican manumission policy see the pioneering study by Harold A. Bierck, Jr., "The Struggle for Abolition in Gran Colombia," *Hispanic American Historical Review*, XXXIII (August, 1953), 365–386.

34. Austria, *Bosquejo*, II, 447 (Margarita, 23 May 1816).

35. *Decretos del Libertador*, I, 55–56 (Carúpano, 2 June 1816). See particularly art. iii.

36. *Decretos del Libertador*, I, 56–57 (Carúpano, 21 June 1816).

37. Austria, *Bosquejo*, II, 448 (Carúpano, 2 June 1816).

38. Lecuna, *Crónica razonada*, I, 460. *Cartas del Libertador*, I, 309–310 (to J. B. Arismendi, 21 August 1816).

39. *Cartas del Libertador*, I, 292 (to Marión, 27 June 1816); I, 322–325 (to president of Haiti, 4 September 1816).

40. See the complaint of Merced de la Vega, *Archivo General de la Nación*, Gran Colombia–Intendencia de Venezuela, XXXII (1821), 43–46; that of Pablo Delgado, LXIII (1822), 184; and that of Bartolomé Manrique, IV (1822), 190–193. Also of interest are the remarks of Tomás José Hernández de Sanavria, *Fomento de la agricultura, Discurso canónico-legal sobre la necesidad de una ley que reduzca los censos en Venezuela* (Caracas: Domingo Navas Spínola, 1823).

41. *Materiales para*, I, 297 (Correspondencia de un grupo de hacendados, 6 August 1821); I, 314–315 (Resolución sobre los esclavos que abracen el servicio de las armas, 14 October 1821).

42. *Materiales para*, I, 171–178 (El Ayuntamiento de Caracas contra Morillo sobre esclavos, 25 September 1815).

43. Ibid.

44. *Materiales para*, I, 164–170 (Memorial de José Ambrosio Llamozas, 31 July 1815).

45. *Materiales para,* I, 208–210 (Observaciones de Ignacio Xavier Vzelay sobre alistamiento de esclavos, 7 November 1817).

46. *Materiales para,* I, 200 (Instrucciones reservadas de Morillo a sus comandantes, 13 August 1817). For another Royalist slave disposition see the *Disposiciones gubernativas circulares a todos los tenientes justicias mayores de la provincia de Venezuela que manda publicar, cumplir y puntualmente egecutar el Sr. Capitán General de ella, a consequencia de lo dispuesto por el Escmo. Sr. D. Pablo Morillo en su cuartel general de Maracay a 3 de los corrientes* (Caracas, 1817).

47. For various examples of slave enlistment see the series of expedientes in *AGN,* Gran Col.–Int. de Ven., IV (1822), 338; and IX (1823), 24–119.

48. Austria, *Bosquejo,* II, 448 (Carúpano, 2 June 1816). For an interesting glimpse of the local operation of slave recruitment and desertion see Arturo Santana, *La campaña de Carabobo (1821). Relación histórica militar* (Caracas: Litografía del Comercio, 1921), pp. 192, 194.

49. For all the slave enlistment decrees see Austria, *Bosquejo,* II, 447 (Margarita, 23 May 1816); *Decretos del Libertador,* I, 55–56 (Carúpano, 2 June 1816); *Las fuerzas armadas de Venezuela en el siglo XIX* (Caracas: Publicaciones de la Presidencia de la República, 1963–1965), II, 169 (Ocumare, 6 July 1816); *Decretos del Libertador,* I, 125 (Villa de Cura, 11 March 1818), and I, 214 (Ceiba Grande, 23 October 1820). The long correspondence with Santander over slave policy in Colombia is very enlightening on the reasons behind Bolívar's public abolitionist attitude. *Cartas del Libertador,* II, 223 (1 November 1819); II, 273 (8 February 1820); II, 305 (14 April 1820); II, 307 (20 April 1820); II, 309 (20 April 1820); II, 323 (7 May 1820); II, 328 (10 May 1820); II, 344 (30 May 1820); II, 348 (1 June 1820); II, 351 (8 June 1820); II, 361 (19 June 1820); II, 369 (25 June 1820); II, 379–380 (11 July 1820); II, 381 (12 July 1820). For Santander's side of the exchange see *Bolívar y Santander, correspondencia, 1819–1820* (Bogota: Estado Mayor General, Ministerio de Guerra, 1940), pp. 139–140 (2 April 1820); pp. 167–169 (5 May 1820); pp. 180–182 (19 May 1820); pp. 183–185 (21 May 1820); pp. 230–231 (9 September 1820); p. 238 (26 November 1820). Bolívar's opinions later on in the war can be seen in *Cartas del Libertador* (Caracas: Litografía y Tipografía del Comercio, 1929), V, 11 (to Santander, 28 June 1825); V, 349 (to Santander, 7 June 1826); and VI, 33 (to Páez, 4 August 1826).

50. R. A. Rondón Márquez, *La esclavitud en Venezuela* (Caracas: Tipografía Garrido, 1954), p. 41.

51. The preamble and text of the Angostura Law are most revealing of the fears and rationalizations of the delegates. *Correo del Orinoco,* No. 51, 5 February 1820.

52. *Correo del Orinoco,* No. 51, 5 February 1820.

53. Ibid.

54. For the text of the 1821 Cúcuta Law see *Cuerpo de leyes de Colombia*, pp. 31–32. All citations of this law are from this source.

55. "Art. 1? Serán libres los hijos de las esclavas que nazcan desde el día de la publicación de esta ley en las capitales de provincia, y como tales se inscribirán sus nombres en los registros civicos de las municipalidades y en los libros parroquiales."

56. See art. ii. The force of this article was weakened by the following article which allowed anyone to buy a child for the cost of his upbringing. This was later restricted in the 1830 Law.

57. See art. iv. This provided the legal basis for the nefarious *patronato* system established in 1839.

58. See the third *considerando* of the 1821 Law in which the Cúcuta delegates proclaimed the gradual freedom of slaves without endangering public tranquillity or hurting slave owners' sacred property rights.

59. The taxes on inheritance as established in art. viii were: "1? de un tres por ciento con que se grava para tan piadoso objeto el quinto de los bienes de los que mueren, dejando descendientes legítimos: 2? de un tres por ciento con que también se grava el tercio de los bienes de los que mueren, dejando ascendientes legítimos: 3? del tres por ciento del total de los bienes de aquellos que mueren dejando herederos colaterales: 4? En fin, del diez por ciento que pagará el total de los bienes de los que mueren dejando herederos extraños." These were modified somewhat in 1827 and again in 1830.

60. See arts. viii through xiv.

61. See arts. v, vii, xv. Art. vii, which ended the slave trade, allowed foreigners to enter the country with one domestic slave which they could not sell within the country.

62. *Cartas del Libertador*, III, 96 (to the president of the sovereign Congress of Colombia, 14 July 1821).

63. An easy way to glimpse the administrative confusion caused by the laws is through the collection of resolutions relating to manumission and slavery emitted between 1830 and 1846 in *Colección completa de las leyes, decretos y resoluciones vijentes sobre manumisión, expedidas por el Congreso constituyente de la república y gobierno supremo de Venezuela, desde 1830 hasta 1846* (Caracas: Reimpreso en "La Nueva Imprenta," por Elías León, 1846). See also the outstanding essay on the Colombian period by Bierck, "The Struggle for Abolition in Gran Colombia," *HAHR*, XXXIII (August 1953), 365–386.

64. The failure of the manumission policy in all its incarnations was admitted by almost everyone. For a running account of manumission failures see the following *Memorias* of the Secretario del Interior y Justicia. *Memoria sobre los negocios correspondientes a los despachos del Interior y*

Justicia del gobierno de Venezuela, que presenta el encargado a ellos al Congreso constitucional del año 1831 (Valencia, 1831), pp. 81–85; *Exposición que dirige al Congreso de Venezuela en 1836 el secretario del Interior y Justicia* (Caracas: A. Damirón, [1836]), pp. 36–37; *Exposición que dirige al Congreso de Venezuela en 1837 el secretario del Interior y Justicia* (Caracas: A. Damirón, 1837), pp. 12–14; *Exposición que dirige al Congreso de Venezuela en 1838 el secretario del Interior y Justicia* (Caracas: A. Damirón, 1838), pp. 9–10; *Exposición que dirige al Congreso de Venezuela en 1839 el secretario del Interior y Justicia* (Caracas: A. Damirón, 1839), pp. 11–15; *Exposición que dirige al Congreso de Venezuela en 1840 el secretario del Interior y Justicia* (Caracas: George Corser, 1840), pp. 14–16; *Exposición que dirige al Congreso de Venezuela en 1841 el secretario de lo Interior y Justicia* (Caracas: Valentín Espinal, 1841), pp. 32–33; *Exposición que dirige al Congreso de Venezuela en 1845 el secretario de lo Interior y Justicia* ([Caracas]: Domingo Salazar, 1845), pp. 28–31; *Exposición que dirige al Congreso de Venezuela en 1846 el secretario de lo Interior y Justicia* (Caracas: Valentín Espinal, 1846), pp. 23–24; *Exposición. que dirije al Congreso de Venezuela en 1849 el secretario del Interior y Justicia* (Caracas: Fortunato Corvaïa, 1849), pp. 19–21; *Exposición que dirije al Congreso de Venezuela en 1850 el secretario del Interior y Justicia* (Caracas: Fortunato Corvaïa, 1850), pp. 18–20; *Exposición que dirige al Congreso de Venezuela en 1851 el secretario del Interior y Justicia* (Caracas: Diego Campbell, 1851), pp. 20–21; *Exposición que dirige al Congreso de Venezuela en 1852, el secretario del Interior y Justicia* (Caracas: Franco y Figueira, 1852), pp. 39–41; *Exposición que dirige al Congreso de Venezuela en 1853, el secretario del Interior y Justicia* (Caracas: Felix E. Bigotte, 1853), pp. 29–31; and *Exposición que dirige al Congreso de Venezuela en 1854 el secretario del Interior y Justicia* (Caracas: Imprenta Republicana de Eduardo Ortiz a cargo de Federico Madriz, 1854), pp. 54–56.

65. For the text of Bolívar's decree see *Decretos del Libertador*, II, 345–352.

66. For a good example of the impossible tax system see the records of Valencia's Junta de Manumisión for the years 1821–1827. AGN, Gran Col.–Int. de Ven., L, 336–362.

67. See art. x.

68. See art. viii.

69. The reasons for the failure of the 1821 Law, plus Bolívar's additional revisions, are clearly evident from the relevant sections of José Rafael Revenga's, *Hacienda pública*, p. 106 and passim.

70. For the text of the 1830 Manumission Law see *Colección completa*, pp. 1–6.

71. Although the tax structure of the 1830 Law was an improvement

on the 1821 Law, another section virtually negated the tax increase. Paragraph 3 of art. x, sec. 4, let the value of slaves freed by testament be used to cancel the manumission tax.

72. The text of the 1848 variation on the Manumission Law can be found in the *Gaceta de Venezuela*, No. 913, 7 May 1848.

73. Some of the most pungent and picturesque criticisms of the manumission system are in Joaquín Mosquera, *Memoria sobre la necesidad de reformar la ley del Congreso constituyente de Colombia, de 21 de julio, de 1821, que sanciona la libertad de los partos, manumisión, y abolición del tráfico de esclavos y bases que podrían adoptarse para la reforma* (Caracas: Tomás Antero, 1829); *Los propietarios de la provincia de Guayana a los propietarios y hombres imparciales del mundo* (Caracas: Tomás Antero, 1838); and *El Observador Caraqueño*, No. 4, 22 January 1824.

74. See *La Bandera Nacional*, No. 89, 9 April 1839; *Correo de Caracas*, No. 19, 14 May 1839; and *El Liberal*, No. 158, 7 May 1839, and No. 201, 3 March 1840.

75. See note 64 above.

76. For the text of this fascinating law see *Collección completa*, pp. 26–28.

77. The characteristically low level of marriages among Venezuelan slaves can be amply seen in the extraordinary series of *padrones* conserved in the *Archivo Arquidiocesano* of Caracas in the Sección Parroquias.

78. A useful summary of the labor sections of various representative police codes can be found in Fernando Ignacio Parra Aranguren, *Antecedentes del derecho del trabajo en Venezuela, 1830–1928* (Maracaibo: Universidad del Zulia, 1965), pp. 283–351.

79. See for example *El Eco Popular*, No. 5, 3 March 1840, and No. 6, 10 March 1840.

CHAPTER 3

The Manumission System

ALTHOUGH the reorganized Republican slave system of 1821 and 1830 was meant to end servile labor in Venezuela and provided various mechanisms to hasten its end, slaves soon discovered the weakness of the law's principal administrative arm. In theory, the Juntas de Manumisión—established in each canton and staffed by local residents—collected death dues, selected slaves to be freed, and paid the owners. Unfortunately, these poorly organized and impotent committees met infrequently, collected few taxes, and freed only a small number of slaves.[1]

The Department of the Interior, to be sure, had the last word on slave matters; yet by virtue of a predisposition towards local administration of local problems, the Congress of 1821, as well as those of 1830 and 1848, left the regulation of slavery in local hands. This, as it turned out, was an unfortunate decision, practically nullifying the Manumission Law. The intricate legal-administrative structure it established collapsed in the first years of implementation, but, strikingly enough, absolutely no serious effort made to improve the system succeeded, and the same localistic administrative plan survived a major revision of the law in 1830 and a reenactment in 1848.

SLAVE OWNERS AND GOVERNMENT

Before beginning this analysis of failure, it is well to have a clear idea of the various interests involved. No one after 1830 seriously attempted to justify slavery as either a positive or even a relative good. No one claimed Biblical authorization for slavery.[2] Liberty, acquired at such a high cost during the wars for independence, should not be stained by the evil institution of slavery. But Venezuela could not ignore the existence of some 40 thousand slaves,[3] nor could it abolish the odious institution without seriously affecting the sacred right of property, since the state could not pay for so many chattel. Slave owners, who had lost many slaves in the war, whose haciendas and *hatos* (stock raising establishments) were seriously damaged by marauding troops, and who could reconstruct their fortunes only with heavy debts and usurious interest rates, saw no reason to acquiesce in the confiscation of their remaining slave property.[4] But, as we have seen, political and military necessity irrevocably implanted the principle of manumission on the nation, and so the slave owners' only recourse was to the tactics of delay and obstruction to reduce the impact of the manumission law.

The government and the party in power worked for self-perpetuation. While sincerely concerned with the economic health of slave owners, they worried much more about the possibility of slave violence. Not that they expected a spontaneous uprising of the oppressed black man; rather they feared the political potential of adequately led rebellions promising black freedom. To keep the peace, all governments from 1821 to 1854 advocated the policy of gradual but effective manumission of slaves.[5]

This conflict of interest was quite clearly demonstrated in the actions of the two groups throughout this era. Regardless of party affiliation, each government's efforts on behalf of manumission appeared practically identical. Each Secretary of the Interior sent directive after directive to local officials and

Juntas de Manumisión in the futile effort to make the gradual abolition of Negro slavery a reality. Year after year they pleaded with the Congress for money to free slaves, for laws to make manumission more effective, or for clarification of confusing sections of the old law. It made no difference whether the government was Liberal or Conservative, although the imminence of revolution seemed to spur all governments to greater efforts on behalf of slaves. On the other side, slave owners in or out of government had no intention of sacrificing their property interests for stability of government. With admirable consistency they resisted every effort to organize an efficient manumission program. Moreover, they fought all interpretations or decisions of local Juntas that threatened to take their slaves. This division of forces in the struggle over manumission prevailed right up to the passage of the Abolition Law in 1854.

As the conflict evolved, it became evident that both sides tacitly accepted a set of rules governing their dispute. Both agreed that the manumission system established in 1821 and revised in 1830 would form the ground rules. The government issued no decrees fundamentally changing the manumission system, and the slave holders paid what taxes they could not avoid. But property owners felt free to obstruct or influence the Juntas, avoid or delay paying death dues, appeal every decision in slave matters, and complicate manumission through prolonged litigation. The government, on the other hand, had the power to decide on petitions against Junta decisions, order Juntas to operate, veto modifications of the law, and influence the Juntas. Any attempt by one side or the other to change the rules met defeat until conditions had changed sufficiently to permit abolition in 1854. The slave, as the object of the controversy, had little or no influence on the operation of manumission. Equally ineffectual, public opinion (the little that existed) alternated between pious denunciations of slavery and ringing defenses of private property.

The only apparent exception to this situation involved the provinces of Guayana and Apure. During the wars for independence Bolívar had declared all slaves in Guayana and Apure free, whether or not they took up arms in favor of the cause of independence. That is, he abolished slavery in these provinces.[6] Naturally, most slave owners refused to accept Bolívar's fiat at face value and continued to believe their Negroes slaves.[7] Nonetheless, once separated from the Colombian Confederation, Venezuelan authorities tried to enforce the Bolivarian abolition decrees. In this effort they had to fight most of Guayana from the governor on down.[8]

The whole affair began when an ex-slave was reenslaved by order of a Guayana court. Naturally, she appealed the decision to the Department of the Interior, which supported her contention and ordered Guayana courts to protect her in the exercise of her rights.[9]

In spite of this initial defeat, guayanés officials stuck to their guns, claiming that Bolívar's decree was illegal, unconstitutional, and in any case had been rescinded by the laws of manumission passed in 1821 and 1830.[10] However, after a number of exchanges along these lines the Department of the Interior had its way, and Guayana and Apure slave owners found themselves pretty much without slaves.[11]

But why did the government take such pains to defend Guayana's blacks? Clearly, it was a matter of public order. Most of Guayana's supposed slave population had, in effect, been free since about 1817. Had the guayanés slave owners' pretention prevailed, all the free blacks would have had to be reenslaved via judicial cases and armed police methods. There did not seem to be the remotest possiblity of carrying out this operation peacefully. Conscious of the unstable conditions in Venezuela during these early years of the Páez regime, the government had no desire to allow a slave or ex-slave rebellion to disturb the peace. While recognizing the justice of Guayana's claims, they could not permit reenslaving without seriously endangering internal security.[12]

Although apparently an exception to the tacit slave owner–government agreement, the decision to keep Guayana free actually is consistent with official slave policy. As explained above, the guiding principle in all slave matters was slow and gradual change of the status quo. For the government to authorize reenslaving would have caused a radical and instantaneous change in the status quo prevailing in Guayana. The only recourse for the guayaneses was to try to get paid for their confiscated property.

But not only Guayana was involved. If guayanés slave owners were allowed to reenslave black freemen liberated by the wars for independence, there is little doubt slave owners of Caracas and other provinces would have followed suit, since some slaves were inducted into the armies in practically all the provinces. Needless to say, it is unlikely the freemen would have submitted to servitude without a fight.

In light of this conflict between slave owners and government, it is easy to see the importance of the Junta de Manumisión. Given the rules of the game—the government could not contemplate expropriation without previous payment and the slave owners could not contemplate a complete return to colonial slavery—the action had to be played out within the framework of the manumission system. Although the slave owners staged a number of major campaigns to revise the whole program of manumission, none succeeded, and the battle degenerated into a long series of guerrilla actions centering around the administration, interpretation, and evasion of the Manumission Law. The Junta de Manumisión provided the battlefield. Due primarily to its local nature, the slave owners managed to intimidate the majority of Juntas. The government found it extremely difficult to have its decisions enforced by the Juntas over the enormous pressure and resources of local citizens.[13] The best perspective, then, on this test of wills is from the Junta de Manumisión, its operation and its failure.

THE JUNTA

In the minds of Colombian legislators meeting in Cúcuta in 1821, the Junta de Manumisión was to be all things to all men. Although in theory slavery was as good as abolished, an impressive number of black Venezuelans would remain slaves until the beneficent effects of the philanthropic manumission law could take effect. The Junta, devised as a temporary local institution charged with the pleasant task of overseeing the liquidation of slavery in Venezuela, not only administered the apparatus of manumission but also regulated and controlled the moribund slave system.[14]

One of the peculiarities of the Venezuelan manumission system was the way the Junta was formed. Since its duties were difficult and at times disagreeable, the only way to fill the membership was by appointment. The governor of a province appointed the members of the local Juntas under both the 1821 and the 1830–1848 laws. Since members received no pay for the many services they performed in the Junta, the legislators provided that the first civil magistrate of each canton, along with the highest ranking local priest, would always form the nucleus of the group, which could be filled out by a couple of respectable citizens and a responsible treasurer.[15]

Juntas, however, had some difficulty getting together. Not only did the respectable citizens seem unwilling or reluctant to take up their duties, but also they had the disagreeable habit of leaving town before meetings or forgetting about them altogether.[16] But even with all the members present, nothing happened without the secretary-treasurer. The meeting could not be officially recorded without him and, more important—since the main business of the meeting was the collection and disbursement of funds—nothing could be accomplished without the presence of the man responsible for all the money. With no reward for attendance at the meetings nor penalty for absenteeism, discipline was impossible.[17]

Nor was impartiality assured by the Junta's composition. By and large the most respectable citizens turned out to be the richest, and the richest citizens turned out to own many slaves. Furthermore, the presence of a Church representative hardly guaranteed impartiality, since the extinction of slavery was bound to hurt the labor force on the various *obras pías* sublet or administered by the Church, not to mention the large amounts put out in *censos píos* with slaves as collateral.[18]

As if these obstacles to the proper functioning of the manumission system were not enough, there was the paperwork controversy over who would pay for paper, pens, ink, copies of laws, and the like. It would certainly be asking too much to expect the unpaid secretary-treasurer to supply his own materials. But by law, the money collected for the purpose of manumission could not be used for anything else. Quite obviously the Juntas could not function correctly, let alone efficiently, until this problem was settled. After much confusion and delay, the Department of the Interior decided that these costs would be borne by the office of the presiding officer.[19]

Two other officials directly concerned with manumission were the *comisionado* and the *síndico municipal*. The first official was appointed by the local Junta to keep track of the dead and dying whose estates would have to pay taxes to the manumission fund. The job was probably not very taxing, since only a small number of people with estates died in any parish in one year. Judging by the lack of complaints about comisionados, they probably performed their small task well.[20] The síndico municipal, on the other hand, had no official connection with the Junta except as the legal defender of slaves. The efficiency and dedication of the síndico depended almost entirely on his independence from the local slave owners. Evidently, few independent síndicos denounced abuses and fixed responsibility. This became increasingly evident after 1840 when the apprenticeship system went into effect. Supposedly, the síndico represented the manumiso being contracted and saw that the price and conditions were fair. Yet, of all the abuses of the manumission and apprenticeship systems denounced to the government, very few came from zealous síndicos.[21]

Throughout the long, dreary history of the Juntas de Manumisión, hundreds of problems arose about the application of the law. Few local Juntas had the courage, inclination, or audacity to decide any of these questions. And so, whether it had to do with how to tax property left to a man's *soul* (which was done on at least one occasion) or how to determine the age of a slave whose birth certificate had been lost, any and all questions went from the local Junta first to the Junta Superior and from there to the Department of the Interior. Indicative of the poor coordination of the system and the tenacity of the slave owners, the same *consultas* were made time and again, although the first decision of the Department of the Interior had been publicized in the *Gaceta de Venezuela*.[22] This constant questioning and answering obviously represented another tactic of delay fully exploited by slave owners. No progress in the gradual abolition of slavery was possible until questions concerning manumission and apprenticeship could be settled, and since the questions were so numerous and sometimes so detailed, very little progress occurred.

These men and institutions, then, had the awesome task of eliminating slavery from Venezuela. While many of the reasons for their failure stem from the organization of the system described above, other reasons can be found in the inadequacy of the instruments provided by law.

THE TAXES

The weakest part of the entire manumission program was the tax system. Even if those taxes assigned by law had been collected assiduously and promptly, they probably would only have begun to free Venezuela's slaves.[23] But collecting taxes proved to be one of the Junta's least efficient operations.

From 1830 to 1854 only some nine hundred slaves received their freedom through the manumission fund, an average of twenty-five slaves a year.[24] Although this number fulfilled the letter of the law, few public functionaries thought the system operated as designed.[25] Nonetheless, as noted above, no one was able to change the system.

Thanks to the poorly constructed collection procedures used

by the Juntas, many debtors managed to avoid the tax entirely or else defer payment almost indefinitely. The stratagems were many and reasonably effective.

The most useful dodge employed by debtors was plain ordinary delay. The first tactic, almost always, was failure to show up when cited by the Juntas to pay or explain lack of payment. This, of course, resulted in only a temporary delay, but some stubborn individuals managed to stretch this out over ten or fifteen years. After all, much could happen in that period to eliminate any need to pay.[26]

Once compelled by the threat of court action to appear, slave owners found unfortunate conditions that prevented payment of the tax. Perhaps the estate was in litigation, in which case no payment was possible until the legal problems were straightened out.[27] Or it could happen that the inheritance took the form of houses leased to third parties, in which case payment of the tax would have to wait until the lease lapsed and the houses could be sold.[28] Some people contended that the inherited hacienda had changed value since the Junta assessed the tax and should therefore be reevaluated, thus postponing payment some time longer.[29]

More philanthropic debtors to the manumission fund proposed paying their tax by manumitting enough slaves to take care of the amount. Although the effect of this procedure was much the same as if the Junta had collected the money, it had the advantage of letting the hacendado choose the slaves he wanted freed.[30] Although there is no direct evidence, one suspects many hacendados freed old or injured slaves they would have had trouble selling, while receiving a tax credit plus a citation for philanthropy.[31]

Of course, it is not fair to blame the failure of the manumission system entirely on the unpaid and overburdened Juntas. After all, they had almost no coercive power and, in any case, after 1840, were so busy with the apprenticeship program they had time for little else. These problems, together with the infrequent meetings of the Juntas, lead one to marvel that they managed to free the minimal two or three slaves in each province every year.[32]

THE SLAVES

With the infinitesimal sums collected the Juntas had to free some slaves. The selection of the favored few caused no serious problems. The 1821 Law provided only for the selection of the most honorable and industrious slaves,[33] a situation not much to the liking of the slave owners since the most industrious and honorable slaves were also the best workers. But this criterion lasted only until 1827, when Bolívar decreed a new and more detailed standard for selection. First preference went to the slaves from the estate paying the tax, the oldest first. Second came the most industrious and honorable slaves in the canton, the oldest first. If, by chance, all the slaves in one province were freed before the money ran out, the excess funds would go to the *Dirección de Manumisión* for disbursement to other provinces.[34]

This revision of standards probably took some of the sting out of the strict tax payment rules included in Bolívar's decree.[35] But when the Venezuelan reaction of 1830 came, the tax enforcement was dropped while the selection standards remained.[36] Venezuelan slave owners got the best of both laws.

It is not clear exactly how the local Juntas went about choosing the privileged few slaves freed by the manumission funds. Many times the tiny sums available reduced the possibility to almost nothing. And so the Juntas gladly freed old slaves or those whose masters were willing to take less than the standard price.[37] A number of slaves petitioned the Junta to be considered in the annual manumission, but the Juntas never took them into consideration.[38]

Another problem, posed by slaves over sixty-three years old, required considerable consultation. Since the oldest slave on the tariff was sixty-three years old and worth 5 pesos, the Juntas wondered if they could free all slaves over sixty-three without paying anything. Or, perhaps, since a slave's value was nil after sixty-three years, all such people were automatically free. The government, with visions of ancient and indigent ex-slaves wandering around with no skills and no place to go, decided that no slave over sixty-three could be freed against his will and that no slave could be freed without paying at least 5 pesos no matter how old. They also promised to ask Congress for a new law on the subject.[39]

By and large, the selection process did not cause the litigation and delay involved in tax collection. Still, a few slave owners complained that the Junta did not pay enough for their confiscated property.[40]

The pressure of the tax and the threat of slave expropriation drove many slave owners to take advantage of paragraph 3, article ten of the 1830–1848 Law.[41] In their wills they freed some slaves and with their value cancelled the tax due the manumission fund. Although the records are by no means complete, perhaps some two hundred slaves were freed by this means.[42]

Since only nine hundred slaves, more or less, ever received their freedom by virtue of the selection and payment mechanism administered by the Junta de Manumisión, it is hardly worthwhile to try to track down each problem presented the Junta.[43] Nevertheless, it is well to keep in mind that the Junta did just what had been planned. It freed old slaves, it provided a very small escape valve, and it proved to the world by its very existence that Venezuela was indeed a philanthropic, liberal-minded republic.[44]

After the passage of Páez's Apprenticeship Decree of 1840, the Junta de Manumisión took on a new role and function. Although the same problem of personnel and expenses plagued the Junta, its efforts on behalf of the eighteen- or twenty-one-year-old free-slave belied the inefficiency of its manumission procedures. Statistics on *aprendizaje* are good and regularly compiled. The reason for this increased efficiency is not difficult to divine. The manumission system failed because of the conflict between slave-owner interests and government interests; the aprendizaje scheme achieved considerable success precisely because these two groups had much the same interests. Both wanted the freeborn slave child to fit into the existing social structure as a docile and industrious worker. Both wanted to see him in fixed employment. What conflict existed generally arose over the greater or lesser extent to which these principles should be carried out in practice.

NOTES

1. From the very beginning of the manumission system some farsighted individuals saw that the law would never succeed. See Mosquera, *Memoria*, pp. 22–24.

2. The last impassioned defense of slavery occurred in 1824 in a long article in *El Observador Caraqueño*, No. 4, 22 January 1824.

3. According to the statistics available, there were about 40,000 slaves in Venezuela. The distribution by provinces and the sources of these figures are in Appendix 1, Table 7 of this work. See also Revenga, *Hacienda pública*, p. 106.

4. The article in *El Observador Caraqueño*, No. 4, 22 January 1824, cited above, gives a very good indication of the Venezuelan farmers' reaction to manumission and abolition. The relationship between slavery and agriculture, as well as between slavery and finance, are studied in another section of this book.

5. Perhaps the best guide to Venezuelan government views on manumission and slavery is the collection of *Memorias* of the Department of the Interior listed in the bibliography. The question of Negro slaves' revolutionary potential is discussed later on in this study.

6. It is well to keep in mind that the Venezuelan government of the 1830s had a rather poor collection of decrees by Bolívar. To support their point of view on Guayana and Apure they mentioned only the decree issued on Margarita, 23 May 1816, *Gaceta de Venezuela*, No. 221, 4 April 1835. In fact there was a whole spate of Bolivarian decrees abolishing slavery in parts or in all of the territory of Venezuela. See for example *Decretos del Libertador*, I, 55–56 (Carúpano, 2 June 1816), and *Las fuerzas armadas*, II, 169 (Ocumare, 6 July 1816).

7. When a padrón of slaves was taken in Guayana in 1832–1833, the freed slaves were all listed as still belonging to their old masters. Many of

them were identified as runaways. For the *expediente* of slave lists from Guayana see AGN, Int. y Just., XLVI (1832), 244–261. There were some four hundred to five hundred slaves in these padrones, at least half listed as runaways.

8. The brunt of the fight was borne almost exclusively by Guayana. This is most likely due to the greater number of slaves in Guayana than in Apure. Evidently Apure claimed between one hundred and two hundred slaves in 1834. AGN, Int. y Just., XC (1834), 370; Agustín Codazzi, *Resumen de la geografía*, I, 245; and AGN, Int. y Just., CCXCI (1843), 121–127.

9. AGN, Int. y Just., LXVI (1833), 190–213, has the original expediente on reenslaving. This problem, however, dates from before 1830. Evidently José Antonio Páez had to make it clear to the slave owners of Guayana and Apure that their slaves had been freed by Bolívar, for on 15 March 1828 he issued a decree exempting all slaves freed in Guayana and Apure from his Fugitive Slave Decree (3 September 1828). A second decree confirmed the freedom of Guayana slaves on 6 May 1829. AGN, Int. y Just., CV (1835), 235. See also the *oficios* of Interior y Justicia to Guayana in *Gaceta de Venezuela*, No. 70, 9 May 1832.

10. See the oficio from the Secretario del Interior y Justicia of 28 March 1832 in *Gaceta de Venezuela*, No. 70, 9 May 1832. For a full exposition of Guayana's position see the pamphlet published by the governor of Guayana, *Los propietarios de la provincia de Guayana;* and AGN, Int. y Just., CXXXI (1836), 180–183.

11. By 1840 the Secretaría del Interior y Justicia had ceased mentioning the problem, and evidently the matter was ended. See also the oficio sent to the governor of Guayana in *Gaceta de Venezuela*, No. 359, 10 December 1837. Although the government won this test of wills, Guayana's case was considerably more logical, albeit less wise. It claimed Bolívar had freed all the slaves in Venezuela, so why pick on Guayana to enforce the law? *Los propietarios de la provincia de Guayana,* and AGN, Int. y Just., CV (1835), 194–248. This was quite true; see Bolívar's oficio of 16 June 1818 to the Alta Corte de Justicia, *Cartas del Libertador*, II, 43–44, where he makes the amazing statement "Nadie ignora en Venezuela que la esclavitud está extinguida entre nosostros."

12. See Int. y Just., 1836, *Memoria*, pp. 36–37; 1837, *Memoria*, pp. 12–14; and especially 1838, *Memoria*, pp. 9–10. The Secretaría felt the 1830 law was unjust because it gave owners whose slaves were freed after 1830 first claim on money collected, while those whose slaves were freed before 1821 had to await the treasury. After all, "loable es la intención de libertar al esclavo, pero es sagrado el deber de pagarle al dueño. . . ."

13. Perhaps the best example of Juntas coinciding with slave owners against the government occurred in Ocumare de la Costa over the inter-

pretation of the Aprendizaje Decree. *AGN*, Int. y Just., CCLVI (1842), 7–34. Then there was the case in Guayana, where the manumission fund had a considerable sum of money but no slaves were freed at all. *Gaceta de Venezuela*, No. 875, 22 August 1847.

14. See *Materiales para*, I, 289–291 (Ley de 19 de julio de 1821), especially arts. ix, x, xi, and xii. The Venezuelan congresses of 1830 and 1848 kept much the same Junta system. See *Colección completa*, pp. 1–6 (Ley de 2 de octubre sobre manumisión), arts. xv, xvi, and xvii; and *Gaceta de Venezuela*, No. 913, 7 May 1848 (Ley de 28 de abril de 1848), arts. xv, xvi, and xvii.

15. See note 14 above.

16. See, for example, *Colección completa*, p. 54 (Resolution of 25 September 1844). Not only was absenteeism a problem, but the Juntas were hard to form in the first place. Int. y Just., 1839, *Memoria*, pp. 11–15. A report of failure to hold meetings can be seen in *El Republicano*, No. 6, 27 June 1844.

17. Unfortunately, almost none of the records of the Juntas de Manumisión between 1830 and 1854 have reached the national archives, most probably because they were considered municipal or at best provincial documents. Nonetheless, a good number of records for the 1821–1827 period are available. Since the 1821–1827 manumission program operated about as badly and with much the same problems as the 1830–1854 program, it is safe to draw certain conclusions about the later period from the manumission records of the former. Furthermore, the problems resolved by the Department of the Interior relating to secretary-treasurer difficulties bear out this assumption. For some examples of the 1821–1827 Junta records see the following expedientes in AGN, Gran Col.–Int. de Ven., L, 336–362 (Valencia, 1821–1827); XCII, 237–240 (Obispos, 1822–1826): LXXIX, 181–206 (Nutrias, 1822–1827); LVI, 334–345 (Guanare, 1822–1827); CXCV, 74–107 (Caracas, 1824–1827); and CLXV, 516–525 (Aragua, 1824–1827). See also Int. y Just., 1831, *Memoria*, pp. 81–85; 1834, *Memoria que presenta el secretario del Interior de los negocios de su departamento al Congreso de 1834* (Caracas: Damirón y Dupuy, [1834]), pp. 37–38; 1839, *Memoria*, pp. 11–15; *Colección completa*, pp. 29–30 (Resolution of 28 April 1840); Int. y Just., 1841, *Memoria*, pp. 32–33; *Colección completa*, p. 54 (Resolution of 25 September 1844).

18. See Antonio Leocadio Guzmán's demogogic denunciation of property interests controlling the Juntas de Manumisión in Int. y Just., 1849, *Memoria*, pp. 19–21. The Church's interest in slavery is hard to document specifically without recourse to the extensive section in the *Archivo Arquidiocesano de Caracas* relating to obras pías and censos. Nevertheless, a good indication of religion's slave-holding can be seen in the debates over

the reduction of censos which occurred soon after abolition in 1854. *Diario de Debates*, Senado, No. 66, 2 May 1855; No. 67, 3 May 1855; No. 68, 3 May 1855; No. 69, 4 May 1855.

19. See the *Memorias* and resolutions cited in note 17 above.

20. In any case, the Juntas were hard pressed to collect taxes on those estates reported by the comisionados. For the duties of the comisionado see the manumission laws of 1821, 1830, and 1848 cited in note 14 above.

21. Antonio Leocadio Guzmán's *Memoria* (Int. y Just., 1849, pp. 19–21) accuses the majority of síndicos of being property owners and often slave holders. Although there is little evidence to prove the síndicos were crusaders for slave and manumiso rights, there are indications that some of them did help slaves. See, for example, AGN, Int. y Just., LXIV (1833), 193–197. Some people, however, felt the síndicos could be doing better. See, for example, *Informe de la comisión de mejoras dirigido a la honorable Diputación de Caracas en su décima nova reunión* (Caracas: Imprenta de "El Patriota" por Andrés A. Figueira, 1849), pp. 15–16. Then there is the extraordinary case of the síndico who defended a slave-servant's right to change masters because she, as a good Catholic, felt she could not possibly live in the same house as her master, a Jew. The síndico felt proud of his defense of religious freedom and denounced those who charged him with anti-Semitism. After all, he pointed out, some of his best friends were Jews. *El Liberal*, No. 125, 3 May 1838.

22. This is best seen in the collection of resolutions published in 1846, *Colección completa*.

23. The impossibility of the manumission tax ever amounting to enough to eliminate slavery from Venezuela before death did the job is evident from the debates over the abolition law of 1854, when a much more productive tax schedule was established over the protests of those who felt even this was inadequate for the job. See *Diario de Debates*, Nos. 7, 8, 10, 17, and 22, 4 March 1854 to 16 March 1854.

24. See Appendix 1, Table 1 for a list of slaves freed.

25. The official charged with manumission in the Department of the Interior was more sanguine than most public officials when he reported that, as of 1843, the manumission law had been complied with satisfactorily, since a little more than twenty slaves had been freed each year. AGN, Int. y Just., CCXCI (1843), 122–127. However, most other officials thought differently. See, for example, AGN, Int. y Just., CCXCI (1843), 119–121 (Observaciones del gobernador de Cumaná sobre la ley de manumisión); CLXXX (1838), 101–112 (Memoria del gobernador de Apure a la Diputación Provincial); CLXXX (1838), 84–92 (Memoria del gobernador de Margarita); CXCV (1839), 51 (Memoria del gobernador de Barcelona); and the *Memorias* of Interior y Justicia cited in the Bibliography.

26. Perhaps the best collection of information on delinquent debtors is the expedientes formed about the funds owed since 1828. Some of the cases ran from 1828 to 1847 before they were settled. AGN, Int. y Just., XLIX (1832), 266–279 (Fondos de Manumisión, Barcelona); 284–295 (Fondos de Manumisión, Trujillo); 307–323 (Fondos de Manumisión, Guayana); 324–326 (Fondos de Manumisión, Cumaná); AGN, Int. y Just., LI (1832), 249–265 (Fondos de Manumisión, Coro); LXXXVIII (1834), 391–397 (Fondos de Manumisión, Margarita); LXXXVIII (1834), 406–506 (12 expedientes about unpaid taxes, 1828–1847); CLXI (1837), 324–333 (expediente on the Castro estate). In this last case Castro's heir, a priest named Giménez, was more astute than most tax evaders. After avoiding payment for a number of years Giménez died, leaving a will declaring he had no worldly goods. By this stratagem his heirs could not be required to pay the manumission tax. One wonders how many more people were farsighted enough to give their property away before death.

27. *Al Público* (Caracas: George Corser, 1845). This *hoja suelta* justified a delay in paying the manumission tax on the Chávez estate. One man left his soul some money. When asked by the Junta how such an inheritance should be taxed, the Department of the Interior responded that the practice was probably illegal, but the estate should be charged 10 percent as in "Legatarios estraños." *Colección completa*, p. 30 (Resolution of 15 July 1840).

28. AGN, Gran Col.–Int. de Ven., CXCIX (1824), 332 (*La Guaira*).

29. AGN, Int. y Just., LXV (1833), 403–424.

30. AGN, Gran. Col.–Int. de Ven., CXXIII (1822), 246 (Caracas). AGN, Int. y Just., CCCLIV (1847), 28–34. The government, however, warned that such slaves should be of "*edad provecta*," *Colección completa*, p. 59 (Resolution of 5 March 1845). See also the series of expedientes on *Fondos de Manumisión* cited in note 26 above.

31. The settlement of the estates of Monsón and of Machado in 1848 showed a list of slaves freed in payment of the tax. Of the fourteen slaves liberated, ten were either over sixty years old or suffered from some injury or disease that made them worth less than the legal price. *Gaceta de Venezuela*, No. 947, 11 February 1849. For the legal tariff of slaves see Appendix 1, Table 5.

32. See the manumission statistics in Appendix 1, Table 1.

33. *Materiales para*, I, 289–291 (Ley de 19 de julio de 1821).

34. *Decretos del Libertador*, II, 345–352, arts. viii and ix.

35. *Decretos del Libertador*, II, 345–352, arts. i, ii, iii, iv, v, and vii.

36. *Colección completa*, pp. 1–6 (Ley de 2 de octubre de 1830). The tax system is in art. x and the selection criteria are in art. xx.

37. See the *Acuerdos* of the Junta de Manumisión of Guanare (1822–

1827), AGN, Gran Col.–Int. de Ven., LVI, 334–345; and those of Nutrias (1822–1827), LXXIX, 181–206, for some examples of this sort of transaction. An even clearer indication of the ages of slaves freed under the manumission system can be seen in some of the reports from cantons and provinces listing freemen, their ages, and their values. Although by no means complete, these records show very clearly that the slaves freed by manumission probably were around fifty years old or had some infirmity that made them worth as much as a fifty-year-old slave. Some of these lists can be seen in Gaceta de Venezuela, No. 438, 9 June 1839; No. 546, 27 June 1841; No. 552, 9 August 1841; and No. 916, 28 May 1848. For a complete list of manumissions see Appendix 1, Table 1.

38. For examples of the petitions submitted see AGN, Gran Col.–Int. de Ven., CXCIX (1824), 52; and AGN, Int. y Just., CDXI (1849), 258–259.

39. This touchy problem caused the government no end of headaches. The expediente on this subject began in 1838 and was not finally resolved until 1844. The Department of the Interior forbade freeing old slaves without providing them with maintenance and denied that any slave could ever be automatically free whatever his age. Int. y Just., 1844, Exposición que dirige al Congreso de Venezuela en 1844 el secretario de lo Interior y Justicia (Caracas: Valentín Espinal, 1844), p. 60. The final resolution is in Int. y Just., 1845, Memoria, pp. 77–78, with the suggestion that the old slaves be persuaded to stay slaves. For the original expediente which contains the advice of the Consejo de Gobierno see AGN, Int. y Just., CLXXI (1838), 260–276.

40. See the complaint of Pablo A. Pichardo (31 March 1846) in Colección completa, p. 62–64. The government reaffirmed the validity of Bolívar's tariff and recommended Pichardo go to court if he did not like it.

41. Colección completa, pp. 1–6 (Ley de 2 de octubre de 1830), art. x. Gaceta de Venezuela, No. 913, 7 May 1848 (Ley de 28 de abril de 1848), art. x.

42. Unfortunately, there are no records of ages or values of slaves freed under this clause, so no estimation of average ages can be made. The few individual cases for which information of this sort does exist are not representative enough for a solid generalization. For an estimate of the number of slaves freed under paragraph 3 of article x see Appendix I, Table 2. Evidently, the Department of the Interior doubted the philanthropy of some heirs, for it required the Junta to either see the freed slaves in person or else to obtain legal certification of the slave's actual freedom before allowing the heirs a tax credit. Colección completa, p. 9 (Resolution, 11 April 1834); and Gaceta de Venezuela, No. 234, 4 July 1835. One heir wanted to count the price of manumisos freed in a will, but this

was denied with the obvious comment that manumisos were born free and could not be freed in a will. Int. y Just., 1854, *Memoria*, pp. 87–88.

43. Although the statistics on manumission are a bit contradictory and apparently incomplete, the 900 figure for freed slaves would seem reasonably close. It must be remembered that the publication of manumission figures could only redound to the greater glory of the provincial or cantonal official who sent them in. For the chart of those freed see Appendix I, Table 1.

44. The self-congratulatory smugness of some Venezuelans where slavery was concerned can be seen in *El Observador Caraqueño*, No. 4, 22 January 1824, and *Correo de Caracas*, No. 7, 20 February 1839. See also the report in PRO, FO 84/481, 207–216 (B. H. Wilson, Caracas, 4 August 1843). The *Memoria* of Interior y Justicia for 1850 (pp. 18–20) leaves no doubt about the escape-valve function of manumission.

CHAPTER 4

Manumisos
and Aprendizaje

ALTHOUGH the effects of the 1821 Manumission Law on the existing institution of slavery could be delayed and minimized, such was not the case with the free-birth provision of the law.[1] The child of a slave mother entered the world free; well, almost free.

MANUMISOS

According to the 1821 Law of Manumission, the slave child, although born free, could not exercise any part of his freedom until he reached eighteen years of age.[2] The reactionary Congress of 1830 extended the period to twenty-one years in the interests of good morality.[3] So that no one could possibly mistake the freeborn slave child for a free man, a new term was invented to classify this semiservile group; they were to be known as manumisos. During the eighteen or twenty-one years a manumiso served his mother's master, he toiled to pay back the costs of his upbringing. After all, reasoned the legislators, they could hardly deprive slave owners of their property rights over slave children and then expect them to raise and educate the children free of charge. The theory, of course, envisioned solicitous slave owners paying special attention to the education of manumisos to prepare them for the arduous responsibilities of citizenship.[4]

In spite of the legalisms and terminological distinctions, manumisos lived much the same as slaves. The main difference was that the manumiso's term as a slave ended legally at age eighteen or twenty-one. Otherwise, the slave and manumiso suffered the same fate. Although technically a manumiso could not be sold (he was a free man!), his services could be sold. This rather fine distinction fooled no one, and interested parties, from the government on down, bought and sold manumisos as they did slaves.[5] Of course, a manumiso—or his services, if you will—brought considerably less than the services of a slave. In fact, the official tariff stipulated that a manumiso was worth half a slave of the same age.[6]

As with slaves, manumisos fled their masters and had to be hunted down and returned.[7] Not that a manumiso had no hope of escaping servitude before reaching legal age: the legislators, in their overriding concern for morality and the family, provided that a manumiso's legitimate and free ascendants or elder brothers and sisters could take him out of servitude, providing they paid the master.[8] This undoubtedly affected few manumisos, for the incidence of legitimate births was extremely low among slaves. Furthermore, the *liberto*, or freed slave, with both the legitimacy requirement and the requisite sum to free his enslaved relations must have been rather rare.[9] Nevertheless, the few parents who tried this procedure ran into stiff opposition. Some masters claimed the parents led such immoral lives that the manumiso was sure to lose the high moral character instilled by his benevolent owner should he be given over. But alas, morality lost out to the law, and the Department of the Interior recommended that the police see to the morality of both child and parents after the manumiso joined his family.[10]

By and large, however, the situation of the manumiso posed few problems. He lived and worked as a slave. The only difficulty lay in the provisions for his freedom at eighteen or twenty-one. In the early years of Gran Colombia and the Venezuelan republic, few slave masters worried much about the fate of their manumisos who attained the legal age, but with the approach of 1839, when the first crop of freeborn slave children would acquire their rights, there was considerable concern. With one voice the owners of manumisos warned of the consequences that would befall Venezuela when the manumisos left the control of their patrons. These eighteen-year-old children would throw off the mantle of good customs and industriousness in which the master had clothed them at no small effort and expense. Grave social changes would result and Venezuelans would regret their leaders' lack of foresight.[11] Such a well-founded plea did not go unheeded in the councils of government, and the Páez administration soon issued the extraordinary Apprenticeship Decree of 1840.

APRENDIZAJE

Rather than allow manumisos of eighteen or twenty-one to lead their own lives and find their own jobs, the government thought it wise to keep them under surveillance for a while longer. Since lengthening the period of service owed the master was out of the question and prohibited by law, the administration hit on the ingenious idea of changing the manumiso's legal status while leaving his actual condition much the same. So it decreed that when a manumiso finished paying his master for the cost of his upbringing he be obligated to remain in tutelage until his twenty-fifth birthday.[12]

Since at eighteen or twenty-one the manumiso, no longer a semislave, got the full exercise of his freedom, the decree instructed the Junta de Manumisión to allow the newly freed to choose their own masters for the remaining years of servitude. Yet, to avoid unnecessary changes and to guarantee the preservation of good character traits, the manumiso should be encouraged to choose his old master.[13] The extended period of enforced servitude carried the euphemistic designation of apprenticeship, although the number of manumisos actually assigned to learn a trade was few.[14] Since *master* connoted slavery, the masters of apprenticed manumisos were called *patrons*. Venezuelan authorities took a good deal of comfort from the thought that the system of apprenticeship provided the poor benighted manumiso with a benevolent father-substitute who would see to his welfare and his much talked-about morality. Morality, of course, rarely took hold without adequate means of coercion, so the authorities recommended the patrons exercise the duty of correcting their young charges as a father would correct his children.[15]

Although the manumiso's change in status from an unpaid forced laborer to a paid forced laborer may seem relatively unimportant, the aprendizaje system proved rather difficult to operate. Even though run considerably better than the related manumission system, aprendizaje met with resistance and evasion by owners of manumiso service and by the manumisos themselves. Before tracing this chronicle of deviousness, a detailed knowledge of the mechanisms of apprenticeship is necessary.

For the apprenticeship of manumisos to take place, accurate birth records had to be available. To this end parish priests sent a register of all manumisos to the local Juntas. From these registers the Junta could tell which manumisos had reached the legal ages of eighteen or twenty-one and should, therefore, be put out in contract. Once the Junta discovered which manumisos should be contracted, they told the proper owners to present them to the Junta with a report of conduct.[16]

With the formality of presentation over, the manumiso was contracted to his former owner if possible. If not, the manumiso could find another patron of means to contract his services. Sometimes a manumiso would have free and legitimate ascendants, in which case he was turned over to them, thus avoiding the onerous apprenticeship.[17]

To prevent frauds and coercion, all contracts involving manumisos were made in the presence of the Junta, which had the responsibility of seeing that they conformed to local standards. The purpose of this provision was to avoid conflicts and disagreements about contracts. The manumiso, in this as in all similar transactions, was not considered capable of representing himself but was spoken for by the síndico municipal.[18]

In case any doubt remained about the nature of the contract, article nine of the 1840 Decree explained that any manumiso leaving the services of his patron would be returned by the police: objections to police authority would be handled through regular channels; nor could a manumiso hope to be quit of his patron before his twenty-fifth year, since the law commanded the Juntas to relocate any manumiso whose contract lapsed; nor could anyone accept the services of an underage manumiso outside the apprenticeship system.[19]

PROBLEMS OF ADMINISTRATION

Such, then, are the outlines of Venezuela's system for the moralization of the manumiso population. Obviously designed to keep freeborn children of slaves in servitude a few more years, it worked rather well. Nonetheless, since the possibility always existed of a manumiso finding his way out of the control of his original master, clever hacendados devised numerous ways of either circumventing the law altogether or at least of making it work more to their advantage.

Needless to say, failure of presentation appeared to many manumiso owners the easiest way of avoiding the law. After all, the Juntas, as we have seen, met irregularly and their means of compulsion were weak. Furthermore, manumisos rarely knew their rights or how to claim them. The evidence strongly suggests that the masters of manumisos delayed presenting their charges until the last possible moment. Many manumisos remained as slaves long past their eighteenth or twenty-first birthday.[20] Another circumstance aiding chicanery was the absence of parochial birth registers in many towns. Fire, revolution, and the weather in the turbulent period after 1821 wreaked havoc in the local Church archives. Many conscientious masters worriedly asked the Juntas how they could know the ages of those manumisos whose birth records no longer existed. No easy solution to this problem appeared, so the Department of the Interior recommended a group guessing session in which the master and his neighbors with the assistance of the síndico municipal estimated the age of the manumiso.[21]

Nevertheless, this stratagem could not hold off presentation indefinitely, and so the reluctant owners eventually presented their charges to the Junta to be contracted. But rather than allow the years spent training their manumisos in good character traits to be wasted, many masters assiduously endeavored to contract their own manumisos. By and large they succeeded, since a large majority of the contracts reaffirmed the old slave-master relationship.[22] But a certain number of brave manumisos absolutely refused to have anything to do with their old masters. Yet, the master's paternal feeling towards the ungrateful manumiso was so strong that he often demanded the contract be made with him anyway. The Juntas, defenders of the legally consecrated right of a manumiso to choose his patron, time and again sided with the master and consulted the government rather than make a decision. After all, they reasoned, unless the manumiso could present well-founded reasons for choosing another patron, it would hardly be just to deprive the master of his services. In weary communication after weary communication, the Department of the Interior responded that this same problem had been resolved many times before and the resolution published in the *Gaceta*; manumisos could contract with whomever they pleased as long as the patron was a man of good character and of means.[23]

In spite of the patron's proclaimed concern with establishing a substitute family relationship for the manumiso, he fought any attempt to allow the real parents to take custody of their child. By first confirming the necessity of legitimacy before a manumiso could be turned over to his parents, the patrons eliminated any serious challenge to their control over the majority of their charges. Yet, even when infrequent parents, free and legitimate, claimed their child, the master would not give it up without a fight. Arguing that the parents led immoral and irresponsible lives, he claimed the years of solid moral training invested in the manumiso would surely be lost if, at the tender age of eighteen or twenty-one, he went to live with his parents. Since the law was very clear on the subject, the Department of the Interior time and again ordered the Juntas to resist the demands of patrons and return manumisos of age to their free and legitimate parents.

Once patron and manumiso agreed on a contract, another sort of battle began. This one, more than the others, pitted master against servant with government officials as a final court. Obviously, the patron wanted to pay the servant as little as possible and make him work as hard as possible. The contracted manumiso wanted the opposite. Some clever patrons saw that withholding payment until the end of the contract improved discipline and the manumiso was less likely to run away. Manumisos did not view the question in this light. The indecisive local Juntas avoided all responsibility by forwarding the dispute to the central government. In justification of their practice patrons alleged that holding back all or part of the salary due the forced laborers contributed to the welfare of the manumiso. By this well-intentioned practice the masters, in effect, saved the salary so that the manumiso would have a small capital to start his own enterprise once the contract ended. The Department of the Interior decided such kindness could not be permitted, since the manumisos had contracted at a certain price per month; if they were not paid they could not be considered to have contracted their services freely.[25]

Nor were manumisos less clever in their tactics to avoid work, although their resources were considerably smaller. Some took to the hills, since they knew the contract could last only until their twenty-fifth year. Although pursued and captured by the police, their patrons could not prevent repeated escape. But they tried. They had the Junta pass a query to the government, ask-

ing if a patron could extend the contract past twenty-five years
to make up for time lost while his manumiso ran away. The
government resolved no. By and large, however, contracted
manumisos had few weapons at their disposal not also available
to their parents as slaves—passive resistance, laziness, flight, or
extreme obnoxiousness.[26]

The legal status of the contracted manumiso closely resembled that of the slave. Although guaranteed a salary of 12 to
24 pesos a year, he had few rights to call his own. Not only must
he obey the patron's commands, but also he had no freedom to
choose his residence or order his life.[27] At no time before his
twenty-fifth birthday, for example, could he marry whom and
when he wished. If allowed to marry, the conditions of his contract were revised without his consent to conform to the status
of his spouse.[28] He remained, of course, a free man; so free that
his services could in most cases be willed to his patron's heirs.[29]

SLAVES, MANUMISOS, AND PEONS

Still, it would be unfair not to recognize the shades of treatment
that separated a contracted manumiso from a slave. A slave belonged to an estate and was frequently considered as much a
part of the establishment as the houses or coffee trees. The contracted manumiso, on the other hand, did not belong to an
establishment, although he or his services were inheritable.[30]
This obeyed the legalistic distinction between the slave as
human chattel and the contracted manumiso as a free man
whose services were owned. The Department of the Interior
struggled hard to impress this distinction on the contractors of
manumisos, but with indifferent results. Contracted manumisos,
for example, could not be rented out or subcontracted as were
many slaves, because such a practice would eliminate the bene-
ficial effects expected from making the manumiso's education
and morality the responsibility of a single individual.[31]

Aside from the relatively superficial differences between the
slave, the manumiso, and the free peon, one quality of their

relationship to the master appears crucial in determining the attitudes of Venezuelan employers—permanence. Obviously, the slave was the most permanent worker of all. He belonged, in the fullest sense of the word, to his employer. His master might pay him, give him special privileges, or rent him,[32] but as long as he remained a slave his destiny was his master's will. Next in the scale of permanence came the manumisos and the contracted manumisos. Protected somewhat by the special manumission and apprenticeship laws, their subservience to the master was less than complete. Furthermore, they could count on the end of their formal obligation at their twenty-fifth birthday. Still, until of age and except for the minor limitations mentioned above, the manumiso was as good as a slave. The least permanent member of the Venezuelan work force was the peon or jornalero. Legally free and more-or-less master of his destiny, the peon sold his labor to the highest bidder. But there were limitations on his freedom devised by desperate hacendados unable to hold him to the land.[33] The peon had to register with the local judge and carry a booklet certifying his status. Upon accepting work—and all must work or be considered vagrants— the employer took the book to be returned when the peon paid his debts and ended his period of work. Without the book no peon could be given a job, and any jornalero caught without his book on the roads would be thrown in jail until his employer could be located.[34]

Fortunately for slaves, manumisos, and peons, legal theory rarely conformed to practice. Heavy investments in coffee required many hands for maintenance and especially harvest.[35] Competition for laborers was lively and the strict peonage laws operated badly or not at all. Many peons, playing on the needs of hacendados, collected bonuses or advances at one hacienda only to appear at the neighboring hacienda soon after to claim a new bonus. Employers howled, but as long as their fellows would accept peons without the proper papers, the police regulations had no effect.[36] Slaves and manumisos, too, had their stratagems. Some manumisos made themselves so obnoxious

and useless that their patrons let them roam about unmo-
lested.[37] Others fled their masters, probably presenting themselves as peons in another canton or province. Some undoubtedly joined the *cumbes* and bandit raiding parties infesting
Venezuela during this period. Many slaves, of course, took to
the hills or passed themselves off as free Negroes in other cantons. Some were even accepted as free laborers by needy employers who well knew their slave status.[38] A few tried slave rebellions, generally without success.[39] Many more joined various
political revolts whose leaders let it be known that freedom
could be acquired as in the independence movement.[40] But,
although the existence of these methods of escape contributed
to a slightly greater degree of consideration by employers and
masters, there was little doubt who commanded in Republican
Venezuela.

NOTES

1. One effort to eliminate free birth altogether reached the Senate in
1839 but was rejected out of hand. See *El Liberal*, No. 158, 7 May 1839
for the text of the proposed law along with the names of its authors. The
Senate's rejection can be found in *El Liberal*, No. 201, 3 March 1840.

2. *Materiales para*, I, 289–291 (Ley de 19 de julio de 1821). See
especially art. ii.

3. *Colección completa*, pp. 1–6 (Ley de 2 de octubre de 1830). See
especially art. ii.

4. See the considerandos of the 1821 and the 1830 laws cited above.

5. Evidence of the sale of manumisos or of their services abounds,
ranging from newspaper ads to official government documents. For example,
Colección completa, p. 34 (How to handle manumisos whose residence has
changed because of sale, 17 September 1840); *El Liberal*, No. 217, 23
June 1840 (Letter proposing a new tariff for manumisos); *El Venezolano*,
No. 141, 1 November 1842 (Advertisement asking for manumisos to buy);
Diaro de Avisos, No. 166, 3 August 1850 (Advertisment offering manumisa
for sale at reduced price.)

6. See *Colección completa*, pp. 1–6 (Ley de 2 de octubre de 1830), art.
v. The official slave tariff is in Appendix 1, Table 5.

7. See, for example, the expediente formed by Rafael Diego Mérida

who refused to pay slave-capturing costs for the return of his runaway manumiso because the manumiso was not legally a slave. *AGN*, Int. y Just., CLXXXVII (1839), 399–405. See also the resolution of Interior y Justicia, 9 September 1847, in *Gaceta de Venezuela*, No. 878, 12 September 1847.

8. *Colección completa*, pp. 1–6 (Ley de 2 de octubre de 1830), arts. iii and v.

9. The characteristically low rate of marriage among slaves can easily be seen in the padrones conserved in the *Archivo Arquidiocesano de Caracas*, Sección Parroquias. This is also evident in the population statistics collected in the *Anuario de la Provincia de Caracas* in *Sociedad Económica de Amigos del País. Memorias y estudios, 1829–1839* (Caracas: Banco Central de Venezuela, 1958), I, 179–391.

10. See, for example, the resolution of 19 February 1842 in *Colección completa*, pp. 41–43; and that of 29 July 1843 in *Gaceta de Venezuela*, No. 655, 6 August 1843.

11. For an example of how some Venezuelan legislators expected to solve this grave problem see the "Proyecto de patronato en favor de los manumisos," in *La Bandera Nacional*, No. 89, 9 April 1839. The considerandos prefacing the project are especially interesting. The law, along with the government's veto message, are in *AGN*, Int. y Just., CLXXXVII (1839), 391–397.

12. *Colección completa*, pp. 26–28 (Decreto de 27 de abril de 1840 sobre aprendizaje), arts. iv, vi, and x.

13. *Ibid.*, arts. iv and vi.

14. That most manumisos were hired as laborers at a small monthly wage can easily be seen in the surviving registers of manumiso contracts in *AGN*, Int. y Just., CCCLXXX (1848), 58–96 (Guárico and Aragua); CDXXXII (1850) 285–364 (Carabobo); CDXXXIII (1850), 344–422 (Barinas); CDXXXIV (1850), 147–234 (Barcelona); CDXXXV (1850), 369–435 (Mérida); DVI (1853), 46–109 (Barquisimeto); CXCII (1839), 326–402 (Coro); CCXIV (1840), 65–136 (Caracas).

15. See, for example, the directive from Interior y Justicia to the governors of provinces on 30 April 1840 stressing the importance of closely supervising manumiso conduct, *Colección completa*, pp. 28–29. The right of punishment is confirmed in a resolution of 9 October 1841, *Colección completa*, pp. 36–38. One wonders how many Venezuelans punished their children aged eighteen to twenty-five with a whip.

16. *Colección completa*, pp. 26–28 (Decreto de 27 de abril de 1840), arts. i, ii, and iii.

17. *Ibid.*, arts. iv, v, and vi.

18. *Ibid.*, arts. vii and viii.

19. *Ibid.*, arts. ix, x, and xi.

20. For some examples of presentation problems see the following: *Colección completa*, p. 34 (Resolution of 17 September 1840); *El Republicano*, No. 6, 27 June 1844 (Article on failure of Junta de Manumisión to meet and dispatch manumiso business); Int. y Just., 1845, *Memoria*, pp. 78–79 (Resolution of 21 August 1844); *Gaceta de Venezuela*, No. 917, 4 June 1848 (Resolution of 26 May 1848); *Informe de la comisión de mejoras*, p. 5 (Recommends police see if there are manumisos of age on haciendas who have not been presented, 1849); and ibid., pp. 15–16 (Recommends that síndico municipal employ someone to check on unpresented manumisos in the province of Caracas, 1849).

21. For the resolution of a number of birth record problems see: *Colección completa*, pp. 35–36 (25 January 1841); *Gaceta de Venezuela*, No. 917, 4 June 1848; AGN, Int. y Just., CCCLXXIII (1847), 210–214; CCCLXXXIII (1848), 4–7.

22. See the registers of *manumisos contratados* cited in note 14 above.

23. For examples of this long series of resolutions see: Int. y Just., 1844, *Memoria*, p. 61; *Gaceta de Venezuela*, No. 917, 4 June 1848. However, the Department of the Interior started out requiring the manumiso to give good reasons why he should not be contracted to his former master, *Colección completa*, p. 48 (Resolution, 30 June 1841). For an example of how completely Juntas identified with owners of manumisos see the expediente formed over the report by a síndico municipal that manumisos were being coerced into contracting their services to their former master. AGN, Int. y Just., CCXLIII (1841), 183–195.

24. For some examples of this controversy see: AGN, Int. y Just., CCXXXIII (1841), 438–445; CCLVI (1842), 1–45; *Colección completa*, pp. 41–43 (Resolution, 19 February 1842); *Gaceta de Venezuela*, No. 655, 6 August 1843 (Resolution, 29 July 1843). The Department of the Interior yielded on one point when it decided natural mothers could not claim their children, *Colección completa*, pp. 51–53 (Resolution, 21 August 1844); AGN, Int. y Just., CCCLII (1847), 179–193. When the owners of manumisos saw they could not count on the Department of the Interior to uphold their contention about manumisos going to the parents, they tried another dodge by attempting to require that manumisos be contracted only to the same kind of work they did before legal age, AGN, Int. y Just., CCLXXIV (1843), 212–226.

25. See, for example, *Colección completa*, p. 36 (Resolution, 8 March 1841). Patrons of manumisos were firm believers in withholding salaries. They included such a provision in their proposal for an apprenticeship law, *La Bandera Nacional*, No. 89, 9 April 1839 (Proyecto de patronato en favor de los manumisos), especially art. v.

26. *El Venezolano*, No. 104, 12 April 1842 (Remitido from Guanare); Int. y Just., 1844, *Memoria*, p. 61 (Circular to the governors of provinces,

12 September 1843); *Colección completa*, p. 67 (Resolution, 5 August 1846); *Gaceta de Venezuela*, No. 878, 12 September 1847 (Resolution, 9 September 1847).

27. The salary received by manumisos contratados varied with the type of work and the locality. The range of 12 to 24 pesos a year is from the registers of contracts cited in note 14 above. Obedience to the patron was probably enforced by the methods usual on slave plantations, although the only correction permitted legally was what a father would apply to his child, *Colección completa*, pp. 36–38 (Resolution, 9 October 1841). It seems clear, however, that few patrons took their role as parent-substitutes very seriously. The Department of the Interior had to caution the governor of Carabobo that patrons were required to feed, clothe, and provide medical care for their manumisos free of charge. Evidently, some patrons deducted these costs from the small salary, thus acquiring a debt-peon. Int. y Just., 1845, *Memoria*, pp. 80–81 (Resolution, 26 September 1844); for the original expediente see AGN, Int. y Just., CCCVII (1844), 1–14.

28. *El Venezolano*, No. 85, 21 December 1841 (Resolution, 18 November 1841).

29. *Colección completa*, pp. 57–58 (Resolution, 8 November 1844); Int. y Just., 1845, *Memoria*, p. 77 (Resolution, 22 June 1844).

30. See the sources cited in note 29 above and the resolution of 23 July 1847 in *Gaceta de Venezuela*, No. 871, 25 July 1847.

31. *Colección completa*, p. 48 (Resolution, 30 June 1841); Int. y Just., 1845, *Memoria*, p. 77 (Resolution, 22 June 1844).

32. For evidence of paid slaves see the accounts of the Hacienda Chuao in AGN, Int. y Just., CDXII (1849), 270. Evidence of slave rentals can be seen in the padrones of slaves in Guayana, AGN, Int. y Just., XLVI (1832), 244–261.

33. Representations by hacendados are legion. See, for example, *El Eco Popular*, No. 5, 3 March 1840 (gricultura. Policía); No. 6, 10 March 1840 (Agricultura. Policía); *El Venezolano*, No. 104, 12 April 1842 (Remitido from La Victoria); *El Liberal*, No. 583, 31 January 1846 (Estractos de la Memoria del gobernador de Guayana. Atraso de la Agricultura); Carabobo, 1847, *Exposición que dirige a la honorable Diputación de la provincia de Carabobo sobre los diversos ramos de la administración municipal, el gobernador* (Valencia: Juan de Sola, 1847), p. 3.

34. This restrictive but rarely effective legislation is collected in the *Reglamentos de policía* issued by the various provinces of Venezuela. The sections relative to Jornaleros, Peones, y Esclavos are selected and collected in Parra Aranguren, *Antecedentes del derecho de trabajo*, pp. 283–346. See also the relevant sections of the police codes listed in the Bibliography.

35. *El Liberal*, No. 205, 31 March 1840 (Inmigración); No. 366, 19

July 1842 (Crisis de 1842); *El Observador*, No. 65, 31 March 1844 (Section from a petition sent by the Concejo Municipal of Canton San Luis: Peonage).

36. *El Venezolano*, No. 85, 21 December 1841 (Avisos: Jornaleros prófugos); No. 151, 3 January 1843 (Avisos); *El Observador*, No. 65, 31 March 1844 (Peonage); *El Republicano*, No. 57, 11 June 1845 (Jornaleros).

37. *Colección completa*, p. 48 (Resolution, 30 June 1841); Int. y Just., 1844, *Memoria*, p. 61 (Resolution, 12 September 1843); *Colección completa*, p. 67 (Resolution, 5 August 1846).

38. See, for example, the complaints of runaways infesting the hills and causing trouble, AGN, Int. y Just., CXVII (1835), 304–308. Also indicative of the lack of effective discipline over slaves is the complaint of the *Jefe Político* of Ocumare de la Costa that runaway slaves were being employed knowingly in the Minas de Aroa, AGN, Int. y Just., CLXIX (1838), 154–159.

39. Although the revolutionary potential of Venezuelan slaves and manumisos will be discussed later on in this study, some examples of slave disturbances can be seen in AGN, Int. y Just., L (1832), 487–578; CXCII (1839), 112–125; Carabobo, 1845, *Exposición que dirige a la honorable Diputación de la provincia de Carabobo sobre various ramos de la administración municipal, el gobernador en 1845* (Valencia: Juan de Sola, [1845]), p. 2. Venezuelans, however, were prone to imagine rebellions where none existed, thus keeping everyone in turmoil. See, for example, AGN, Int. y Just., CCXLVIII (1842), 79–86; CCCXCI (1848), 347–369; CD (1849), 122–154; CDLXXII (1852), 344–347.

40. See, for example, *El Liberal*, No. 615, 12 September 1846 (El Guzmancismo en la práctica and Crónica interior: facciosos); No. 617, 26 September 1846 (Editorial).

PART II

* * *

Towards Abolition

CHAPTER 5

The Economy and Slavery

EXPANSION AND PROSPERITY (1830–1842)

WITHOUT some idea of nineteenth-century Venezuela's rapidly changing economy, her slave policy is difficult to understand. The economic situation helped determine each maneuver, tactic, and stratagem. Yet, to attempt an analysis of the development of Venezuela's domestic economy in the quarter-century before abolition is risky indeed. Not only are there few reliable monographs to guide one through the confusion of the periodical press,[1] but also the basic statistical series on population, exports, imports, and the like have yet to be compiled.[2] Nonetheless, with the aid of the reasonably reliable *Memorias* of the Department of the Interior and of the Treasury, and the often extremely perceptive contemporary analyses of the state of the nation, a relatively accurate outline of the structure and development of the Venezuelan economy can be obtained.

Throughout the period under consideration, Venezuela had a model agricultural export economy. With almost no native manufactures she produced coffee, cacao, sugar, hides, and indigo for export along with smaller quantities of other commodities.[3] But the crucial crop was coffee. Not only did it earn the most money, but it was also the item most susceptible to price fluctuations. The discussion that follows is focused on the coffee-producing section of the agricultural economy, for much of the story of Venezuela's development in this period is the story of coffee expansion.[4]

Once the aftermath of the wars for independence had passed, Venezuela—ruled by the firm hand of President-General José Antonio Páez and separated from the Colombian Confederation—the economic recovery begun in the late twenties grew into a full-fledged boom during the thirties. Everything conspired to aid the expanding economy. Planters, whose lands, houses, and slaves had been destroyed or dispersed by the ravages of war, began the task of reconstruction with good prospects for a full and rapid recovery.

Before 1810 Venezuela had concentrated her exports on cacao almost to the exclusion of other crops.[5] However, by the beginning of the nineteenth century, some of the more adventuresome planters began experimenting with coffee, and by 1810 some 6 million pounds of this important crop were being exported from the Caracas province alone.[6] This tendency to shift from cacao to coffee cultivation was accelerated by the independence movement. Not only did these fourteen years of warfare drain the country of manpower needed to care for and harvest cacao, but the most destructive campaigns in Venezuela took place in the major cacao-growing regions of the country: the valleys of Aragua and Caracas and along the coast of Barlovento.[7]

When the planters could safely return to their fields they had to devise some way to effect a quick recovery. Those whose cacao plantations still could be saved continued producing and marketing the valuable seed. But for most planters, all or large parts of their holdings were beyond hope of salvation. New plantings would have to be made. For these men, continued investment in cacao was quite out of the question: the trees were expensive and they took about six years to begin producing.[8] Coffee, on the other hand, appeared much more attractive. In addition to producing a marketable crop within three years of planting, coffee could be planted at almost four times the density. Although only producing one harvest a year, each unit of land generated almost twice as much income when planted in coffee as when planted in cacao.[9]

Given these conditions, plus an expanding world market in coffee which kept prices high for a time, the decision to plant coffee is not surprising. Encouraging expansion, initiated in the late 1820s, planters found speculation and foreign commission houses eager to lend the capital necessary to establish a plantation and maintain it for a number of years, albeit at extremely high interest rates.[10]

This boom, which lasted unabated until the 1840s, was extraordinary from almost every point of view. Based at first on the substitution of coffee for cacao and the rehabilitation of destroyed plantations, the boom expanded, particularly after 1835, as new land was cleared and brought under production.

Indicative of this trend are the export figures. For example, while the total quantity of cacao exported grew very slowly between 1830 and 1840, the production of coffee doubled and then almost tripled in the same period.[11] Such unprecedented growth had profound effects on all aspects of Venezuelan society and economy. Traditional relationships between capitalists, workers, commercial factors, planters, and government could not withstand both the onslaught of war and the exposure to the dynamics of rapid economic expansion.

Unfortunately, expansion proved a very expensive process. In Venezuela, a devastated country with an uncertain future and shaky political institutions, planters with haciendas in relatively well-preserved condition were the best off. In the early years, while the rates of interest remained exorbitantly high, they required money only to hire the men necessary to refurbish their old plantations and collect the first harvests. But many Venezuelan planters had a much greater need for capital. The conversion to or replanting of coffee required not only a heavy initial investment in manpower and trees but also sustained expenditures over several years before the first harvests would permit any substantial repayment. But, on the other hand, laborers were readily available as more and more men were discharged from the armies of independence and drifted back to their homes. Furthermore, planters could count on the relatively high prices being quoted for coffee in the major ports. In any case, planters saw little alternative to rebuilding the plantations ruined by war. Few Venezuelans had either the financial resources or the personal inclination to change their way of life and embark on a career in business or commerce. In addition, most planters had few assets except land, coffee or cacao trees, and slaves. The solution to their financial problems seemed obvious enough: borrow money, rebuild, and hope to repay. Once this decision was taken, expansion in coffee was the only really viable alternative for the majority of planters whose land lay in the coffee zone.

Then came the really difficult question: the money. Traditionally, Venezuelan agriculture had relied on three major sources of investment capital: the Church, Spanish capitalists, and the Venezuelan rich.[12] But the wars for independence ended these relationships. By the end of the eighteenth century large-scale Spanish investment in Venezuela was over, and the individual capitalists remaining were effectively destroyed or driven out by the ravages of war.[13] The same sort of calamities that forced planters to borrow money in the post-war era also ruined or blocked most of the Church's sources of capital. By and large, the Church had sunk most of her resources into agriculture. Censos, obras pías, *capellanías*, and other holy loans were widely distributed among Venezuelan planters, and as their fortunes declined so did the Church's. In equally bad shape, Church-owned and administered properties added little or no revenue to the priestly coffers.[14] Given the expansion between 1825 and 1840, it appears that the Church was never in a position to contribute the large sums needed to support such a boom.

The credit vacuum existing in Venezuela soon after the war

was quickly filled by European and American speculators with an eye on the high prices of coffee and the desperate straits of the local planters. Evidently, there was practically no lack of capital during these years, but the interest rates were phenomenally high. In the late 1820s planters commonly paid 2 or 3 percent a month, although by the end of the 1830s this had fallen to around 1 percent a month.[15] But a more subtle danger for the planter lay in a change in the terms of credit. Long accustomed to the long-term, low-interest agricultural credit supplied by the Church, the planters were ill-equipped to handle the intricacies of short-term, high-interest commercial credit extended by the exporters and their agents. Since the primary sources of capital, that is, banks and commission houses, wanted loans that could be paid off in a year or less, most planters found themselves in the disagreeable position of having to deal with middlemen. Naturally, this raised the cost of money still higher as the middlemen took their cut.[16]

Yet, so desperate were Venezuelans for money that they threw open their arms and welcomed these speculators as the saviours of the fatherland. Agricultural, cattle raising, and commercial interests joined together to remove all the restrictions on moneylenders imposed by Spanish legal tradition. In their gratitude for the contribution of resources to Venezuelan reconstruction, the legislators voted to eliminate the protection Spanish law had placed around the debtor to guard him against exploitation by avaricious capitalists. This famous law, cursed and praised throughout the Páez era as the Ley de 10 de abril de 1834, showed the amount of political control gained by the commercial-mercantile elite under the first years of the Conservative Oligarchy's rule.[17]

Nor were the legislative triumphs of the commercial elite limited to the 10 de abril law. Although this law allowed any rate of interest under any condition, a special court was deemed necessary to avoid unnecessary delay in the settling of commercial and financial claims. A Commercial Tribunal, created in 1836, had special jurisdiction over economic cases and followed few of the formalities usually prevalent in courts of law.[18] Safely sconced behind this legal barricade, the commercial sector created a National Bank in 1841, the height of the coffee boom, to help in its financial transactions and to handle the banking of the federal government.

This series of legislative victories testifies eloquently to the political ascendancy of the financial elite as well as to the necessity and optimism of Venezuelan planters. As long as the price of coffee continued high, and barring political calamities, the planters believed they could get out from under their high debts. By the same token the moneylenders willingly extended, renegotiated, or increased loans as long as the export market held up.

But this happy merry-go-round of debts, expansion, and high interest rates could not last forever. By the end of the 1830s numerous cracks began to appear in the foundations of the coffee boom. The overwhelming ascendance, political and economic, of the financial-commercial sector began to irk the traditional lords of Venezuela; they saw their power slipping as agriculture came to depend more and more heavily on the possessors of capital. More important, however, than questions of prestige and political prominence were the economic consequences of allowing creditors to control much of the administrative and judicial apparatus of the nation.[19] About 1840, planters really began to feel the squeeze of their creditors as coffee prices sagged and loans were called in. When a planter's loan was called and he could not make good on his obligations nor renegotiate the debt, the provisions of the 10 de abril law went into effect, and his goods, land, or slaves were put up in public auction. This arrangement was not very satisfactory for the planter, since he generally lost his holdings for the amount of his debt, which rarely corresponded to its real value.[20]

This type of transaction helped bring about a profound division in Venezuelan society between those identified with the agricultural interests and those who sided with the commercial-mercantile elite. This split was symbolically formalized in 1840 when the planters helped found *El Venezolano*, edited by Antonio Leocadio Guzmán, and then organized the Liberal party later in the same year. Originally concentrating on a change of leaders in the government, the party soon became more concerned with the economic crisis that gripped the nation, particularly the agricultural sector, in the years after 1842. Meanwhile, the Conservatives concentrated on keeping their privileges and control.[21]

CRISIS AND THE ECONOMY (1842–1854)

When crisis struck in 1842 and planters found themselves overextended, each individual quickly enlisted in the ranks of whichever leader promised a way out of his dilemma. Naturally enough, no one—planter or financial oligarch—wanted to acknowledge himself responsible for his own problems. Prominent publicists vied with one another in analyzing the causes of and remedies for the crisis. But before examining the charges and countercharges, we should have a clear idea of how the crisis came about and an understanding of its immediate consequences. There were three major areas of the economy which contributed most to the severity and duration of the crisis: production, labor, and credit.

During the decade of the 1830s, Venezuelan planters were obsessed by the single-minded mania of coffee expansion. So energetically did these men operate that, between 1830 and 1842, coffee production almost tripled. Such a massive increment in exports of this vital crop reflected an equally massive commitment of capital and labor to the clearing, planting, and harvesting of new coffee plantations. Although some of the growth in the export figures can be traced to the substitution of coffee for cacao on already cleared land or to the more intensive cultivation of existing plantations, most of it probably represented new plantings in new areas. This is made particularly clear when we examine the export figures for cacao during the boom period. Had the planters conducted an energetic campaign of conversion from cacao to coffee, we could expect to see a rapid decline in the quantities of cacao exported. But nothing of the kind occurred, and in fact cacao production registered a slight increase during this period.[22] Since cacao was grown at much the same altitude-temperature combination as coffee, it seems safe to assume that most of the coffee growth came from new establishments on virgin land.[23]

Nor does it appear accurate to attribute much of the expansion to improved methods or denser plantings in the coffee fields. Venezuelan planters were very slow to adopt new methods or employ new tools. Indicative of this are the series of articles published in newspapers advocating improvements in pruning, fertilizers, planting, and harvesting. The same ideas were being pushed in 1842 as had been advocated in the twenties. Moreover, denser planting was a self-defeating method of expansion, since the yield of a coffee plantation declined in quantity and quality if the trees were crowded too close together.[24]

From the beginning of the boom, coffee expansion appears to have been a self-generating phenomenon. Since most of the growth in production, particularly after the first years, implied heavy investments in land, trees, and labor, which in turn implied heavy planter indebtedness, the only way for a coffee baron to get out from under his financial obligations was to produce more and more coffee. But at the end of each cycle of borrowing and planting, the planters found themselves in just as bad shape as before, since coffee prices declined slowly throughout the boom period.[25] Yet, in their efforts to get ahead of the cycle, planters did little more than contribute to the lowering of coffee prices by saturating the foreign coffee market.[26]

Of course, sooner or later, this cycle had to end. As the boom decade progressed, most of the readily accessible land came under cultivation, and planters had to go farther afield to find undeveloped land suitable for coffee. As they moved outside the traditionally cultivated areas their costs of production rose sharply, primarily because of Venezuela's abominably bad roads. Although Congress studied many projects for roads, none of them were backed by sufficient interest or cash to become realities. Thus, as they expanded farther and farther from the ports, and as the price of coffee declined, planters saw much of their small margin of profit absorbed by transportation charges. With the sharp drop in coffee prices in 1842 this small margin of profit probably disappeared, and the cycle of expansion had to end.[27]

At the beginning of the boom plantation workers were easy to find. The relative stability established and guaranteed by the Páez regime, plus the return of discharged soldiers, encouraged better organization of rural labor. Perhaps even more important, peons found planters willing to pay well on the basis of the high price of coffee. It seems clear that rural laborers found it more advantageous to trade their work for the wages offered by planters than to remain occupied in subsistence agriculture.[28] Since coffee production is a seasonal operation, the growers needed large numbers of workers only at harvest time. For the duration of the growing season only a small maintenance force could be kept busy with the cleaning and pruning operations. Thus, with a large floating work force readily available, few planters worried much about labor problems.[29]

As coffee production soared and more and more land came under cultivation, a large percentage of the labor force became occupied with maintenance, with a corresponding reduction in the number of men available for seasonal harvest work.[30] In addition, falling coffee prices made it harder for planters to attract any but the most temporary workers to their plantations, since they could no longer afford to pay the peons more than could be made in subsistence agriculture.[31] This explains the sudden burst of interest in labor problems evidenced by planters and their supporters in the late thirties and through the forties.[32] Deeply concerned with the morality of the peon population, planters devised codes of conduct that, if enforced, would have registered and controlled every rural worker's movements. As it turned out, Venezuela's level of police efficiency was so low that almost none of the elaborate ordinances succeeded in subjugating the peons.[33] And though provincial legislatures might pass and repass restrictive labor rules, no one could push through a law that would improve the conditions and wages of peons, the only remedy with any possibility for success.[34]

As the commercial agricultural sector shifted from overpopulation to underpopulation in the late 1830s, the Congress and the Department of the Interior became more and more interested in the possibilities of immigration.[35] Venezuela's population grew only 25 percent[36] during the decade of expansion, and many statesmen saw immigration as the answer to labor shortages. Unfortunately, Venezuela had little to offer prospective citizens, and government support of immigration remained limited.[37] By and large, most of the immigration to Venezuela in this period came from Spanish possessions, particularly in the Canary Islands, and these people were more interested in commerce than in agriculture.[38]

Although planters had a hard enough time coping with labor difficulties and land shortages, these problems appeared secondary when compared to the credit squeeze that set in with the crisis. Since the entire coffee boom depended on credit for its existence, restrictions on the amount of money available or any rise in the rates of interest were bound to wreak havoc among planters mortgaged far beyond their ability to pay. As we have seen, throughout the boom period, and particularly in the early years, credit was readily available although at exorbitantly high rates of interest. But as the country stabilized and coffee production soared, interest rates fell from 1 or 2 percent monthly to about 9 percent yearly between 1830 and 1840.[39] Nevertheless, as planters never tired of pointing out, few agricultural enterprises could boast of returning even 6 percent a year on capital invested.[40]

The obvious result of this type of credit arrangement was that most planters were heavily in debt to commission houses, financial middlemen, the Church, or all three. Counting on continued coffee prosperity, growers evidently placed their hopes for economic survival on the income from increased coffee plantings. But as prices declined slowly throughout the late 1830s, the average planter's margin of profit had to decline as well. In hopes of postponing the day of reckoning, planters borrowed more money to make more plantings or to pay off insistent creditors, thereby increasing their debt.[41] When the crisis of 1842–1843 hit, these hacendados were in desperate straits as creditors began calling in loans and demanding payment of back interest. When payment was not forthcoming, the moneylenders put their cherished debt laws into effect and auctioned off the delinquent's property.[42] Naturally enough, planters found little favor with this sort of operation and clamored for some kind of relief or protection from the federal government. But that body, long dominated by the financial elite, appeared to have little interest in bailing out the desperate planters.[43]

Each group affected by the crisis of 1842–1843 developed elaborate schemes for economic recovery. As one might suspect, each analysis of the causes of depression reflected rather clearly the analyst's interests. For example, the moneylenders saw the major cause of crisis in the sloppy management, extravagance, and improvidence of the majority of agriculturalists. After all, they said, these men had entered their contracts with capitalists with open eyes. If they now found themselves unable to fulfill their obligations, there was no one to blame but themselves. In any case, a short crisis was probably a good thing, since it tended to weed out the weak planters and would serve to strengthen the economy in the long run.[44]

Such equanimity in the face of crisis was not shared by the hacendados. They identified the high cost of money and the ruthless methods of moneylenders, sanctified by the iniquitous 10 de abril law, as the major cause of trouble. Although admitting that some farmers might have been a bit improvident in agreeing to loans with interests far beyond their abilities for repayment and acknowledging the extravagance of a very few planters, the agricultural bloc claimed that the vast majority of coffee growers were honest, hardworking, frugal, and far-sighted men. Such an exemplary group could hardly have brought this crisis on itself. The blame for the whole mess, they claimed, could be laid squarely at the door of the parasite class of moneylenders and their puppet government. While the agriculturalists produced the crops that made Venezuela rich, the usurers collected all the money and took no risks.[45]

Directly opposing projects for stimulating recovery were pro-pounded by the two groups. The Conservatives, firm believers in liberal economic doctrines, called for belt tightening and government aid to road building and immigration. By this sound method, the long-term prosperity of Venezuela would be secured. By leaving intact the enlightened free-credit laws, Venezuela would remain an attractive place for the foreign investment so necessary for her development.[46]

Not enough, cried the planters. Roads and immigration were fine, but the crisis was now, and more direct and drastic measures must be used. Since the major illness of Venezuelan agriculture, they believed, was financial instead of structural, the most effective remedies would be aimed at changing the financial climate. First, they proposed, the iniquitous law of 10 de abril should be repealed, as it legalized the worst forms of extortion and exploitation under the guise of freedom of con-tracts. Once the money power lost its stranglehold over the country, adequate credit laws could be passed regulating the amount of interest legally collectible. But even these reforms would have little effect on the immediate predicament of the only productive class in society. What all growers needed more than anything else was money—money to employ peons to harvest their crops, money to tide them over until the price of coffee turned upward, but most of all money at a low interest rate so the planters could get out of their credit bind. The best plan, they thought, would be to establish an agricultural credit institution whose capital would be provided by a foreign loan guaranteed by the nation. Since few agricultural enterprises made more than 6 percent on their capital, loans to farmers should be fixed at 6 percent interest per year and should be available only to those with agricultural properties to mortgage. According to its proponents, this scheme would be self-support-ing, since agriculture was a good investment at 6 percent.[47]

Special-interest legislation, cried the Conservatives, the major beneficiaries of the pro-creditor laws of the 1830s. It just was not fair, they protested, for the entire nation to pay for the relief of a small group of backsliding farmers. All the country needed was more honesty and industriousness among the agri-cultural population. In any case such a plan would never pay for itself, and the nation would eventually have to pay off the foreign loan. Besides, the nation already had the *Banco Nacional* whose wise policies since its founding in 1841 had resulted in a steadily declining interest rate.[48] The solution to Venezuela's ills, they reiterated, was morality, industry, and prudence coupled with an energetic road program and increased en-couragement to immigrants.

As the crisis begun in 1842 lingered on through 1843 and 1844, the discussion over these issues grew more and more strident and the dividing line between money men and planters grew sharper. By the elections of 1844, the planter-dominated Liberal party scored a number of triumphs at the polls prompt-ing them to present a plan for their agricultural bank to the Congress. After much public controversy, the Liberals forced a vote and passed the measure. But Conservative President Carlos Soublette vetoed the bill and sent it back to Congress. Although the Liberals counted one vote more than the two-thirds needed to repass the measure over the presidential veto, the defection of two members of the Liberal majority allowed the Conserva-tives to defeat this sensitive measure. Outraged Liberals, cry-ing bribery, began laying plans for victory in the next elections scheduled for 1846.[49]

In the supercharged atmosphere fostered by the bitter legisla-tive battles, no one could hope for a peaceful election. Liberals, fighting in a campaign marred by violence and fraud, were severely handicapped by divisions within the party over the

choice of a presidential candidate. Conservatives, united behind
Páez's choice, General José Tadeo Monagas, enjoyed all the
advantages of controlling most public offices. Given such a
situation it is not too surprising that the Conservatives, by dint
of fraud and force, captured the presidency. With all avenues
of peaceful conquest of power closed, desperate planters
turned to armed rebellion in some of the richest agricultural
districts of Venezuela. For most of 1846 and the first part of
1847, the outgoing Conservative administration of President
Soublette had to chase down the rebels.[50]

Evidently, the desperation and strength of the Liberal rebels,
as well as the social and economic prominence of some of the
leaders, enlightened Monagas on the gravity of the depression.
By late 1847, soon after taking office, Monagas decided to cut
himself loose from the political tutelage of Páez and began
bringing more and more prominent Liberals into his administration. By January of 1848 this shift to Liberal dominance was so complete that the Conservative caudillo, Páez,
rose in rebellion against the president he himself had elected.[51]

Although short-lived, this rebellion contributed one more
blow to the already sagging economy. While the price depression continued to plague coffee growers, their peons were
drafted by one side or another to fight out the rebellions.[52]
Nor did the military defeat of Páez in 1849 end the problem,
because the Conservative exiles kept up an unending stream of
propaganda and subversion from the neighboring islands, always a haven for out-of-favor Venezuelans.[53]

Enjoying almost complete support from the planter elite, the
Monagas government proceeded to pass into law much of the
Liberal program. The major pieces of pro-creditor legislation,
such as the 10 de abril law, were abolished and replaced by
more lenient credit arrangements. Unfortunately, however, the
agricultural credit bank lacked the resources to become a
reality, and the only two commercial banks in the country
folded in the early 1850s.[54]

Thus, the Liberals' political triumph could not be transformed into economic recovery. Civil war and its attendant disorganization of agriculture, together with continued low coffee prices, prolonged the depression through the 1840s and into the 1850s. Further complicating the planter's problems, the administration of José Gregorio Monagas, (successor to his brother, José Tadeo Monagas), was forced to abolish slavery in 1854 without prior compensation.

SLAVES AND THE ECONOMY (1830–1854)

By and large, the Negro slave was counted twice in the planter's economic calculations. First of all, of course, the slave was a laborer, subject to servitude, but nonetheless influenced by the same conditions governing the free peons. In the second place, a Negro slave served as a financial cipher in every planter's calculations.

As mentioned above, the Venezuelan founding fathers had thought it expedient to declare the slave trade ended in law, as it had already ended in fact.[55] In 1810 there apparently existed a sufficient labor force for the relatively limited needs of the predominantly cacao-oriented agricultural sector.[56] Before marveling at such philanthropy by Venezuelan slave holders, consider that by 1810 the slave population in Venezuela could hardly have exceeded 5 percent, and in the major agricultural provinces it probably approached 9 or 10 percent of the population.[57] From these figures it would seem evident that Venezuelan planters no longer saw slavery as the future labor system. The wars for independence established the principle of gradual emancipation and free birth as a military and political necessity.

Thus, by 1830 and the beginning of the coffee boom, the continuance of slavery as a prospering institution had ceased to be possible without grave risks to social and political tranquillity. It is also well to note that most slaves were concentrated in the traditional cacao and sugar regions, particularly along the coast of Barlovento. For this reason the subsequent coffee expansion, when it occurred in new lands, drew less on slave labor than the proportion of slaves in the population would suggest. Moreover, most plantations had few slaves to spare for new operations. If the slaves were shifted from an established plantation to a new area, peons would have to be hired to maintain the old plantation, and the additional cost to the planter would remain the same. Furthermore, overpopulation in the subsistence agricultural sector for most of the period of expansion helped reduce the importance of the Negro slave as a laborer.[58] As the years passed, the number of healthy slaves available for field work declined as the free-birth provision of the manumission laws took effect.[59] In addition, there was a tendency for more and more slaves to be absorbed into domestic service, reducing even further their importance to agriculture.[60]

By the late 1830s, then, when planters began to feel the pinch of a labor shortage, slavery was long past the point of no return. Nonetheless, labor-hungry planters did the next best thing to reestablishing slavery by tying the legally free children of slaves to their masters until they reached age twenty-five. The care lavished on the apprenticeship system is eloquent testimony of the planters' desperate need for labor, as are the efforts spent trying to avoid the laws mitigating the servitude of these freeborn slave children.

But why did slavery last until 1854, if the institution was moribund from the mid-1830s? In Venezuela's elaborate credit structure, slaves played a role all out of proportion to their contribution to the agricultural work force. Each slave, as chattel, could be used as collateral for much needed loans. Many slaves, of course, had already been mortgaged to the Church since long before independence, thus creating a strong institutional defender of property rights.[61] Other slaves had been put up as collateral for more secular loans. Moreover, a planter's slaves probably represented a high percentage of his total capital. Since land alone was worth relatively little, slaves and coffee trees were the major capital resources of the planter.[62] The case was much the same for owners of domestics. This situation was reinforced by the institutionally established slave tariff. The Department of the Interior authorized a schedule of prices for slaves based on their ages which was maintained until abolition and formed the basis for all evaluations used in administering the manumission laws. Few slave owners wanted to sell much below this price, since their inheritance taxes could be cancelled on this basis. In any case, the Caracas slave market was none too active. Although many transactions occurred, most involved the transfer of one or maybe two individuals, probably bought for domestic service. The institutional price was not totally fictitious, as a sample from the notorial records shows.[63]

This state of affairs clearly explains the absence of debate over slavery, except as a financial matter. No one worried much about slaves since their fate was determined by laws and treaties long sanctioned by time, custom, and necessity. On the other hand, most of the elite, Conservative or Liberal, could generate a good deal of steam about the iniquity of abolishing slavery without adequate and prompt compensation. Church officials and defenders became some of the best advocates of the complete-payment principle. The only energy expended over slaves, other than as financial ciphers, concerned their revolutionary potential. As the years progressed and the number of workable slaves declined to insignificance their political and social importance grew greater, particularly as depression and attendant discontent grew after 1844. The revolutions of 1846 and 1848 brought the slaves more into prominence. In 1854, the Monagas dynasty decided slavery was more of a social and political liability than an economic advantage and ordered the institution abolished.

NOTES

1. Practically nothing has been written analyzing Venezuelan economics during this period with the exception of the relevant chapters in David

Bushnell's *The Santander Regime*. By and large the most helpful Vene-zuelan efforts have been in the genre of the interpretive historical essay. See, for example, Carrera Damas, *Tres temas*, especially the essay entitled "Algunos problemas relativos a la organización del estado durante la segunda república venezolana." Also containing useful insights is Federico Brito Figueroa's *Ensayos de historia social venezolana* (Caracas: Universidad Central de Venezuela, 1960), especially chaps. 3 and 5. On the other hand, political studies of this era are legion. Particularly useful in this respect are the fifteen volumes of documents *Pensamiento político vene-zolano del siglo XIX*.

2. The statistical information on population and exports included in the Appendices are preliminary tables designed to provide the reader with an idea of the relative orders of magnitude involved. I am particularly grateful to Dr. James A. Hanson, Brown University–Yale Economic Growth Center, for his assistance in the preparation of the export tables and for his val-uable comments and suggestions on this chapter.

3. See the export figures in Appendix 2, Tables 1–7.

4. Although coffee accounted for only about 40 percent of total exports, its importance was exaggerated by the relative price stability of the other major export, cacao. Since coffee producers were the most heavily indebted sector of the economy, price fluctuations were bound to have disastrous results.

5. See Humbolt, *Viaje*, III, 137–139 and Hussey, *La compañía de Caracas*, passim and especially Apéndice II. Also of interest are the figures and discussion of the agriculture of the province of Caracas by José Do-mingo Díaz in *Semanario de Caracas* (Sesquicentenario de la Independ-encia, No. 9 [Caracas: Academia Nacional de la Historia, 1959]), passim.

6. See *Semanario de Caracas*, No. 9, 30 December 1810 (Estadística: Provincia de Caracas); Humboldt, *Viaje*, III, 42–43; and Depons, *Viajes*, II, 38–39.

7. Evidence of large-scale destruction is widely scattered throughout the records of the Department of the Interior. See, for example, AGN, Gran Col.–Int. de Ven., XXXII (1821), 43–46 (Excuse of Merced de la Vega for not paying forced loan); LXIII (1822), 184 (Pablo Delgado complains about disruption of agriculture caused by the war). One of the hardest trials for most planters was the disorganization of the labor force of slaves and peons due to levies and general instability. This situation was extremely aggravating since it began in the earliest years of the war and lasted past the fall of Puerto Cabello in 1823. See, in addition to the letter from Merced de la Vega cited above, AGN, Gran Col.–Int. de Ven., IV (1822), 190–193 (Bartolomé Manrique complains about insubordination of his slaves); and CXLVIII (1823), 31 (a similar complaint from a Brother on behalf of his Order's plantation); Porter, *Caracas Diary*, pp.

141, 354, 432, 596; and Robert Ker Porter (Caracas) to Colonel Campbell (Bogota), 6 February 1829, *Lilly Library* (Indiana University), 1828–1840, Porter Mss., Sir Robert Ker Porter, Autograph Letter Books, I, 48–50.

8. There is an excellent chart included in Codazzi's treatise on Venezuelan political and economic geography that shows relative maturation times, yields, and similar information for Venezuela's major crops, Codazzi, *Obras*, I, 154–155.

9. Of course, this income-producing estimate is based on 1825–1835 coffee prices which tended to be higher in relation to cacao prices than they would be in the 1840s and 1850s. Codazzi, *Obras*, I, 154–155; and Appendix 2, Tables 1–2.

10. Until more detailed information can be extracted from the statistics in the *Memorias* of Hacienda we must rely on contemporary analyses. See, for example, *El Liberal*, No. 366, 19 July 1842 (Remetidos. Crisis de 1842) and the answer in the same paper, No. 367, 22 July 1842. Also useful are *El Venezolano*, No. 174, 26 April 1843 and No. 177, 9 May 1843 (Crisis de 1843); Alberto Rojas, *Influencia de la ley de 10 de abril de 1834 sobre la propiedad territorial en Venezuela* (Caracas: Imprenta Boliviana por Domingo Salazar, 1844); *El Liberal*, No. 605, 4 July 1846 (Venezuela en 1830 y 1846); and the classic pamphlet by Fermín Toro, "Reflexiones sobre la ley de 10 de abril de 1834," *Pensamiento político*, I, 107–225; U.S. Dept. State, Diplomatic, Venezuela, No. 79, I (J. G. A. Williamson to Sec. State, Caracas, 12 April 1838); PRO, FO 80/14, 36 (D. F. O'Leary, Caracas, 22 February 1841), FO 80/22, 46–51 (D. F. O'Leary, Puerto Cabello, 30 June 1843).

11. See Appendix 2, Table 1.

12. See Brito Figueroa, *La estructura económica*, pp. 285–300. Also very revealing are the nostalgic commentaries of hard-pressed planters about the happy days of Church-dominated credit and lenient cacao factors. See for example *El Venezolano*, No. 234, 13 April 1844 (Francisco Aranda. Un pensamiento para ser examinado), a fragment of which was published earlier in *El Agricultor*, No. 2, 28 February 1844. Also helpful for understanding the Church's financial operations is Michael P. Costeloe, *Church Wealth in Mexico: A Study of the "Juzgado de Capellanías" in the Archbishopric of Mexico, 1800–1856* (Cambridge: Cambridge University Press, 1967).

13. See, in addition to the article by Aranda cited directly above, *El Venezolano*, Nos. 274, 275, 276, 29 March to 26 April 1845 (Cuestión económico-política).

14. Churchmen were forever bewailing the decline of their terrestrial goods, particularly when someone suggested reducing the interest on holy loans. See, for example, AGN, Gran Col.–Int. de Ven., IV (1822), 190–

193 (letter from the administrator of obra pía of Chuao); CXLVIII (1823), 31 (letter from another obra pía); *Representación dirigida al soberano Congreso sobre que se reduzcan los réditos de los censos constituidos al dos y medio por ciento* (1831) in Sociedad Económica de Amigos del País, I, 141–152. The Church answered this last challenge in *El Patriota Venezolano*, No. 6, 26 January 1832 (Comunicado: dos amigos). Also *Archivo Arquidiocesano, Obras Pías*, carpeta 15 (Marcos Borges compra esclavos de San Nicolás a censo), 1833. Particularly helpful in this respect is the publication of part of the documents from the Church-owned Hacienda Chuao, Eduardo Arcila Farías, et al., *La Obra Pía de Chuao, 1568–1825* (Caracas: Universidad Central de Venezuela, 1968), I.

15. It is, of course, extraordinarily difficult to chart the fluctuations of interest rates. While the material for such a task exists in such places as the *Registro Principal de Caracas* and the *Archivo Arquidiocesano*, the organization and analysis of this widely scattered data is a job for a trained economist or economic historian armed with the might of computer technology. Nevertheless, it is possible to glean enough information from the contentious periodical press to hazard an interpretation of the trends. It is well to note that the 1 percent per month figure is probably what planters paid for their money; merchants and moneylenders most likely paid less. See, in addition to the sources cited in note 10 above, *La ley de 10 de abril y el comercio de Venezuela* (Valencia: Bartolomé Valdés, 1838); *La Bandera Nacional*, No. 60, 18 September 1838 (Banco de la Sociedad de Agricultores); *El Promotor*, Nos. 4 to 10, 15 May to 26 June 1843 (Crisis); *El Venezolano*, No. 177, 9 May 1843 (Crisis de 1843); No. 234, 13 April 1844 (Aranda. Un pensamiento); *El Agricultor*, No. 1, 21 February 1844 (Representación de los agricultores al Congreso); and *Gaceta de Venezuela*, No. 888, 14 November 1847 (Sociedad Económica de Caracas); PRO, FO 80/25, 84–91 (Belford H. Wilson, Caracas, 13 March 1844); FO 80/25, 151 (Belford H. Wilson, Caracas, 20 April 1844).

16. See, for example, some of the discussions of the credit problem in Tomás Lander, "Continuación del apego sacerdotal a los bienes terrenales," *Pensamiento político*, IV, 143–159; *El Liberal*, No. 366, 19 July 1842 (Remetidos: Crisis de 1842); *El Manzanares*, No. 3, 28 March 1843 (Banco Nacional); *El Promotor*, No. 4, 15 May 1843 (Crisis); Rojas, *Influencia*; *El Relámpago de Marzo*, No. 1, 9 March 1844 (Cuestión agrícola), in *Pensamiento político*, IV, 620–622; and *El Venezolano*, Nos. 274, 275, 276, 29 March to 26 April 1845 (Cuestión económico-política).

17. This short but crucial law is worth copying here. "Considerando: que la libertad, igualdad y seguridad de los contratos son unos de los medios poderosos que puede contribuir a la prosperidad de la República, Decretan. Art. 1° Puede pactarse libremente, que para hacer efectivo el

pago de cualquiera acreencia, se rematen los bienes del deudor por la cantidad que se ofresca por ellos el día y hora señalados para la subasta. Art. 2? En todos los demas contratos, así como en el interés que en ellos se estipule, cualquiera que sea, también se ejecutará estrictamente la voluntad de los contrantanes. Art. 3? Para el remate de que habla el Art. 1? se observarán las formalidades prescriptas en las leyes de procedimiento ejecutivo. Art. 4? En los remates que se celebren a virtud de lo dispuesto en el Art. 1? de esta ley, cesa el privilegio de retracto, y ninguna corporación ni persona podrá reclamar lesión ni restitución *in integrum*. Art. 5? El acreedor o acreedores pueden ser licitadores en la subasta. Art. 6? El rematador por el acto del remate y posesión subsecuente, se hace dueño de la propiedad rematada. Art. 7? Se derogan todas las demas leyes que se opongan a las disposiciones de la presente." See also González Guinán, *Historia*, II, 298–300.

18. Particularly useful are the revealing polemics conducted by Tomás Lander over his being persecuted by those he called "logreros." See his series of articles in *El Venezolano*, Nos. 194, 197, 199, 202, 206, and 207, 8 August to 24 October 1843 in *Pensamiento político*, IV, 627–667.

19. In addition to the Lander polemics cited above see *La ley de 10 de abril y el comercio*; *La Bandera Nacional*, No. 60, 18 September 1838 (Banco de la Sociedad de Agricultores); *El Relámpago*, No. 2, 2 November 1843 (Diálogo), in *Pensamiento político*, IV, 590–592.

20. There are numerous denunciations of this system. Perhaps the best and most significant, coming from a Conservative, is Fermín Toro's "Reflexiones sobre la ley de 10 de abril de 1834," *Pensamiento político*, I, 107–225. See also *El Agricultor*, No. 4, 13 March 1844 (Legislación); and *El Venezolano*, No. 264, 10 December 1844 (Ojeada histórico-política sobre Venezuela).

21. In addition to the sentiments expressed in the articles cited in the three notes directly above, see the suggestive essay by Brito Figueroa in his *Ensayos de historia social*, pp. 233–277.

22. See Appendix 2, Table 2.

23. Of course, some of the increase in coffee production must have come from planters impressing food-producing lands into coffee cultivation. Indications of this can be seen in the discussion of food shortages in *El Liberal*, No. 367, 22 July 1842.

24. For example, an 1809 treatise on coffee and cacao cultivation methods was thought valid enough in 1833 to be reprinted. *Memoria de los abonos, cultivos y beneficios que necesitan los diversos valles de la provincia de Caracas para la plantación de café. Presentada al Real Consulado por un patriota que se interesa en la prosperidad de la agricultura, en 26 de octubre de 1809. Adicionada por un amigo de la agricultura con una instrucción para el gobierno de las haciendas de cacao* (Caracas: Tomás

Antero, 1833), a typescript copy in possession of Don Pedro Grases, Caracas. In 1836 a long series of articles encouraged farmers to import machinery to increase the efficiency of their plantations. *El Liberal*, Nos. 10 to 14, 2 August to 30 August 1836. Then, in 1839, another series on improving cultivation repeated the same ideas expressed since 1809. *Correo de Caracas*, Nos. 24 and 25, 18 June and 25 June 1839. See also *El Liceo Venezolano*, No. 3, March 1842 (Fermín Toro. Ideas y necesidades), in *Pensamiento político*, I, 103–105.

25. See Appendix 2, Table 1.

26. Contributing to the abundance of coffee on the world market and thus to the decline in the world coffee price were Ceylon and Brazil. See Donald Snodgrass, *Ceylon: An Export Economy in Transition* (Homewood, Ill., Irwin, 1966), p. 20 and Brazil, Instituto Brasileiro de Geografia e Estatística, Conselho Nacional de Estatística, *Anuário estatístico do Brasil Ano V, 1939–1940* (Rio de Janeiro, [1940?]), pp. 1374–1375.

27. Without embarking on a major project, it is difficult to arrive at an accurate estimate of transportation costs. Nevertheless, few Venezuelans doubted that the rising cost of transportation hurt the planters severely. Complaints about the badness and impassibility of the roads were heard from the beginning of the boom and grew in frequency and urgency. Lander, *Fragmentos Semanales*, "A los cuidadanos del a provincia" in *Pensamiento político*, IV, 174–181; *El Liberal*, No. 367, 22 July 1842 (Analysis of the 1842 crisis); Carabobo, 1845, *Memoria*, pp. 7–11; *Instituto de crédito territorial* (Caracas: George Corser, 1845). See also PRO, FO 80/11, 33–35 (R. K. Porter, Caracas, 29 March 1840). O'Leary estimated that it cost as much to transport goods from the Valles de Aragua to the Port of La Guaira as it did to ship goods from La Guaira to Liverpool via the Cape of Good Hope. PRO, FO 80/14, 36 (D. F. O'Leary, Caracas, 22 February 1841).

28. Overpopulation, as used in this chapter, means a situation where agricultural workers find it more attractive to transfer from the subsistence sector to the commercial sector of the agricultural economy, because their wages can buy more than they can realize in subsistence farming. In this kind of situation, employers find it relatively easy to attract workers to their fields. Underpopulation, of course, is just the reverse situation. I am grateful to Dr. James A. Hanson for the elaboration of this concept.

29. It would be too much to expect planters to ever be satisfied with their workers. However, the complaints registered during boom times were mainly about behavior, not shortages or excessive cost. See, for example, Caracas, 1833, *Memoria que presenta el gobernador de la provincia de Caracas a la honorable Diputación de la misma reunida en sus sesiones ordinarias de 1833* (Caracas: Damirón y Dupuy, 1833), p. 21; and *Memorias de la Sociedad de Amigos del País*, No. 23, 15 November 1834 in *Sociedad Económica de Amigos del País*, II, 345–356.

30. Indicative of this shift is the increasing scarcity of foodstuffs, as laborers became more and more occupied in commercial agriculture and spent less and less time on the production of food crops. Not only were considerable quantities of foodstuffs imported; duties on corn, rice, and beans were suspended as early as 1837. U.S. Dept. State, Consular, No. 84, IV (B. Renshaw, La Guaira, 12 March 1837) and No. 84, VI (B. Renshaw, La Guaira, 12 January 1841).

31. It is, of course, almost impossible to figure out the real wage of a plantation worker, since the figures quoted as salaries were only part of the compensation. Nonetheless, there are indications that the planters were aware of the greater gain in subsistence farming. See, for example, El Eco Popular, Nos. 5 and 6, 3 March and 10 March 1840 (Agricultura. Policía); El Liberal, No. 205, 31 March 1840 (Inmigración).

32. Indicative of planter concern was the inclusion, in ads offering plantations for sale, of information about available peon populations. See El Liberal, No. 75, 17 October 1837(Se vende); El Venezolano, Nos. 51 and 113, 31 May 1841 and 31 May 1842 (Avisos).

33. An accurate reflection of the growing concern with labor can be obtained from the list of police codes included in Parra Aranguren, Antecedentes del derecho del trabajo, pp. 465–468, and in the list of police codes included in the bibliography of this study. Also of considerable interest are the following articles on the labor problem: El Venezolano, No. 104, 12 April 1842 (Remitido. Algunos agricultores); No. 151, 3 January 1843 (Aviso); No. 181, 30 May 1843 (Representación. Sociedad Agricultora de Caracas); Toro, "Reflexiones sobre la ley de 10 de abril de 1834," Pensamiento político, I, 107–225; El Liberal, No. 541, 19 April 1845 (Rojas. Votos salvados); Protesta razonada (Caracas: Valentín Espinal, 1845); Gaceta de Venezuela, No. 826, 15 November 1846 (Memoria del gobernador de Caracas); Carabobo, 1847, Memoria, p. 3; PRO, FO 80/8, 171 (Mackay, Maracaibo, 7 April 1838); FO 80/11, 33–35 (R. K. Porter, Caracas, 29 March 1840); FO 80/22, 51 (D. F. O'Leary, Puerto Cabello, 30 June 1843).

34. This radical proposition received little support when it was put forward in El Republicano, No. 57, 11 June 1845 (Jornaleros).

35. See Gonzales Guinán, Historia, II, 185, 220, 259, 297, 427; III, 29, 60, 79, 121, 135–136, 140, 176–177, 183–184, 223, 326–327, 379; IV, 17, 31–32, 88, 139, 256, 366, 371–372, 435; V, 183, 204, 217, 265, 327 where the various efforts at encouraging immigration are listed. Also useful are the relevant sections in the Memorias of Interior y Justicia listed in the Bibliography.

36. See Appendix 1, Tables 7 and 8.

37. All parties agreed with the principle of immigration but many only wanted workers, not new citizens, and few could afford to pay immigrant laborers more than they paid their Venezuelan peons, not a very attractive

proposition to the immigrants. *La Bandera Nacional,* Nos. 22 and 24, 26 December 1837 and 9 January 1838; *El Liberal,* No. 205, 31 March 1840 (Inmigración); *El Venezolano,* No. 51, 31 May 1841 (Avisos. Un canario prófugo); and *El Liceo Venezolano,* No. 2, February 1842 (Mendoza. De la inmigración en Venezuela) in *Pensamiento político,* XII, 403–413.

38. See the list of Spanish nationals resident in Venezuela and their occupations in *Gaceta de Venezuela,* No. 918, 6 June 1848. An exception to this rule was the group of Scotsmen who came to Venezuela in the late 1820s. Privately financed, these people were so unsuccessful in setting up an agricultural colony in Venezuela that the British government had to pay their passage out of Venezuela. Porter, *Diary,* pp. 10, 24, 45–46, 51, 59–60, 146–147, 157, 170, 213–214, 236, 237, 253, 270, 281, 337–338.

39. See notes 10 and 15 of this chapter.

40. See, for example, the series of articles on interest rates in *El Promotor,* Nos. 4 to 10, 15 May to 26 June 1843 (Crisis). Also useful are the following: *El Venezolano,* No. 177, 9 May 1843 (Crisis de 1843); *El Agricultor,* No. 4, 13 March 1844 (Legislación); and *El Venezolano,* No. 234, 13 April 1844 (Aranda. Un pensamiento). However, there is some evidence that *El Promotor* pleaded the case of agricultural distress to stir up ill will against the British Colonial Bank branch operating in Venezuela. The purpose envisioned by the friends of the Banco Nacional in Caracas who put out *El Promotor* was to discredit the British Colonial Bank and get a monopoly for the Banco Nacional. The scheme backfired, evidently, and the campaign produced ill will against *all* banks. PRO, FO 80/25, 84–91 (B. H. Wilson, Caracas, 13 March 1844); FO 80/25, 151 (B. H. Wilson, Caracas, 20 April 1844).

41. This pattern is denounced often in the periodical press. See, for example, *El Liberal,* No. 366, 19 July 1842 (Remetidos: Crisis de 1842).

42. The best information on the operation of this system is in the impassioned articles by Tomás Lander about his difficulties with the financial powers. *El Venezolano,* Nos. 194, 197, 199, 202, 206, and 207, 8 August to 24 October 1843 (Logreros, Tribunal Mercantil, Administración de justicia) in *Pensamiento político,* IV, 627–667.

43. For some planter pleas see Rojas, *Influencia; El Eco de Venezuela,* No. 2, 1 March 1846 (Proyecto del Instituto de crédito territorial); and *Gaceta de Venezuela,* No. 890, 28 November 1847 (Informe de la Sociedad Económica). The hardheaded reaction of Conservatives can be seen in Santos Michelena, "Movilización del crédito territorial," *Pensamiento político,* XII, 434–444; *Instituto de crédito territorial* (1845); and *Protesta razonada.*

44. *El Liberal,* Nos. 366 and 367, 19 July and 22 July 1842 (Remetido: Crisis de 1842 and Editorial); No. 583, 31 January 1846 (Auxilio a la agricultura); No. 605, 4 July 1846 (Venezuela en 1830 y 1846); *Protesta razonada.*

45. These ideas can be found in the series of articles in *El Venezolano* and *El Agricultor* as well as the polemics of Tomás Lander and Fermín Toro cited in the notes to this chapter.

46. Conservative views are found principally in the columns of such papers as *El Liberal*. See, for example, the items cited in note 44 and the second part of note 43 above.

47. This theory was propounded by most all the defenders of agriculturalists. The classic exposition of this theme is Francisco Aranda's "Un pensamiento para ser examinado" in *El Venezolano*, No. 234, 13 April 1844. See also the supporting articles by Antonio Leocadio Guzmán in *El Venezolano*, Nos. 274, 275, and 276, 29 March to 26 April 1845 (Cuestión económico-política). The best arguments on the question of legal interest rates are in Toro, "Reflexiones sobre la ley de 10 de abril de 1834," *Pensamiento político*, I, 107–225; *El Nacional*, Nos. 1 to 4, 4 May to 24 May 1848; and the revealing debates over the reduction of interest on Church loans in *Diario de Debates*, Nos. 65, 94, and 98, 28 March to 9 May 1849.

48. These arguments were developed primarily to refute the proponents of an agricultural bank. See *El Liberal*, No. 541, 19 April 1845 (Rojas. Votos salvados); *Instituto de crédito territorial*; *Protesta razonada*; and *El Liberal*, No. 583, 31 January 1846 (Auxilio a la agricultura).

49. For the best available account of these events see González Guinán, *Historia*, III, chaps. 40–48, passim. Also useful on this period is Ramón Díaz Sánchez' perceptive study *Guzmán*. See also Rafael Agostini, . . . *a sus conciudadanos* (Caracas: Imprenta Boliviana por Domingo Salazar, 1845).

50. Very helpful for the political history of this period is Parra Pérez, *Mariño y las guerras civiles*. See also González Guinán, *Historia*, IV, chaps. 52–62.

51. Ibid., chaps. 1–13. Also very useful are the diplomatic reports (1844–1848) from English and United States officers PRO, FO 80/26, 109–111 (B. H. Wilson, Caracas, 1 July 1844), FO 80/32, 117–121 (B. H. Wilson, Caracas, 31 March 1845); FO 80/33, 201–205 (B. H. Wilson, Caracas, 7 December 1845); FO 80/39, 322–324 (B. H. Wilson, Caracas, 21 August 1846); FO 80/40, 20–26 (B. H. Wilson, Caracas, 19 September 1846); FO 80/40, 153–158 (B. H. Wilson, Caracas, 21 October 1846); FO 80/44, 84–86 (B. H. Wilson, Caracas, 4 February 1847); FO 80/44, 185–188 (B. H. Wilson, Caracas, 4 March 1847); FO 80/45, 156–158 (B. H. Wilson, Caracas, 20 May 1847); U.S. Dept. State, Diplomatic, No. 79, II (A. A. Hall, Caracas, 25 May 1844); No. 79, II (A. A. Hall, Caracas, 27 June 1844); No. 79, II (A. A. Hall, Caracas, 28 October 1844); No. 79, II (V. Ellis, Caracas, 10 December 1844); No. 79, III (B. G. Shields, Caracas, 30 September 1846); No. 79, IV (B. G. Shields, Caracas, 7 January 1848); No. 79, IV (B. G. Shields,

Caracas, 29 January 1848); No. 79, IV (B. G. Shields, Caracas, 17 February 1848).

52. González Guinán, *Historia*, chaps. 7–13; V, chap. 14; and *El Centinela de la Patria*, No. 8, 9 December 1846 (Editorial. Guzmancismo).

53. González Guinán, *Historia*, V, passim. An excellent idea of the state of public order prevailing in the provinces during this period can be gained from the following reports. AGN, Int. y Just., CCCLXI (1848), 1–187 (Coro); CCCLXI (1848), 358–494 (Carabobo); CCCLXII (1848), 1–106 (Caracas); CCCLXII (1848), 162–252 (Barinas); and DXI (1853), 185–358 (Papers on expected invasion by Páez). From 1845 through at least 1847, political agitators introduced and spread the false rumor that England or English abolitionist societies had authorized the British minister in Caracas to offer the government 4 million dollars for the abolition of slavery in Venezuela. PRO, FO 84/592, 187–190 (B. H. Wilson, Caracas, 1 February 1845); FO 84/642, 157–168 (B. H. Wilson, Caracas, 21 March 1846); FO 84/642, 202–216 (B. H. Wilson, Caracas, 5 September 1846); FO 84/642, 262–297 (B. H. Wilson, Caracas, 29 September 1846); and FO 84/686, 232–235 (B. H. Wilson, Caracas, 1 June 1847).

54. González Guinán, *Historia*, V, chaps. 14–20.

55. See Chapter 2 of this study.

56. This is borne out by the very low level of slave imports during the years before independence as well as by the indifference displayed by planters over the elimination of the trade. See Brito Figueroa, *La estructura económica*, pp. 93–138.

57. These estimates of proportions are based on the information in Appendix 1, Table 7 and on the estimate by Humboldt, *Viaje*, II, 234.

58. It would be reasonable to suppose that the overpopulation of Venezuela during the 1830s would have made slave investments only marginally profitable, if at all, since slaves had to be maintained all year while the hired peon could be discharged at slow times and need be paid a wage only barely above subsistence.

59. Assuming that a slave became a fully productive field hand at about fifteen years old, the first reduction in the work force would have occurred in about 1836 and would have grown steadily worse as the years went by.

60. See the discussion of this phenomenon in the next chapter of this study.

61. *Sociedad Económica de Amigos del País*, I, 141–152; *El Patriota Venezolano*, No. 6, 26 January 1832; AGN, Int. y Just., CLXIX (1838), 154–159 (Obra pía de Cata); *Diario de Debates*, Nos. 65, 94, and 98, 28 March to 9 May 1849 (Reducción del interés de los censos píos); and Brito Figueroa, *La estructura económica*, pp. 285–300.

62. It is impossible to be precise about the value of slaves in contrast

to other forms of agricultural capital, but it is probably safe to say that slaves were second only to cacao or coffee trees in any planter's capital stock. See, for example, the evaluations in the *Registro Principal*, Escribanías (Hernández Guerra), 1838, f. 16–23; and *Archivo Arquidiocesano*, Obras Pías, Carpeta 15, María de la Torre (1823). Also helpful are the inventories found throughout *La Obra Pía de Chuao*, I.

63. Although it is not possible at this time to establish the prices actually paid for slaves, a spot-check of the Caracas *Registro Principal* shows that the official tariff was not just a figment of the imagination. On the other hand, there were almost no sales that exceeded the official price. Moreover, there were few transactions involving more than one or two slaves. For some specific examples of transactions see *Registro Principal*, Escribanías (Juan A. Hernández), 1830, f. 23–153; (Hernández Guerra), 1836, f. 1–4, 16–23.

CHAPTER 6

Slaves in Society

BEFORE we can understand what Negro slavery meant to Venezuela, we must try to recapture its impact on the rest of society and on the slave himself. We need to know how many slaves there were, and where they lived. We must discover who they worked for, and what they did. Questions such as these must be answered if we ever hope to understand why slavery lasted until 1854 and why the institution took the form it did. The following analysis of the proportion of slaves in the total population, their distribution throughout the country, their ownership, and their occupations relies heavily on population statistics whose completeness and accuracy leave much to be desired. Although local authorities were required by law to submit complete and comprehensive statistics on the institution of slavery, compliance was poor and incomplete.[1]

NUMBERS

One of the best indicators of the impact of slavery on society is the percentage of total population represented by slaves. In the period under discussion here, 1820 to 1854, the absolute number of slaves declined continually, simply because the children of slave mothers were technically born free. Perhaps the best census taken during these years occurred in 1844; it showed that a little less than 2 percent of the population was legally

122

enslaved. In 1837–1838 the famous Venezuelan geographer Agustín Codazzi estimated that slaves represented a bit over 5 percent of the population.[2] If we take 1844 as a base year and work backward using the detailed birth and death figures collected by the government, we see that at the beginning of Venezuela's independence in 1830, Negro slaves totaled only a bit over 5 percent of the population. Now, from the foregoing information, it appears that in the first part of our period, from 1821 to 1844, Negro slaves never totaled more than 6 or 7 percent at the most and were probably closer to 5, 4, or 3 percent during most of these years. Moreover, it would seem reasonable to assume that slaves, being attached to persons of some means, were more completely counted in the various census-taking operations than were the legions of legally free peons without permanent residence or fixed employment.[3]

For the later period, from 1844 to 1854, the birth and death figures are somewhat more complete, and the liquidation of slavery in 1854 required reliable census information to carry out the payment provisions. From this information it becomes clear that the percentage of total population represented by slaves had shrunk to about 1 percent by the time of abolition.[4]

But these figures tell only part of the story. While three provinces had slave concentrations at much the same level as the national average, four had higher percentages, and six had lower. Perhaps a better way of expressing these differences is to point out that the four provinces with a concentration of slaves higher than the national average contained about 58 percent of the population and 77 percent of the slaves, while the six provinces with concentrations of slaves under the national average accounted for 25 percent of the population and 10 percent of the slaves. Yet, before attaching too much significance to these disparities, keep in mind that no province had slaves equaling more than 3 percent of its population. It is, of course, no surprise to find the highest concentrations of slaves in the four most agriculturally developed provinces of Venezuela: Barquisimeto, Carabobo, Caracas, and Coro.[5]

In addition to considering the above information, it is useful to try and make some sense out of the confused set of records known as *Padrones de esclavos*. Formed at the canton level by order of the federal government once in the early thirties and again in the early fifties, these slave lists were supposed to provide the government with the sound statistical information needed to formulate an effective slave policy. Although the census takers were evidently supposed to include such information as the slave's name, owner, age, occupation, and conduct, few local officials had enough energy or ambition to carry out their assignment in full. In fact, the Department of the Interior found it extremely difficult to get any information at all. In spite of these problems, however, a fairly good sampling of slave lists was collected and has survived the ravages of civil war and other natural disasters.[6]

For the 1830s there is useable information on seven provinces representing about one-eighth of the total slave population. Although the sample is rather small, it has the advantage of including two of the provinces with the highest percentages of slaves and some of those with the lowest. Taking this group as a whole, we find that the average number of slaves per owner is just over two and one-half. If, however, we separate those owning ten or more slaves, we find that they average just over twenty slaves apiece, while those owning under ten slaves average about two and one-quarter apiece. Or, looking at it from another angle, the owners of over ten slaves (about 2 percent of all slave holders) controlled 15 percent of the slaves. These figures, of course, show that, at least for the provinces sampled, the average slave owner held only two or three slaves, and that the large owners were relatively few.[7]

Unfortunately for the symmetry of this presentation, the foregoing breakdown contains one glaring fault: the province of Caracas is not included. As we will see, Caracas not only had the largest number of slaves but the highest number of slaves per owner as well. Fortunately, the 1850 slave lists include the province of Caracas. Moreover, although the 1850 lists are not complete, they do duplicate a number of provinces included in the 1830 lists, allowing a comparison of ownership patterns over the years.

From the 1850 data we find that the average number of slaves per owner was just under four. Furthermore, owners of ten or more slaves averaged just under twenty slaves apiece, whereas those owning under ten averaged about two and one-half apiece. In other words, in 1850 the owners of over ten slaves (about 9 percent of all slave holders) controlled 43 percent of the slaves. The averages for 1850 are not greatly different from those for 1830, but the number of slave owners with over ten slaves, as well as the percentage of all the slaves controlled by these individuals, is significantly greater. This, naturally, is the result of adding Caracas into the balance. This province contained the largest single owners of slaves. In fact, the average number of slaves per owner in Caracas province alone was over seven.[8]

The characteristics of Venezuelan slavery that can be gleaned from this maze of statistics, percentage points, and numerical comparisons are significant. The first and most important characteristic is the relatively low number of slaves in the total population. Ranging from around 4 or 5 percent of the population in the early years of independence from Spain, Negro slaves as a group shrank in significance to 1 or 2 percent of the population during the critical decade of the 1840s. A society with this small a percentage of slaves can hardly have been characterized by the institution and was by no means dependent upon it for survival. Moreover, the proportion of the population actually possessing slaves must have been considerably smaller, since each owner held two to four slaves. Even assuming a one-to-one ratio between owners and slaves, the largest percentage possible, only about 4 percent of the population had any direct interest in slavery in our base year of 1844, and by the time of abolition in 1854 only about 2 percent of the population could have been directly affected by the measure. Of course, even these estimates are too high, since most owners held more than one slave.

The numerical insignificance of the group directly involved in slavery is tempered somewhat by the fact that slave owners were all persons of property, often of very much property, and tended to belong to the governing, financial, or agricultural oligarchies. A glance at a list of owners of over ten slaves will reveal such prominent Venezuelan names as Monagas, Sotillo, Arismendi, Lecuna, Ward, Macero, Herrera, Monjas Dominicanas, Manrique, Palacios, Mijares, Alderson, and Echandía.[9] With such men as these financially interested in the future of slavery, it is not so very strange that Venezuela's vaunted liberality took so little interest in freeing the slaves.

Before moving on to the nonstatistical aspect of slaves in society, we must consider one more numerical topic. As noted above, slavery in Venezuela was doomed to die by the free-birth laws of 1821 and 1830. Since no slave could be born after 1821, by 1833 there could be no slaves under eleven, in 1844 none could be under twenty-two, and by 1853 none could be under thirty-one. Slaves were old by forty and few survived longer than fifty or fifty-five. After forty-five a slave was unlikely to be able to work a full day. If we take fifty years as the age when a slave ceased to be worth his keep to his master, it becomes clear that slavery as an institution could not have survived past the 1860s. This is, of course, the outside limit of existence for the system. Most likely, slavery would have become untenable in the late fifties, as the burden of supporting old unproductive slaves more than canceled out the profit earned by the younger slaves.

Indicative of this situation are age profiles compiled from the slave lists used above. While the sample is not as large as one would like, the age profile does not appear to be subject to the geographic difficulties that complicate the owner-slave ratios. Although field hands probably lived shorter lives than domestics, the sample includes a fair cross section of Venezuelan slave occupations. In 1833–1835, when no slave should have been younger than eleven or thirteen, about a quarter of the slave population was under twenty, a bit over half was between

twenty and thirty-nine, while the rest were forty or over. Some
twenty years later, just before abolition, over half the remaining
slave population was over forty. This calculation is further
borne out by the fact that in 1854, when slavery was finally
abolished, the average age of the newly freed men was about
forty-five.[10]

POSITION IN SOCIETY

With a clear idea of the numerical characteristics of Venezuela's
slave population, it is possible to consider the place and personality of the Negro slave. Since slaves formed such a small
part of the population, they rarely appeared in the press except
as advertisements of one kind or another. Because just about all
the elite in Venezuela agreed on the slave question, there was
little need to discuss such probems as the evils of servitude or
the benefits of abolition. And since all agreed that slavery in
principle was an evil thing and should eventually be abolished,
an abolitionist would have had a hard time stirring up any enthusiasm. In fact, Venezuela officially considered herself abolitionist, because she had passed a free-birth law which would,
in time, produce total abolition through the agent of death.
While the slaves waited for the grim reaper to set them free,
they were supposed to work hard for their masters, always keeping in mind that if they lived long enough and honorably
enough they might be freed by the manumission system. Although slave owners never tired of pointing out the beneficence
of their labor system when compared with the United States
or with the free European peasants,[11] slaves somehow remained
unconvinced. Even the masters were amazed at the sacrifices a
slave would endure to collect enough money to free his wife
so their children would be born free of all servitude.[12]

Before freedom came, of course, the slaves would have to
labor at the various tasks designated by their owners. Although
the available information is not good enough to allow a statisti-

cal breakdown of the various jobs filled by slaves, it is possible to divide most bondsmen into four occupational groups: field hands, artisans, domestics, and runaways. Of course, the traditional occupation of slaves was field work on cacao, coffee, or sugar plantations. Yet, by the time of the 1830 census, common laborers were becoming a minority among slaves. The job of clearing and harvesting had shifted, it would seem, from owned hands to hired hands. Moreover, as the century wore on, this tendency became established tradition, as fewer and fewer plantations had enough slaves to handle the tasks. The coffee boom, with its attendant expansion into newly opened land, intensified the shift to peon labor, as the steadily declining and aging slave population filled fewer and fewer jobs.

This process, most likely, accounts for the high concentration of domestics among slaves. Most owners of one, two, or three slaves evidently preferred to keep their property constantly occupied in housework or cooking rather than send them out as field hands. Rare indeed were the owners of under four slaves who listed their slaves' occupations as other than housework. A few owners were privileged to own one of the slave artisans, usually shoemakers or carpenters, perhaps a stevedore or sailor, who presumably paid their master all or part of their wages. But since most slave holders owned three or four slaves, it comes as no surprise that domestic work seems to have been the favorite occupation. There were, of course, all kinds of domestics. Some washed, others ironed. Some cooked, others arranged the house. A few seemed to have no fixed duties at all.[13]

Although domestic service and field work absorbed most slave energies, a significant group of bondsmen opted for the life of a fugitive. The exact number of runaways is impossible to determine and most likely varied with the political and economic climate, but in a country as sparsely populated as Venezuela, with rugged mountains cutting through the areas of highest slave concentrations, it is not surprising that slaves found it easy and attractive to take to the hills. Evidently, slave supervision was not as close as masters and majordomos might have liked, for slaves seemed to disappear with relative ease into the neighboring mountains. Nevertheless, life as a fugitive could not have been much fun, albeit better than slavery. Survival was generally assured by subsistence agriculture. To supplement this meager existence, slaves apparently passed themselves off as free peons to work by the day on plantations or, more commonly, in the mines of Aroa.[14] Much of this sort of thing had to be done with the connivance of employers, hard pressed for labor. In any case, fugitives managed to eke out a reasonable existence on the fringes of society, often teaming up with free-born outcasts in bandit bands or communities. Runaways often grouped together for safety and defense.[15] Some of the better located slaves found they could easily flee to Trinidad where they were protected by the British government, much to the self-righteous indignation of the Venezuelan government.[16]

Slave catching was a rather hazardous operation. All police officials in Venezuela were authorized and duty bound to capture runaways, but were singularly ineffective at this as well as at their other duties. Individuals, too, were legally empowered to lay hold of any fugitives they might find. But these slave catchers proved so poorly motivated that some owners employed hungry peons to hunt slaves in their spare time, a job reputed to be both dangerous and distasteful.[17] Now and then a runaway community, or *rochela*, would become so large and its members so bold as to threaten the nearby communities, or at least to make the respectable people fear for their property and lives. When this occurred, letters from panic-stricken citizens would issue forth to the local, provincial, and national governments, crying for help. An expedition would be formed, guns would be distributed, and the defenders of society would sally forth to deal with the threat to their safety. Often the expedition would find no one around, sometimes one or two individuals might be caught, and rarely some determined resistance would be encountered. In any case, the rochela was destroyed, and the runaways were either captured or dispersed.[18]

There is no way to even guess how many runaways were eventually captured. But many must have been caught or masters would have stopped advertising fugitive slave descriptions as a futile expense. Nevertheless, throughout this period, slaves continued to escape their servitude, preferring the precarious life of a rochela to the security of a slave hut.

Yet, in spite of the futility of slave existence, few slaves opted for violent rebellion. From the end of independence to abolition, there is no record of any large-scale organized rebellion of slaves.[19] This does not mean that slaves were always peaceful nor that they never took up arms for their freedom. What is significant, however, is that the enslaved population never found the leadership nor the occasion to mount a major effort for freedom. There were a number of conditions making slave rebellions a rather unattractive proposition. First of all, slaves were outnumbered. In addition, they were spread out over quite a large geographic area. The organization and communication problems attendant on a massive uprising were almost insurmountable.[20] Third, the facility with which slaves could flee to the hills provided an escape valve for those ambitious and courageous slaves who might have provided the leadership. Moreover, a whole generation of such leaders had acquired their freedom fighting in the armies of the independence. Naturally, there were individual instances of slave violence directed against overbearing overseers or brutal masters, but none of these incidents seemed to spark any wider response.[21]

Perhaps the greatest deterrent to slave violence, however, was the periodic violence led by the master class. The wars for independence fixed on the country the policy of admitting Negro slaves to the political battles of their masters. Although no one much wanted to acknowledge complicity in recruiting slaves for the purpose of overthrowing a government, both Liberals and Conservatives indulged in the practice. Rumors of Negro slave uprisings abounded during the short-lived rebellion in 1835, but little came of it, probably because of the short duration of the revolt.[22] However, the crisis of 1842 lengthened, the ruling Conservative Oligarchy refused to help (as the Liberal elite thought it should), and, in the wake of the evidently fraudulent elections of 1846, revolt broke out. Horror-struck Conservative oligarchs pronounced lengthy and self-righteous condemnations of the Liberal oligarchs' tacit endorsement of freedom for all slaves joining the rebellion. Although relatively few atrocities were attributable to slaves seeking freedom, the profoundly shaken government accused its opponents of extraordinary irresponsibility and immorality in unleashing a race war.[23]

Somehow this righteous indignation rang a bit hollow, especially when we find the ousted Conservatives inciting slave rebellions in the late forties and early fifties.[24] It is almost impossible to assess the influence and magnitude of slave participation in these uprisings, but there is no question they did participate and in sufficient numbers to seriously scare all the oligarchs concerned.

The Liberal elite was no less frightened of slave rebellions than their Conservative enemies. The reports of the Department of the Interior on the efficacy of the manumission system leave no doubt about the Monagas dynasty's fears. Manumission must be speeded up, they believed, to free enough slaves to give the others hope. Otherwise, the consequences would be terrible to behold.[25] Moreover, officialdom was exceedingly jittery about slave conspiracy. Any rumor was sufficient to call out troops to put down imagined uprisings. Exiled Conservatives exploited this nervousness by propagating false alarms.[26]

On the basis of the information available, we can conclude that Venezuelan Negro slaves were disinclined to revolt on their own. Most slaves opted for passive resistance or flight. On the other hand, freedom was such a worthwhile goal that many slaves were willing to serve their masters as cannon fodder in the civil wars for the often vain hope of liberation. Yet, ironically enough, it was the slave's disruptive potential, real or imagined, that finally brought him freedom.

NOTES

1. An indication of the difficulties encountered by official census compilers can be seen in the series of circular letters sent to local officials pleading for information. *Gaceta de Venezuela*, No. 153, 14 December 1833; No. 1084, 7 October 1852; No. 1091, 5 December 1852.

2. However, Codazzi's figures for slaves were probably inflated, since he evidently included manumisos, the freeborn children of slaves, with the slaves. See Codazzi, *Obras*, I.

3. Moreover, as property, slaves were more fully registered with local authorities, since proof of ownership was needed to conduct any transaction involving slaves.

4. Tables and a description of the sources used to compile these statistics are included in Appendix 1.

5. On the other hand, some evidence exists which shows a number of small towns scattered throughout the agricultural zones having over half their population made up of slaves. See the census returns in the *Archivo Arquidiocesano de Caracas*, sección parroquias, where there are returns scattered throughout the years 1780–1830 from at least 250 parishes.

6. See Appendix 1, Table 3 for a list of the padrones de esclavos used in this analysis.

7. Exceptional cases, such as the famous Hacienda Chuao, occurred where an institution might own one or two hundred slaves, but these were relatively rare. See Arcila Farias, et al., *La Obra Pía de Chuao*, passim.

8. The rise in the average number of slaves per owner in 1850 is not only a function of the higher concentration of slaves in the province of Caracas. Since large numbers of owners held only one or two slaves in 1830, by 1850 many of them would have ceased to be slave holders as their property died in the intervening years. This process would tend to reduce the number of small slave holders while increasing the percentage of slaves owned by the large holders.

9. These names are all in the padrones de esclavos cited in Appendix 1, Table 3.

10. This estimate is derived from the average prices assigned the slaves in a census taken of all the slaves freed by the 1854 law. Int. y Just., 1856, *Exposición que dirige al Congreso de Venezuela en 1856 el secretario del Interior y Justicia* (Caracas: Imprenta y Litografía Republicana de Federico Madriz, 1856), pp. 48–51.

11. *El Correo de Caracas*, No. 17, 30 April 1839 (Fermín Toro: Europa y América); *El Observador Caraqueño*, No. 4, 22 January 1824; *Diario de Avisos*, No. 101, 17 May 1850.

12. *El Observador Caraqueño*, No. 4, 22 January 1824.

13. Indications of this trend, aside from those cited in the chapter on economics, can be found in those slave lists that include occupations.

14. Accounts of runaways are legion. See, for example, Caracas, 1833, *Memoria*, pp. 18–20; *Memorias de la Sociedad de Amigos del País*, No. 23, 15 November 1834 in *Sociedad Económica de Amigos del País*, II, 345–356; AGN, Int. y Just., CXVII (1835), 304–308 (list and description of fugitive slaves, fourteen men and seven women plus some children). Accounts of runaways working as freemen can be seen in AGN, Int. y Just., CLXVI (1837), 93–94 (Letter from a slave owner about runaways in Mines of Aroa); CLXIX (1838), 154–159 (Official letter from Ocumare de la Costa about runaways at Aroa); and CLXXVI (1838), 47–56.

15. In addition to the sources cited in note 14 above see AGN, Int. y Just., LVI (1832), 24–29 (Novedades con algunos esclavos); CVIII (1835), 365–369 (Persecución de malhechores y esclavos prófugos en Caucagua); CLVIII (1837), 367 (Lista de esclavos prófugos); CLXXXII (1838), 215–275 (Amotinados en Pto. Cabello); and Carabobo, 1845, *Memoria*, p. 2.

16. AGN, Int. y Just., CCLVII (1842), 322–335 (Impida que los esclavos se fugan para la isla de Trinidad).

17. Caracas, 1832, *Proyecto de reglamento general de policía* (Caracas: Valentín Espinal, 1832); Caracas, 1833, *Memoria*, pp. 18–20; Caracas, 1839, *Ordenanzas, resoluciones y acuerdos de la Diputación Provincial de Caracas en sus reuniones ordinarias de 1838 y 1839*, Edición oficial (Caracas: George Corser, 1839), p. 60; *El Liberal*, No. 665, 21 August 1847 (On need for police measures against slaves); AGN, Int. y Just., CCCXCVI (1849), 83–101 (Denuncia sobre conspiración de clases).

18. Accounts of these expeditions can be found in the following expedientes, AGN, Int. y Just., LVI (1832), 24–29; CVIII (1835), 365–369; CLXXVI (1838), 47–56.

19. This is not to say that slaves were never involved in violent rebellions, only that rebellions in which slaves took part were always organized and led by nonslaves who proffered freedom to acquire troops.

20. An idea of the communications problem can be seen in the expediente on a slave disturbance that was feared to have ramifications in other areas, AGN, Int. y Just., CD (1849), 122–154.

21. For an example of a small altercation, blown all out of proportion by nervous government officials, see AGN, Int. y Just., CCCXCI (1848), 347–369.

22. AGN, Int. y Just., CLII (1836), 1–7; CXXXVIII (1836), 251–276; and Williamson, *Caracas Diary*, p. 72.

23. Information on slave participation in the revolution of 1846 is scattered throughout the press. See, for example, *El Republicano*, No. 6, 27 June 1844 (Diabólica invención); *El Centinela de la Patria*, No. 8, 9 December 1846 (Editorial on Guzmancismo); *Diario de la Tarde*, No. 60, 6 August 1846 (J. V. González, Carta X to A. L. Guzmán); *El Liberal*, No. 615, 12 September 1846 (El Guzmancismo en la práctica); No. 615, 12 September 1846 (Crónica interior: facciosos); No. 617, 26 September 1846 (Editorial); No. 622, 24 October 1846 (Description of attack on hacienda of Angel Quintero); No. 624, 7 November 1846 (Facción de Charallave); *El Centinela de la Patria*, No. 8, 9 December 1846 (Breve juicio). See also PRO, FO 80/40, 20–26 (B. H. Wilson, Caracas, 19 September 1846); U.S. Dept. State, Diplomatic, Venezuela, No. 79, III (Benjamin G. Shields, Caracas, 30 September 1846).

24. AGN, Int. y Just., CCXCI (1848), 347–369 (Denuncia un plan negricida); CCCXCIII (1849), 299–300 (False alarm of rebellion); CCCXCVI (1849), 83–101 (Denuncia sobre conspiración de clases).

25. *El Republicano*, No. 252, 7 November 1849 (Circular letter to governors urging pressure for abolition). Nothing could be more explicit on this point than the Department of the Interior's reason for urging effective manumission. By ". . . haciendo efectiva la manumisión de los esclavos, asegurando las naturales esperanzas de estos, acercando el día de la emancipación de todos y respetando el derecho de propiedad de sus dueños, quedará destruido un poderoso elemento de ajitación, de zozobra y de disgusto, de que se hace uso cuando así conviene a los partidos políticos con notable perjuicio del órden, de la tranquilidad y de la dicha de la patria," Int. y Just., 1850, *Memoria*, pp. 19–20.

26. In addition to the pieces cited in note 24 above see AGN, Int. y Just., CD (1849), 122–154 (Se denuncia una revolución); CDLXXII (1852), 344–347 (Esclavos trastornando el órden).

CHAPTER 7

The Abolition of Negro Slavery

THROUGHOUT this discussion of the operation and decline of Venezuela's slave system, I have mentioned the official act of abolition without explaining or discussing it. But now it is time to come to grips with the problem posed by the formal abolition of Negro slavery in Venezuela on 24 March 1854. In view of the small number of slaves in Venezuela and the administrative and disciplinary problems they caused, one wonders why the institution was not done away with long before the presidential term of José Gregorio Monagas. There are two major reasons why slavery lasted as long as it did. First of all, no one much cared whether a few thousand blacks belonged to a small band of powerful men, and second, no one regarded it either convenient or expedient to assume the costs of emancipation before 1854.

From the wars of independence to abolition, Venezuela never suffered any kind of moral crisis over her slave problem. By means of her elaborately contrived manumission system and her widely publicized belief in the gradual abolition of slavery, Venezuela avoided the bitter and divisive controversies that characterized the abolition process in other countries. This ideology of gradual freedom for all men was born of the neces-

sity of war, and once confirmed on the battlefields of the republic this precious principle of liberty could not be revoked.

Venezuelans, insofar as we are able to tell from the periodical
press, were pretty much of one mind on slave matters. Slavery,
they realized, was an economically decadent institution in their
own country; they were also aware that it was viewed with dis-
taste by the most enlightened countries of Europe. Moreover,
few individuals could find much fundamentally wrong with
an official policy that espoused the gradual freedom of slaves.[1]
In any case, it would have been surprising indeed had Venezuelans allowed themselves to become worked up over the fate
of such a small minority of their countrymen.

Yet, while almost everyone agreed that slaves should be
freed, almost no one thought they should be freed now. Freedom carried such awesome responsibility that much preparation would be necessary before any slave or child of a slave could
be allowed to exercise the privileges and responsibilities of a
free man.

Underneath this charade of pious platitudes lay a number
of unpleasant facts little discussed in the press. The first of
these facts was that the institution of slavery represented a
considerable amount of money. Although only 4, 3, or 2 percent
of the population was enslaved, its value was considerable. By
the time of abolition in 1854 slave property equalled 3 million
pesos, about the same amount earned by Venezuelan coffee
exports the same year.[2] Since abolition without indemnifica-
tion was almost never considered, any government would think
twice before assuming the burden of 3 million pesos. Moreover, the abolition of slavery would almost certainly cause a
temporary but sudden reduction in the labor force, as the
newly freed Negroes began to exercise their rights.[3] As we have
seen in an earlier chapter, after the 1840s the amount of labor
available to planters at the price they were willing and able
to pay was severely limited. Thus, the political risk to any
government attempting to abolish one of the few institutions
that kept some of these scarce laborers on the land would

indeed have been high. Moreover, given the unstable political conditions prevalent in Venezuela after about 1840 and the severe economic depression that hit about the same time, no governing party could have wanted to add the expense and problems of abolition to their difficulties.

Had the Conservative Oligarchy been able to maintain its hold on the reins of power for another decade, or had the Liberal Oligarchy got a firmer grip on the reins in 1848, Venezuela probably would have stuck with her ineffectual but philanthropic manumission system until death brought about the abolition of slavery sometime in the 1860s. But this was not to be. The Conservatives lost control of their handpicked president when he defected to the Liberals. In turn, the Liberals, inexperienced in government and racked by internal feuds, were unable to gain complete control of the country. Conservative-led bands harassed the government, spreading rumors of impending slave uprisings, as government troops rushed hither and yon looking for nonexistent revolts. Conservative caudillos let it be known that freedom would be one of the first orders of business for their government come the restoration of their leader, José Antonio Páez.

In view of these events, it is little wonder that the Liberal government began to think seriously about some way of eliminating the possibility of a Conservative-led slave rebellion. Their first proposal was to revitalize the creaky manumission system by an infusion of some 50,000 pesos into the fund. This might convince doubting Negroes that there was some hope of freedom within the legal system. And so the directive went out. Each province was assigned an amount in proportion to the number of slaves believed to be in the province. Unfortunately, the money Congress authorized could not be used for freedom, because the expenses of putting down various uprisings drew too heavily on the treasury. So the government urged the provinces to free those slaves whose masters would take an I.O.U. on the basis of the government's good intentions. The stratagem had little success.[4]

From 1849 on, the number of individuals willing to come out openly in favor of some sort of abolition scheme rose dramatically. The governor of Apure, Rafael Acevedo, sent out a circular letter to his fellow governors urging them to support an abolition plan. The benefits would be great, he believed, and they would much outweigh any problems such a beneficent measure could cause. It was only right that the slaves should be free, since most of them had more than paid their price in services. Moreover, he said, the day the abolition law is passed will be the ". . . day on which will be decreed definitively the high and great destiny of Venezuela, the day on which we shall all embrace one another with unheard of cordiality; and this can not be the day on which a threat of public disorder is thrust into the bosom of the fatherland."[5] Other Liberals with a sharper business sense pointed out that if the institution of slavery was not abolished soon, slave owners would find themselves without capital and without slaves as their property died or became useless. Better to abolish slavery now and get a little something for the capital that they would lose in a few years in any case.[6]

Lest anyone misunderstand the situation, the Department of the Interior reminded Congress of the precariousness of its position. By making manumission effective, that is, by freeing a significant number of slaves, ". . . by assuring their natural hopes, by bringing closer the day of freedom for all, and by respecting the property rights of the owners, a powerful element of agitation, of anxiety, of disgust will be destroyed, which has been used when convenient by the political parties with a notable prejudice to public order, tranquility. . . ."[7]

As nothing much was done about these gentle hints, and the political situation continued to worsen, Congress moved to consider an abolition proposal in 1854 which had evidently been introduced some years before.[8] The first days of debate dragged on, with congressmen exchanging worthy statements on the relative sacredness of property and of liberty. One delegate, notable for his concern for property rights, set the tone of the debates when he announced his dedication to the principle of freedom for all men. However, he continued, such freedom could not come at the expense of that other great Liberal principle: property. Unless someone could come up with a viable tax scheme offering a chance of paying slave owners within a reasonably short time, he could not be expected to vote in favor of abolition.[9] Evidently, he felt that the rights of some men to property were more precious than the rights of other men to liberty. Following up this line of thought, this Liberal champion pointed out that if the abolition project did not include some system of apprenticeship, the newly freed slaves might forget how to work.[10]

But these arguments appear to have been no more than window dressing for the major objection of most of the law's opponents. Slaves represented capital invested in workers and usually had been mortgaged to the full amount of their value. Thus, no slave owner could view abolition with equanimity unless he was assured prompt and adequate payment. Congressional skepticism about the various taxation schemes proposed by abolition advocates was not without foundation. One has only to remember the fate of the 50,000 pesos destined for manumission to understand the slave owner's lack of enthusiasm for payment plans. At this point in the debate the proposed law was sent back to committee for a major revision.

When the committee reported out the revised law, the political climate had changed somewhat. On the same day the new law reached the floor, President José Gregorio Monagas sent a special message to Congress putting the full weight of the administration behind the abolition of Negro slavery—now. With this message, tantamount to an order, on their desks, the legislators got down to the serious business of producing an abolition law. The slave owners on the revising committee had devised an abolition decree that was exceptional for its complexity and conservatism. Being ardent Liberals they stood fully behind the principle of abolition, but once slavery was abolished all the ex-slaves should be held to their former owners for three years, with time added for bad behavior. This plan, naturally, was devised for the benefit of the freemen who might otherwise get distracted by their new-found liberty. Moreover, the manumisos, those unfortunate freeborn slave children, would be required to serve out their contracts.[11]

In the discussion that followed, it became increasingly evident that everyone knew abolition had arrived. The defenders of slave property could only try to achieve better terms. One such individual, a cleric, bemoaned the timing of the measure. Why turn loose these people during a period of internal unrest and revolution? Furthermore, there was no adequate police force to make the newly freed work and to prevent them from bringing ruin on Venezuela. Nonetheless, this representative of the Church would vote for complete abolition.[12] After some other representatives made their speeches to much the same effect, abolition of Negro slavery was approved and the continuance of any kind of apprenticeship system was defeated.[13]

Of course the battle was far from over, for the legislators now had to face the real problem: how to pay for the slaves. In the ensuing debates over a variety of complex tax plans and revenue schemes, more heat was generated than in any of the pro forma speeches on abolition. Yet, with the presidential message in mind, the payment sections of the abolition bill were discussed and approved in short order.[14] By 16 March the bill was ready to be sent to the Senate, less than a week after the presidential message. The Senate, too, cooperated in this historic endeavor and promptly approved the whole bill, with one exception. They vetoed a provision giving freedom to slaves fleeing other countries. Such a provision, as one senator pointed out, was not only immoral but would encourage the wrong kind of immigration to Venezuela.[15] On 20 March the Senate returned the bill to the House for final approval. On 23 March the House took up the abolition measure; they had been prevented from doing so on 22 March by a discussion of whether to include inscriptions on the portraits of José Tadeo and José Gregorio Monagas to be hung in the chambers of Congress. Naturally, the House quickly sanctioned the Senate revision.[16]

The next day a congressional commission presented the bill to the president for his signature. Such a momentous occasion called forth numerous speeches to an enthusiastic crowd. Accompanied by music and fireworks, the 24 March 1854 Abolition Law went into effect. The grateful people hoisted a banner reading: "If the Liberator, Simón Bolívar, through various decrees and resolutions, provided for the freedom of the slaves in Venezuela, the Congress of 1854 made it effective and the Eastern Genius signed the *EXEQUATUR*."[17]

Although we have little direct evidence, it is not too difficult to guess the motives of the administration's demand for abolition. The Conservatives were increasing their revolutionary activity, and the continual drain on the treasury caused by sporadic uprisings in one province or another was becoming serious.[18] Moreover, the coffee depression continued to hang on and planters remained in desperate straits. The Monagas administration undoubtedly knew that the twelve or thirteen thousand slaves liable to be freed by an abolition decree would have a relatively small effect on the economy as a whole. The Liberal ministers most likely calculated that the risk of allowing the Conservatives to capture the banner of abolition was greater than the risk of alienating a small number of slave owners. Conservatives, of course, accused the Monagas government of freeing the slaves to acquire a few loyal soldiers and prevent a general uprising of slaves on behalf of the Conservative cause.[19] And in a sense they were probably right. It is, of course, impossible to determine what effect abolition had on the course of the ensuing civil disorders since, with abolition, slaves ceased to be identifiable as such.

In any case, the abolition of Negro slavery in Venezuela came as an anticlimax to over a quarter century of gradual disintegration of the slave system. By 1854 slavery as an institution was barely profitable, if at all. It was maintained mostly out of inertia and from slave holders' attempts to derive as much profit as possible from their doomed investment. Slavery ended only when the cost of maintaining the institution was calculated to be greater than the cost of eliminating it.

With the abolition of slavery in Venezuela, the ex-slave disappears from view and merges into the mass of nonwhites. Thus it is almost impossible to trace his activities after March 1854. To be sure, the elaborate tax system designed to pay the slave master full value for the property lost through abolition required the ex-slave to present himself before a local committee, thereby testifying to his master's right to compensation. But without a major research effort we cannot determine how many slaves presented themselves nor whether the masters were ever paid in full.

It is equally difficult to estimate the effect of abolition on the subsequent economic and political history of Venezuela, since the actions of the freemen are rendered invisible by their free status. Not until a well-researched study of the period from 1850 to 1880 appears will we be able to comprehend the political and military battles of the Federal Wars, not to mention the significance of the economic and social transformations begun during the wars for independence and continued through the nineteenth century. Thus, for an understanding of Venezuela, this study represents only the beginning of what must be a long and sustained effort to discover the dynamics of Venezuela's social, political, and economic development.

NOTES

1. See the interesting comments by the Venezuelan agent in England in PRO, FO 80/29, 19–22 (Alejo Fortique, London, 9 April 1844).

2. For the evaluation of slave property as of 1854 by cantons see Appendix 1, Table 6. The value of coffee exports can be seen in Appendix 2, Table 1.

3. When calculating the effect of abolition on agriculture, Venezuelans were quick to point out that the loss of labor would be greater than the loss of slaves alone because the manumisos, legally free, could not be held any longer than the slaves. One newspaper placed the financial cost of replacing these laborers at two million pesos. *Diario de Avisos*, No. 72, 22 April 1854.

4. *Gaceta de Venezuela*, No. 1094, 26 December 1852 (Circular, 21

December 1852); Int. y Just., 1854, *Memoria,* pp. 54–56; and *Gaceta de Venezuela,* No. 1105, 16 April 1853 (Circular, 14 March 1853).

5. The Acevedo letter can be seen in *El Republicano,* No. 252, 7 November 1849 (Letter dated 17 October 1849). Other examples of the sudden interest in some sort of abolition measure can be seen in articles on slavery in the United States and Great Britain. The Calhoun-Webster debate of 4 March 1850 on slavery was printed without comment, along with a piece from the "Memorias Postumas" of Chateaubriand on the slave problem in the United States, in the *Diario de Avisos,* No. 101, 17 May 1850. An article on the abolition of slavery in the English colonies wondered why Republican Venezuela could not do what aristocratic England had done, *El Alerta,* No. 23, 28 February 1850.

6. See the two editorials in *El Republicano,* No. 236, 25 August 1849 and No. 237, 3 October 1849. Also of interest is the notice of a pamphlet by F. Bolívar from Valencia with the title "Cuestión política y filantrópica" which advocated the extinction of slavery within six years. *Diario de Avisos,* No. 4, 22 January 1850.

7. See Int. y Just., 1850, *Memoria,* pp. 18–20. Some provincial governments also came out in favor of abolition. See the "Decreto de la Diputación Provincial de Barquisimeto" of 29 November 1851 in *Pensamiento político,* XII, 278–280; and the resolution of the Diputación Provincial of Caracas on 10 December 1852 in Caracas, 1852, *Ordenanzas, resoluciones y acuerdos de la honorable Diputación Provincial de Caracas en 1852* (Caracas: Oficinas Tipográficas de Briceño y Campbell, 1852), pp. 126–127.

8. The records of congressional debates leave much to be desired, but it appears clear that the abolition of slavery was introduced sometime in 1850 by José Silverio González. See *Diario de Debates,* No. 8, 7 March 1854 (House debates of 4 March 1854).

9. *Diario de Debates,* No. 8, 7 March 1854 (Speech by Sr. Amengual in session of 4 March 1854).

10. *Diario de Debates,* No. 10, 8 March 1854 (Speech by Sr. Amengual in session of 4 March 1854). In this same speech, Sr. Amengual cautioned his colleagues that to sanction abolition without adequate compensation was the same as bringing communism to Venezuela.

11. *Diario de Debates,* Nos. 16 and 17, 11 March 1854. These issues carry both the president's speech and the "Informe" of the commission revising the abolition bill, with the text of the revised bill.

12. *Diario de Debates,* No. 19, 14 March 1854 (Speech by Prbo. Dr. Cabrales on 13 March 1854).

13. *Diario de Debates,* Nos. 20, 21, and 22, 14 March and 16 March 1854.

14. For the entire record of the abolition debates in the House see

Diario de Debates, Nos. 7, 8, 10, 16, 17, 19–24, 26, 1, and 7–9, 4 March to 25 March 1854. This covers the sessions from 3 March through 24 March 1854.

15. *Diario de Debates*, No. 6, 23 March 1854 (Speech of Sr. Henriquez on 22 March 1854). The entire Senate proceedings on abolition are in *Diario de Debates*, Nos. 3, 5, 6, 21 March and 23 March 1854. This covers the sessions from 17 March through 22 March 1854.

16. *Diario de Debates*, No. 7, 24 March 1854.

17. *Diario de Debates*, No. 9, 25 March 1854.

18. As mentioned above, things were so tight the government had to take the 50,000 pesos destined for manumission to put down disturbances in the provinces.

19. This accusation is found in many places. See, for example, *El Eco de los Andes*, No. 8, 28 March 1855.

APPENDICES
GLOSSARY
BIBLIOGRAPHY
INDEX

✳ ✳ ✳

Introduction to the Appendices

SINCE statistical information on most phrases of Latin American history is usually at best fragmentary and at worst totally unreliable, some kind of introduction to the following tables is in order. There are two appendices. The first has a variety of tables on the operation of the manumission system and the aprendizaje system, the distribution of the slave population and the price of slaves, and some estimates of the total population. The second appendix contains a series of charts on the export trade of Venezuela during this period.

In Appendix 1, the first two tables set out the results of the manumission and the aprendizaje systems. They were compiled from the apparently incomplete information included in the annual *Memorias* of the Department of the Interior. It would appear, however, that the information on manumissions is good enough to be taken as a reasonably reliable estimate of the actual number of Venezuelan Negro slaves who acquired their freedom through the mechanism of state-sponsored manumission. The reasons for this conclusion are obvious enough: since the manumission system worked rather poorly, and local officials were importuned time and time again to produce at least a few freemen, it stands to reason that most of the manumissions that eventully took place would be promptly reported to the national government so the local officials concerned could receive credit for their actions. There is always the possibility, of course, that the Department of the Interior's accounting methods were none too accurate. For example, in 1842 the Department published a summary of manumissions which unfortunately did not agree with the total of all the manumissions reported in previous years. The discrepancy was not very large, however.

Much the same sort of qualifications can be made about Table 2. Compiled from the same sources as Table 1, the list of individuals contracted under the apprenticeship system does not appear to be complete. There are a number of reasons for this situation. Although the apprenticeship system was administered by the same local Juntas as the manumission system, the pressure from the central government for numerical results was not as insistent. The law made no provision about how many manumisos should be apprenticed each year, since all manumisos who reached the legal age were to be so taken care of. Moreover, the contracts between patrons and their charges were strictly a local affair and not really subject to close scrutiny by the national government. Given this situation, it appears likely that the Juntas would be little concerned with the completeness and regularity of their reports to the central government. A glance at Table 2 will show the erratic nature of some of the provinces' reporting techniques. Presumably, the number of manumisos being contracted would not vary widely from one year to the next, since the birth rate of slave children probably remained relatively stable. Yet the apprenticeship figures are very erratic for many provinces. This is due in part to the inefficiency of reporting techniques. Some provinces probably only sent in part of the statistics from their jurisdictions in any year. Moreover, late returns were most likely added to the next year's reports. Then, of course, during times of instability and political turmoil, statistics might not even get compiled. With these considerations in mind, it would be safe to assume that the Apprenticeship of Manumisos Table is an underestimation. There is, of course, no way to tell how much an underestimation is involved here. However, for the purposes of this study, the table is important principally for the light it sheds on the number of manumisos given over to their relatives, in comparison to the total number of contracts recorded. The proportion between manumisos contracted to patrons and manumisos released to the custody of their parents is reasonably accurate.

Tables 3 and 4 give a feeling of authority that is not deserved. The neat figures and percentage points inspire more confidence than they should. Yet, there is really no other way of presenting the results of a spot-check of slave age patterns and slave-owner ratios. At the bottom of each of these tables is a list of the manuscript census of slave population from which these figures were derived. A word is in order about the reliability of these figures. The censuses were supposed to be rather complete registers of all the slaves residing in each locality, but unfortunately for historians the completeness of these lists varies widely. Some of the slave lists contain information on occupation, ownership, age, sex, and conduct. Most, however, contain only the age and ownership information. Moreover, the returns from the various cantons within a province vary as well. In any case, the purpose of these tables is not so much to show a definitely established situation as to indicate the types of ownership patterns prevalent in Venezuela during this period, as well as the age profiles that could be calculated. They are included to provide indications of trends and broad characteristics and are not designed to provide specific percentages for all Venezuela.

Table 6 lists the number of slaves and manumisos freed by the 1854 Abolition Law. These are the individuals whose existence was certified to the federal government and whose masters were entitled to compensation under the law. This is probably a rather accurate accounting. However, it does present a number of difficulties. As can be seen by comparing the figures in Table 6 with the population estimates in Table 7, there is a considerable discrepancy between the two sets of figures. It is not possible yet to determine the reasons for this difference, but some educated guesses can be advanced. For one thing, the census information and vital statistics from which the information in Table 7 was compiled were gathered in the place of the slave's residence. The statistics for slaves freed in 1854, on the other hand, were formed by committees in the place of the owner's residence. This fact alone helps explain the larger number of slaves ascribed to the province of Caracas in the abolition census than were calculated for the population projections of Table 7. Probably, the 1854 total number of slaves shown in Table 7 is larger than the number reported in the abolition census of Table 6 because slave deaths went unreported in many parts of agricultural Venezuela. The value figure in Table 6 is the combined value of both manumisos and slaves freed. It is, therefore, of little use in trying to calculate the average price paid for a freed manumiso or slave. An earlier census of slaves freed under the 1854 law did give the average prices, but the census was not official.

The population projections of Table 7 are of the roughest kind. As can be seen from the notes accompanying the table, the 1844 census was used as a base for the calculation of the figures for 1830 and 1854. These last were computed by adding or subtracting the gains in population recorded in the vital statistics—births and deaths—contained in the *Memorias* of the Department of the Interior. The birth and death figures (Table 8) are, unfortunately for the symmetry of this presentation, nowhere as consistent as they should be. In fact there are numerous gaps. In order to have a reasonably complete series of birth and death figures to use in the population projections, it was necessary to make some rather extensive estimates of population growth for a number of years. However, since there is only one year in which these statistics are absent altogether, and since the gaps occur in different places in different years, the construction of reasonable estimates was not too difficult. The census for 1838 is the work of the famous Venezuelan geographer, Agustín

Codazzi. His estimate was based on his extensive travels and on his investigations in the Church registers in a large number of parishes throughout Venezuela. The reasonably close correlation between his estimates and the one based on the birth and death figures would tend to inspire some confidence in the procedures used. However, there is always the danger that his calculations were based on the same, possibly erroneous, data as mine. In any case, these figures are offered as a preliminary and very rough estimate of the magnitude of Venezuelan population growth during the period under discussion here. A project is now under way to process the extensive collection of ecclesiastical population records from the Archivo Arquidiocesano de Caracas. When it is completed, more sophisticated demographic techniques can be brought to the problem of population estimates for Venezuela, and these tentative figures can be revised with considerable confidence.

Appendix 2 contains seven tables showing the export trade of Venezuela in seven major products. These statistics were compiled from the customs information included in the annual *Memorias* of the treasury department. Rather than list the full citations for all these *Memorias* at the foot of each table, the reader is referred to the full list of *Memorias de Hacienda* in the Bibliography. I have been greatly aided in the compilation of these tables by Dr. James A. Hanson (Brown University—Yale Economic Growth Center). It is our conviction that these tables are a good representation of the fluctuations in Venezuela's foreign trade on the export side. The omission of various ports is due primarily to revolutionary activity in those years which made the operation of the customs system impossible. On the whole, however, they provide quite accurate reflections of the fluctuations in prices and quantities of the important export commodities.

APPENDIX 1

Tables Pertaining to Slaves and Manumisos

TABLE 1
Manumissions

Slaves Freed by Provisions of the
1830–1848 Laws[a] *(1830–1854)*

PROVINCE	FREED BY MANUMISSION TAX	FREED IN WILLS TO CANCEL TAX
Apure	39	—
Aragua	2	—
Barcelona	40	49
Barinas	92	8
Barquisimeto	79	26
Carabobo	78	15
Caracas	387	143
Coro	—	—
Cumaná	—	—
Guárico	—	—
Guayana	21	2
Maracaibo	109	12
Margarita	5	3
Mérida	30	25
Portuguesa	—	—
Trujillo	52	6
TOTAL	934	289

[a] Compiled from Int. y Just., 1842–1847, 1850, 1853, Memoria.

TABLE 2

Apprenticeship of Manumisos

Individuals Contracted[a]

PROVINCE	1839	1841	1842	1843	1844	1845	1846	1848	1849	1850	1852	1853
Apure	—	—	4	—	1	2	4	—	—	—	4	—
Aragua									27(3)	3	25(2)	23(1)
Barcelona	38	—	26	—	15	2	5	26(3)	10(1)	9	7	7
Barinas	—	12	16	4	16	16	31	14	10(2)	18(1)	9	—
Barquisimeto	19	81	43	41	12	45	65	70	—	6	5	24
Carabobo	—	10	50	80	66	103	199	55(2)	84	5	—	—
Caracas	12	160	175	357	225	381	258	254	275	87	109(5)	56(4)
Coro	24	2	16	4	34	14	59	12	5	2	19	7
Cumaná	2	—	21	40	—	63	34	13	—	—	—	—
Guárico									82	25	—	—
Guayana	3	—	—	—	—	—	—	1	—	—	3	1
Maracaibo	—	14	—	3	7	6	10	17	—	—	5	2
Margarita	2	4	2	3	—	11	4	—	5	5(1)	12	—
Mérida	3	18	26	13	26	16	28	—	—	—	3	—
Portuguesa											6	
Trujillo	—	52	42	32	20	32	23	13	5(1)	13	12	8
TOTAL	103	353	421	577	422	691	720	475(5)	503(7)	173(2)	219(7)	128(5)

[a] Compiled from Int. y Just., 1842–47, 1850, 1851, 1853, 1854, *Memoria*.

NOTES: Wherever two figures are shown for any province in any year, the first represents the number of manumisos contracted and the second number, within parentheses, indicates manumisos given over to their elder brothers or sisters, parents or grandparents.

The spaces filled with a dash indicate that no returns were received for that province in that year. Blank spaces are for those provinces not established until after 1848.

TABLE 3
Slaves/Owners[a]

DATE OF CENSUS	SLAVES/OWNER	CATEGORY
1833–34	2.6	All owners of slaves
1833–34	20.3	Owners of over 10 slaves
1833–34	2.25	Owners of under 11 slaves
1852–53	3.9	All owners of slaves
1852–53	19.2	Owners of over 10 slaves
1852–53	2.5	Owners of under 11 slaves
1852–53	7.4	Caracas Province overall

[a] This table compiled from the following sources:

PROVINCE	AGN, INT. Y JUST.
Maracaibo	LXIV (1833), 37–47; CDLXXI (1852), 80–83
Guayana	LXIV (1833), 243–252
Cumaná	LXVI (1833), 170–189
Barinas	LXVII (1833), 42–68, 199–204
Margarita	LXXXVIII (1834), 83–89
Barcelona	LXXXVIII (1834), 259–272; CDLXVI (1852), 4–12
Apure	CDLXII (1852), 64–66
Trujillo	CDLXII (1852), 195–201
Caracas	CDLXXVII (1853), 176–243

TABLE 4
Slave Age Profile[a]

YEAR OF CENSUS	PERCENT BETWEEN 11 AND 19	PERCENT BETWEEN 20 AND 39	PERCENT OVER 40
1833–35	25.3	53.2	21.5
1852–53	—	48.6	51.4

[a] The sources for this table are the same as those listed for Table 3 with the addition of Cumaná, AGN, Int. y Just., CDLXXIV (1853), 87–89.

TABLE 5
Tariff of Slave Prices (1821–1854)[a]

AGE	PRICE	AGE	PRICE
8 days	50 pesos	15–39 years	300 pesos
1 month	54	40	290
2	58	41	285
3	62	42	280
4	66	43	275
5	70	44	270
6	74	45	260
7	78	46	250
8	82	47	240
9	86	48	230
10	90	49	215
11	95	50	200
1 year	100	51	180
2	105	52	170
3	110	53	155
4	115	54	140
5	120	55	125
6	130	56	110
7	140	57	95
8	150	58	80
9	160	59	65
10	180	60	50
11	200	61	35
12	230	62	20
13	270	63	5
14	290	64	0

[a] From *Colección completa*, p. 65.

NOTE: Manumisos, or the free-born children of slave mothers, were assessed at one-half the price they would have brought had they been slaves.

TABLE 6
Slaves Freed by the 24 March 1854 Abolition Law[a]

PROVINCE	CANTON	SLAVES	MANU-MISOS	TOTAL VALUE (PESOS)[b]
Aragua	Victoria	796	506	
	Turmero	258	259	
	Maracay	243	216	
	Cura	176	121	
	San Sebastian	34	62	520,725.00
	*Unknown	161	281	72,413.00
		1668	1445	593,138.00
Apure	San Fernando	4	6	2,065.00
	*Unknown	1	0	300.00
		5	6	2,365.00
Barcelona	Barcelona	81	104	
	Aragua	37	82	
	Onoto	7	15	
	Piritu	5	15	
	Freites	1	2	
	Chamariapa	1	0	59,112.00
	*Unknown	20	36	9,862.00
		152	254	68,974.00
Barinas	Barinas	8	0	
	Obispos	3	0	
	Nutrias	6	0	4,361.00
	*Unknown	2	0	585.00
		19	0	4,946.00

TABLE 6 (continued)

Barquisimeto	Barquisimeto	64	18	
	Cabudare	51	3	
	Quibor	25	0	
	Tocuyo	182	76	
	Carora	63	69	
	San Felipe	145	84	159,585.00
	*Unknown	41	100	20,277.00
		571	350	179,862.00
Carabobo	Valencia	962	587	
	Pto. Cabello	127	182	
	Ocumare de la Costa	597	538	
	Montalván	108	172	
	San Carlos	36	15	
	Pao	12	4	
	Tinaco	1	0	651,240.00
	*Unknown	38	266	52,026.00
		1881	1764	703,266.00
Caracas	Caracas	1329	897	
	Ocumare del Tuy	1465	1243	
	Petare	407	377	
	Caucagua	520	577	
	La Guaira	296	281	
	Rio Chico	298	574	
	Guarenas	461	398	
	Santa Lucía	581	489	
	Maiquetía	131	117	
	Curiepe	152	145	
	Guaicaipuro	100	82	2,117,971.00
	*Unknown	256	426	112,768.00
		5996	5606	2,230,739.00

TABLE 6 (continued)

Coro	Coro	370	520	
	San Luís	61	4	
	Cumarebo	35	23	
	Paraguaná	58	125	
	Casigua	11	6	197,479.00
	*Unknown	55	94	24,014.00
		590	772	221,493.00
Cumaná	Cumaná	56	61	
	Carúpano	42	41	
	Cariaco	15	12	
	Rio Caribe	37	25	
	Güiria	1	3	
	Maturín	7	7	
	Aragua	12	12	
	Caños	4	0	63,684.00
	*Unknown	58	64	21,929.00
		232	225	85,613.00
Guárico	Calabozo	15	3	
	Ortiz	29	42	
	Unare	58	74	
	Orituco	158	180	
	Chaguaramas	48	48	
	Sombrero	22	6	117,731.00
	*Unknown	48	125	26,460.00
		378	478	144,191.00
Guayana	Ciudad Bolívar	10	3	
	Upata	1	0	3,595.00
	*Unknown	4	9	1,925.00
		15	12	5,520.00
Maracaibo	Maracaibo	48	18	
	Zulia	2	0	
	Altagracia	7	3	
	Perijá	1	0	17,347.00
	*Unknown	2	1	710.00
		60	22	18,057.00

TABLE 6 (continued)

Margarita	Asunción	35	33	
	Villa del Norte	14	10	18,124.00
	*Unknown	14	4	4,555.00
		63	47	22,679.00
Mérida	Mérida	106	116	
	Mucuchíes	1	0	
	Bailadores	7	4	
	Egido	22	0	
	San Cristóbal	13	1	
	La Grita	11	20	56,504.00
	*Unknown	10	6	2,922.00
		170	137	59,426.00
Portuguesa	Guanare	40	12	
	Araure	18	14	
	Guanarito	5	5	
	Ospino	27	14	28,155.00
	*Unknown	32	27	10,979.00
		122	72	39,134.00
Trujillo	Trujillo	68	8	
	Escuque	50	16	
	Boconó	21	0	
	Carache	3	6	39,501.00
	*Unknown	29	55	14,087.00
		171	85	53,588.00
TOTALS		12,093	11,285	4,432,991.00

a Compiled from Int. y Just., 1858 and 1860, *Memoria*.
b The Total Value column includes the appraised value of slaves freed plus the value of manumiso services terminated by the abolition law.

NOTE: The asterisked figures refer to slaves listed in a supplementary census by provinces rather than by cantons.

TABLE 7
Population Estimates
(in hundreds)

PROVINCE	1830[a]		1838[b]		1844[c]		1854[d]	
	FREE	SLAVE	FREE	SLAVE	FREE	SLAVE	FREE	SLAVE
Apure	200	2	155	2	237	1	266	1
Aragua	—	—	—	—	—	—	—	—
Barcelona	391	13	521	9	655	10	851	8
Barinas	947	12	1095	15	1272	9	1457	8
Barquisimeto	1382	48	1128	23	1769	37	2034	36
Carabobo	1051	47	970	41	1414	33	1713	28
Caracas	2327	242	2429	344	3184	79	3839	32
Coro	549	21	405	15	715	17	822	13
Cumaná	520	14	507	15	744	12	895	11
Guárico	—	—	—	—	—	—	—	—
Guayana	104	1	565	6	136	1	175	1
Maracaibo	319	4	428	6	435	3	486	2
Margarita	133	2	183	2	201	1	241	1
Mérida	626	8	621	7	842	6	1013	2
Portuguesa	—	—	—	—	—	—	—	—
Trujillo	453	11	448	14	585	8	704	7
TOTAL	9002	425	9455	499	12189	217	14496	150

[a] The population estimate for 1830 was calculated by subtracting the net gain of population according to the birth and death figures between 1830 and 1844 from the totals given in the census of 1844. The sources for the birth and death data are listed in Table 8.

[b] The estimate for 1838 is from Codazzi, *Obras*, I. They are included to give a somewhat independent estimate not based on the 1844 official census. It should be noted that Codazzi includes an estimate of some 52,400 independent Indians, mostly in Guayana. Moreover, his slave figures apparently include the free-born manumisos.

[c] The 1844 figures are from the census of that year printed in Int. y Just., 1846, *Memoria*.

[d] The estimate for 1854 was calculated by adding the net population gain

since 1844 according to the birth and death statistics. The provinces of Aragua and Guárico were created from the province of Caracas, the province of Portuguesa was created from the province of Barinas after 1848. The net population gain from these units after their creation has been added to their parent provinces in order to keep the administrative units more or less the same for the purposes of this table.

TABLE 8
Births and Deaths[a]
(in hundreds)

YEAR	BIRTHS		DEATHS			NET GAIN /YEAR
	TOTAL	MANUMISOS	TOTAL	FREE	SLAVE	
1831–1838	3072	229	1417	1283	134	207
1839	435	20	182	165	17	253
1840	459	22	202	184	18	257
1841	470	25	229	212	17	241
1842	468	24	194	181	13	274
1843	509	19	222	213	9	287
1844	484	22	261	249	12	223
1845	486	15	271	262	9	215
1847	526	13	245	233	12	281
1848	502	9	226	218	8	276
1849	500	4	247	242	5	253
1850	550	12	244	237	7	306
1851	573	7	376	370	6	197
1853	571	5	323	318	5	248

[a] Compiled and estimated from Int. y Just., 1841–1847, 1850–1854, Memoria.

APPENDIX 2

Tables of Major Exports

TABLE 1
Major Exports—Coffee[a]

FISCAL YEAR	QUANTITY (000 LIBRAS)[g]	VALUE (000 PESOS)	UNIT VALUE /LIBRA	PERCENT OF TOTAL EXPORTS
1831–32	11544	1063	.092	37
1832–33	11914	1192	.100	39
1833–34	11603	1294	.111	38
1834–35[b]	5953	712	.120	29
1835–36	11591	1467	.127	37
1836–37	16635	1660	.100	34
1837–38	17491	1587	.091	37
1838–39	21881	2254	.103	42
1839–40	19126	1938	.101	33
1840–41	25999	2447	.094	40
1841–42	32994	3350	.102	44
1842–43	29567	2528	.086	37
1843–44	28792	2223	.077	37
1844–45	29035	2373	.082	42
1845–46	39063	3293	.084	46

TABLE 1 (continued)

1846–47c	26663	2432	.091	38
1847–48d	26217	2055	.078	37
1848–49e	39317	2634	.067	48
1849–50f	37995	2888	.076	48
1850–51	37971	2663	.070	42
1851–52	32676	2698	.083	41
1852–53	32085	n.a.	n.a.	n.a.
1853–54	38772	3099	.080	43
1854–55	37745	3111	.082	45

a Compiled from Hacienda, 1833–56, Memoria.
b Excludes Barcelona and Puerto Cabello.
c Excludes Güiria.
d Excludes Maracaibo and Carúpano.
e Value figures for Maracaibo, Carúpano, and Cumaná obtained by multiplying the average price for the country with the quantities for each of these cities. Actual value figures were not available.
f Value figures for Maracaibo, Carúpano, and Güiria obtained by multiplying average price for country with quantities for each of these cities. Actual value figures were not available.
g One libra = 1.0143 pounds.

TABLE 2
Major Exports—Cacaoa

FISCAL YEAR	QUANTITY (000 LIBRAS)g	VALUE (000 PESOS)	UNIT VALUE /LIBRA	PERCENT OF TOTAL EXPORTS
1831–32	7215	975	.135	34
1832–33	5483	812	.148	27
1833–34	5385	706	.131	21
1834–35b	4243	574	.135	24
1835–36	5242	774	.148	19
1836–37	6780	875	.129	18
1837–38	5810	744	.128	17
1838–39	6498	946	.146	18
1839–40	8770	1255	.143	21
1840–41	7656	1327	.173	22

TABLE 2 (continued)

1841–42	9634	1232	.128	16
1842–43	8904	1381	.155	20
1843–44	9065	1351	.149	23
1844–45	7571	1115	.147	19
1845–46	9241	1454	.157	20
1846–47ᶜ	7321	1218	.166	19
1847–48 ᵈ	6666	1208	.181	22
1848–49ᵉ	7495	1199	.160	22
1849–50ᶠ	9198	1692	.184	28
1850–51	8160	1300	.159	21
1851–52	10923	1468	.134	23
1852–53	7677	n.a.	n.a.	n.a.
1853–54	9938	1579	.159	22
1854–55	8713	1192	.137	17

a Compiled from Hacienda, 1833–56, *Memoria*.
b Excludes Barcelona and Puerto Cabello.
c Excludes Güiria.
d Excludes Maracaibo and Carúpano.
e Value figures for Maracaibo, Carúpano, and Cumaná obtained by multiplying the average price for the country with the quantities for each of these cities. Actual value figures were not available.
f Value figures for Maracaibo, Carúpano, and Güiria obtained by multiplying the average price for the country with the quantities for each of these cities. Actual value figures were not available.
g One libra = 1.0143 pounds.

TABLE 3
Major Exports—Hidesª

FISCAL YEAR	QUANTITY (000 HIDES)	VALUE (000 PESOS)	UNIT VALUE /HIDE	PERCENT OF TOTAL EXPORTS
1831–32	77	135	1.77	5
1832–33	61	100	1.64	3
1833–34	53	125	2.36	4
1834–35ᵇ	53	130	2.46	5
1835–36	76	181	2.37	5

TABLE 3 (continued)

1836–37	111	247	2.22	5
1837–38	122	241	1.98	6
1838–39	139	284	2.04	5
1939–40	164	351	2.14	6
1840–41	157	369	2.35	6
1841–42	253	613	2.43	8
1842–43	238	527	2.22	8
1843–44	253	530	2.09	9
1844–45	359	742	2.07	13
1845–46	400	837	2.09	13
1846–47[c]	436	924	2.12	14
1847–48[d]	356	665	1.86	12
1848–49[e]	364	513	1.41	9
1849–50[f]	421	671	1.59	11
1850–51	635	1124	1.77	18
1851–52	545	930	1.71	14
1852–53	536	n.a.	n.a.	n.a.
1853–54	633	1310	2.07	18
1854–55	646	1305	2.02	19

[a] Compiled from Hacienda, 1833–56, Memoria.
[b] Excludes Barcelona and Puerto Cabello.
[c] Excludes Güiria.
[d] Excludes Maracaibo and Carúpano.
[e] Value figures for Maracaibo, Carúpano, and Cumaná obtained by multiplying the average price for the country with the quantities for each of these cities. Actual value figures were not available.
[f] Value figures for Maracaibo, Carúpano, and Güiria obtained by multiplying the average price for the country with the quantities for each of these cities. Actual value figures were not available.

TABLE 4
Major Exports—Indigo[a]

FISCAL YEAR	QUANTITY (000 LIBRAS)[g]	VALUE (000 PESOS)	UNIT VALUE /LIBRA	PERCENT OF TOTAL EXPORTS
1831–32	262	241	.92	8
1832–33	325	270	.83	9
1833–34	422	505	1.20	15
1834–35[b]	282	324	1.15	13
1835–36	375	427	1.14	11
1836–37	448	502	1.12	10
1837–38	384	427	1.11	10
1838–39	458	571	1.25	11
1839–40	544	812	1.49	14
1840–41	546	547	1.00	9
1841–42	351	484	1.38	6
1842–43	377	438	1.16	7
1843–44	353	331	.93	6
1844–45	296	288	.97	5
1845–46	275	242	.88	4
1846–47[c]	367	317	.86	5
1847–48[d]	200	164	.82	3
1848–49[e]	236	170	.72	3
1849–50[f]	175	91	.52	1
1850–51	218	158	.73	2
1851–52	273	170	.62	3
1852–53	352	n.a.	n.a.	n.a.
1853–54	287	178	.62	1
1854–55	326	124	.38	2

[a] Compiled from Hacienda, 1833–56, Memoria.
[b] Excludes Barcelona and Puerto Cabello.
[c] Excludes Güiria.
[d] Excludes Maracaibo and Carúpano.
[e] Value figures for Maracaibo, Carúpano, and Cumaná obtained by multiplying the average price for the country with the quantities for each of these cities. Actual value figures were not available.

f Value figures for Maracaibo, Carúpano, and Güiria obtained by multiplying the average price for the country with the quantities for each of
these cities. Actual value figures were not available.
g One libra = 1.0143 pounds.

TABLE 5
Major Exports—Cattle[a]

FISCAL YEAR	QUANTITY	VALUE (000 PESOS)	UNIT VALUE	PERCENT OF TOTAL EXPORTS
1831–32	1825	25	13.7	1
1832–33	1667	22	13.2	1
1833–34	3461	61	17.6	2
1834–35[b]	4563	94	20.6	4
1835–36	3219	56	17.4	1
1836–37	7912	148	18.7	3
1837–38	9809	187	19.1	4
1838–39	8949	171	19.1	3
1839–40	9968	190	19.1	3
1840–41	11648	208	17.9	3
1841–42	12933	277	21.4	4
1842–43	10979	175	15.9	3
1843–44	14894	179	12.0	3
1844–45	17661	176	10.0	3
1845–46	16127	159	9.8	2
1846–47[c]	15976	131	8.2	2
1847–48[d]	15832	140	8.8	3
1848–49[e]	12001	92	7.7	2
1849–50[f]	13626	89	6.5	1
1850–51	15929	116	7.3	2

TABLE 5 (continued)

1851–52	16155	131	8.1	2
1852–53	12115	n.a.	n.a.	n.a.
1853–54	13187	57	4.3	1
1854–55	13920	101	7.3	1

[a] Compiled from Hacienda, 1833–56, *Memoria*.
[b] Excludes Barcelona and Puerto Cabello.
[c] Excludes Güiria.
[d] Excludes Maracaibo and Carúpano.
[e] Value figures for Maracaibo, Carúpano, and Cumaná obtained by multiplying the average price for the country with the quantities for each of these cities. Actual value figures were not available.
[f] Value figures for Maracaibo, Carúpano, and Güiria obtained by multiplying the average price for the country with the quantities for each of these cities. Actual value figures were not available.

TABLE 6
Major Exports—Cotton[a]

FISCAL YEAR	QUANTITY (000 LIBRAS)[g]	VALUE (000 PESOS)	UNIT VALUE /LIBRA	PERCENT OF TOTAL EXPORTS
1831–32	97	7	.07	—
1832–33	195	16	.08	1
1833–34	421	45	.10	1
1834–35[b]	254	31	.12	1
1835–36	1655	268	.16	7
1836–37	3878	617	.16	13
1837–38	3260	372	.11	9
1838–39	2799	294	.10	6
1839–40	1640	224	.14	4
1840–41	2014	242	.12	4

TABLE 6 (continued)

1841–42	2621	305	.12	4
1842–43	2308	229	.10	3
1843–44	2074	165	.08	3
1844–45	1007	85	.08	2
1845–46	788	64	.08	1
1846–47[c]	684	64	.09	1
1847–48[d]	656	64	.10	1
1848–49[e]	1115	83	.07	1
1849–50[f]	660	44	.07	1
1850–51	733	95	.13	2
1851–52	1764	189	.11	3
1852–53	2078	n.a.	n.a.	n.a.
1853–54	1498	131	.09	2
1854–55	1131	92	.08	1

[a] Compiled from Hacienda, 1833–56, *Memoria*.
[b] Excludes Barcelona and Puerto Cabello.
[c] Excludes Güiria.
[d] Excludes Maracaibo and Carúpano.
[e] Value figures for Maracaibo, Carúpano, and Cumaná obtained by multiplying the average price for the country with the quantities for each of these cities. Actual value figures were not available.
[f] Value figures for Maracaibo, Carúpano, and Güiria obtained by multiplying the average price for the country with the quantities for each of these cities. Actual value figures were not available.
[g] One libra = 1.0143 pounds.

TABLE 7
Major Exports—Sugar[a]

FISCAL YEAR	QUANTITY (000 LIBRAS)[g]	VALUE (000 PESOS)	UNIT VALUE /LIBRA	PERCENT OF TOTAL EXPORTS
1831–32	1406	61	.043	2
1832–33	1141	47	.041	2
1833–34	607	20	.034	1
1834–35[b]	364	10	.027	—
1835–36	n.a.	39	n.a.	1

TABLE 7 (continued)

1836–37	n.a.	54	n.a.	1
1837–38	n.a.	41	n.a.	1
1838–39	n.a.	64	n.a.	1
1839–40	780	59	.076	1
1840–41	879	48	.055	1
1841–42	397	148	.370	2
1842–43	227	12	.053	—
1843–44	648	26	.040	—
1844–45	814	45	.055	1
1845–46	799	46	.058	1
1846–47[c]	1430	62	.044	1
1847–48[d]	1278	61	.048	1
1848–49[e]	1214	52	.043	1
1849–50[f]	934	26	.028	—
1850–51	568	21	.037	—
1851–52	37	2	.054	—
1852–53	78	n.a.	n.a.	n.a.
1853–54	192	7	.038	—
1854–55	158	6	.038	—

[a] Compiled from Hacienda, 1833–56, Memoria.
[b] Excludes Barcelona and Puerto Cabello.
[c] Excludes Güiria.
[d] Excludes Maracaibo and Carúpano.
[e] Value figures for Maracaibo, Carúpano, and Cumaná obtained by multiplying the average price for the country with the quantities for each of these cities. Actual value figures were not available.
[f] Value figures for Maracaibo, Carúpano, and Güiria obtained by multiplying the average price for the country with the quantities for each of these cities. Actual value figures were not available.
[g] One libra = 1.0143 pounds.

Glossary

acuerdos The official acts or decisions of a political body such as the Ayuntamiento or Junta.

aprendizaje Apprenticeship.

Ayuntamiento A town council, also Cabildo.

Banco Nacional The National Bank.

cabildantes Town councilors, members of the Cabildo.

La Campaña Admirable Bolívar's military sweep from Colombia to Caracas in 1814.

capellanías An ecclesiastical benefice carrying certain obligations.

caraqueño A resident of Caracas.

caudillo A charismatic leader characteristic of Latin American popular movements.

censo pío A Church loan contract mortgaging real property at interest.

cimarrones Runaway slaves.

comisionado A commissioner

Consejo de Gobierno The Council of Government.

Consejo de Guerra The Council of War.

Consejo de las Indias The Council of the Indies.

consejero A counselor.

considerandos A preamble.

consultas Requests for advice on how to administer a law.

criollo A Spaniard born in America.

cumbes Runaway slave hideouts or communities in the hills, also rochela.

173

Dirección de Manumisión   Manumission Administration.

edad provecta   Mature in years.

Exequatur   The executive signature which puts a law into effect.

expediente   A file of information or documents.

golpe   A coup d'état.

hacendado   The owner of a large rural agricultural property.

hacienda   A large rural agricultural property.

hato   A large rural stock raising establishment.

hoja suelta   A broadsheet.

independientistas   Partisans of American independence from Spain.

Jefe político   The political chief of a town.

jornaleros   Day workers.

Junta de Manumisión   The committee in charge of administering the manumission law at the local level.

Ley de 10 de abril de 1834   The credit law of 10 April 1834.

Libertador   Simón Bolívar.

liberto   A freed slave.

llanos   Flatlands.

mantuanos   The Caracas aristocracy before independence.

manumiso   A free born child of a slave.

manumiso contratado   A manumiso, over 18 or 21, obligated to be contracted until the age of 25.

Memorias   The annual reports of government bodies such as the Departments of the Federal Government or of State Governments. Also used to refer to reports, white papers, and proceedings of non-government groups.

oficios   The official letters from government authorities.

padrón   A list.

padrones de esclavos   Slave lists.

paecistas   The supporters of José Antonio Páez.

pardocracia   A mulatto dominated government or society.

pardos   Mulattos (a very vague ethnic category).

Patria Boba   The nickname for Venezuela's first republic 1811–1812.

patronato   The tutelage exercised by a man of substance and property over manumisos and manumisos contratados.

reformistas   Reformers, a name given the supporters of the movement against the government of José María Vargas in 1835–1836.

Reglamentos de Policía   Police ordinances.

rochela   A hideout or community of runaway slaves in the hills.

Secretaría de Interior y Justicia   The Department of the Interior and of Justice.

Secretario del Interior y Justicia   The Secretary of the Interior and of Justice.

síndico municipal   The municipal prosecutor.

Tierra de Gracia   Blessed land.

vicario   A vicar.

Bibliography

AS pointed out in the Introduction and in the notes to this monograph, the quantity and quality of specialized works on the period covered by this book are minimal. By and large most of the important works used are mentioned in the notes, but a few words are in order on areas insufficiently treated or totally neglected. Perhaps the most glaring lacuna in Venezuelan historiography of the post-independence era is in the realm of political history. It is difficult, indeed, to study any phase of Republican Venezuela without an adequate analysis of the basic political structure and development. While both González Guinán and Gil Fortoul attempt such an analysis, their efforts are not wholly successful.[1] González Guinán's *Historia*, in spite of its thoroughness and detail, rarely rises above the level of a chronicle, albeit an excellent and accurate one. Gil Fortoul's work, on the other hand, suffers from an excessive concentration on constitutional history and a tendency to slough off problematical historical interpretations in the interests of a symmetrical and balanced narrative. Whatever their faults, these two histories, written at the turn of the century, have yet to be superseded. This fact alone speaks most eloquently of the paucity of adequate research on so many phases of Venezuela's past.[2]

Since González Guinán and Gil Fortoul published their works, most of the efforts of Venezuelan historians have fallen into two categories.[3] First is the work of the elaborators. Perhaps the most successful of these is Ramón Díaz Sánchez, whose romantic biography of the Guzmán family carries the themes evident in González Guinan and Gil Fortoul one step farther. His greater contri-

177

bution is an elaborate description of the baroque complexities of Venezuelan politics through the lives of Antonio Leocadio Guzmán and his son, Antonio Guzmán Blanco. Yet Díaz Sánchez's biographical technique is not quite good enough to allow his work to be considered a significant departure from the earlier studies done on this period. Unfortunately, his work is marred by a total disregard for scholarly apparatus. It is never clear where Díaz Sánchez gets his information, and were it not for the introduction and bibliography, *Guzmán. Elipse de una ambición del poder* might as well be a historical novel.[4]

The second category of historical writing includes the work of the revisionists. In this broad group are those writers who set out boldly to smash traditional molds of Venezuelan historiography, men whose historical speculation and research is predicated on the assumption that much of Venezuelan historical writing has been twisted to show a past carefully filtered for some partisan purpose. Most of the members of this category want to recreate Venezuela's past in its true perspective, but use the same basic source material as the elaborators. They have provided a number of fascinating reinterpretations of nineteenth-century Venezuela but few, in their haste for something new, have been able to present adequately prepared and documented works. The reason for this situation is clear enough. Most revisionists are, or were, deeply involved in the political battles of the present, and few have the time or resources to explore their hypotheses in depth. As a result, many revisionists' works suffer from the same fault as the elaborators' works, political tendentiousness. Where many of the traditionalist elaborators found support for their conservative political beliefs in Venezuela's early nineteenth-century experience, the revisionists, too, find confirmation of their revolutionary doctrines in this same turbulent period.[5]

Yet, in spite of their political orientation and present-mindedness, the revisionists' speculations on and reevaluations of Venezuela's past have injected a new and healthy note of controversy into Venezuelan historiography. It is not yet clear whether the second generation of revisionists will take on the task of exploring in depth the implications of the new hypotheses, or whether they will be allowed the time or be given the support to document their findings in the untapped archival reserves of Venezuela.[6]

One of the tasks the new historians might profitably undertake is a comprehensive analysis of the development of Venezuela's economy during the first half-century of independence. The major chronicle of Venezuelan economic growth is an erratic hodgepodge of unreliable statistics.[7] The primitiveness of most economic history of the early nineteenth century can readily be appreciated when we realize that the export statistics in Appendix 2 are reliably compiled for the first time.

Equally frustrating is the lack of specialized investigations of the most elementary facets of social history. What happened to the pardos after independence? What were the effects of the wars for independence on the race situation in Venezuela? And what relationships were worked out in the countryside between peon and planter? Such fundamental questions as these still remain unanswered.[8]

Given the absence of a wide monographic base to supplement this study, the documentary resources used assume great importance. In general, two types of documents support the findings of this book. First are the manuscript sources, second are the printed sources. This division is somewhat arbitrary but has the advantage of facilitating this discussion.

The largest number of manuscripts examined came from the Archivo General de la Nación.[9] This is the major source of official government documents on all phases of Venezuelan affairs. Particularly important for this study were the sections containing the papers of Interior y Justicia where the letters sent from local and provincial officials are kept. Also in Interior y Justicia can be found letters and petitions from private citizens to the government complaining, requesting, or pleading. For this study the documents in Interior y Justicia covering the years 1830 through 1855 were consulted; a similar collection exists for the Gran Colombia period and was consulted for the period 1820 to 1830. Both of these sections are indexed chronologically; each item or group of related items receives a one-sentence description in the index and the descriptions are arranged in the same order as the documents. Unfortunately, the index is not as helpful as it might be, since the one-line descriptions are often insufficient to give a clear indication of the contents. Also, the accuracy of these descriptions is somewhat erratic, as the indices were compiled over a long period of time by a variety of people. Still, in spite of their deficiencies, these indices provide a useful guide to the material in the Archivo.

The Archivo Arquidiocesano deserves special mention as one of the most important and little used document collections in Venezuela. Here are collected and organized the papers of the Bishopric and Archbishopric of Caracas. It contains extremely valuable information on all aspects of Church activity in Venezuela from the early colonial period to the late nineteenth century. To aid its usefulness the Arquidiocesano has a fine general index.[10] For this study the Arquidiocesano served as a supplementary source of information. Although the Church was vitally involved in slavery through her financial operations and her own plantations, a detailed analysis of these activities from the documents in this archive would require a major research project.

The Registro Principal de Caracas contains documents on all phases of Venezuelan life from the founding of Caracas to the present. In fact, it is still housed in the working section of the present-day public registry office. Unfortunately, it is probably the least cared for and most poorly organized archive in Caracas. It is tragic to view the abandonment of this treasury of Venezuelan history; the part of the Registro which has ceased to be used for legal purposes should be transferred to a separate building under the jurisdiction of a qualified staff that would undertake the organization and preservation of the collection. The Registro was used only supplementarily in this study to spot-check the prices actually paid for slaves during the period under discussion. An elaborate analysis of the economic data available in the Registro would require an extensive project using computer technology. These, then, are the major archives consulted in the preparation of this monograph.

Since diplomatic affairs played such a small role in the decline and abolition of Negro slavery in Venezuela, I confined my research on this subject to the British and United States diplomatic papers available on microfilm. The other archives listed in the Bibliography are smaller in size and were only marginally useful.[11]

Printed documents—newspapers, pamphlets, and broadsides—proved to be exceptionally important for this work. There are two important newspaper collections in Venezuela of approximately equal size and importance: the Hemerotecas of the Academia Nacional de la Historia and the Biblioteca Nacional, which rather neatly supplement each other's collections. Very often a number missing from the Academia can be found in the Biblioteca, and vice versa. Both institutions have their newspapers well-organized and well-catalogued. The importance of newspapers for my work is immediately evident from the Bibliography. Many of those listed are occasional publications issued for a few months to further someone's political ambitions. Nevertheless, for most of the period under discussion the press was reasonably free to say what it pleased, and the vitriolic editorials plus the vindictive personal slander encountered in these periodicals testify to this freedom.[12]

The pamphlets and broadsides in the Bibliography are not a complete list of all those consulted. I chose to include those items that fulfill one of the following two conditions. If the item contained references to slavery or abolition, it was automatically included. The other pamphlets and broadsides listed were chosen to give a representative sampling of the variety of material consulted. This type of document is found primarily in two institutions. First is the Academia Nacional de la Historia. This institution's subdivisions, the Biblioteca and the Archivo, have extensive and valuable collections; however, the index systems of both places are incomplete. Another group of pamphlets is housed in the Biblioteca Nacional.

The following selected list of works consulted in the preparation of this monograph is not intended to be exhaustive. In addition to the items cited in the notes and the printed documents discussed above, I have included works that, while not pertaining specifically to the topic under consideration, still proved helpful as background information.

ARCHIVES

CARACAS

Academia Nacional de la Historia. Archivo.
Archivo Arquidiocesano de Caracas.
Archivo General de la Nación.
Casa Natal del Libertador. Archivo Revenga.
Fundación John Boulton. Sección Venezolana del Archivo de la Gran Colombia.
Registro Principal. Sección Civiles. Sección Escribanías.

ENGLAND

Public Record Office. Foreign Office. No. 80 (Venezuela), 1835–1855; No. 84 (Slave Trade), 1836–1854 (microfilm).

UNITED STATES

File Microcopies of Records in the National Archives, No. 62 (Despatches from United States Consular Representatives in Maracaibo, Venezuela, 1824–1906). 1830–1862. Washington: The National Archives, 1957–1959.
File Microcopies of Records in the National Archives, No. 77 (Diplomatic Instructions of the Department of State, 1801–1906, Venezuela). 1835–1865. Washington: The National Archives, 1946.
File Microcopies of Records in the National Archives, No. 79 (Despatches from United States Ministers to Venezuela). 1835–1855. Washington: The National Archives, 1944–1951.
File Microcopies of Records in the National Archives, No. 84 (Despatches from United States Consular Representatives in La Guaira, Venezuela, 1810–1906). 1810–1857. Washington: The National Archives, 1944, 1961.
Lilly Library. Indiana University. Bloomington. 1828–1840. Porter Mss. Porter, Sir Robert Ker. Autograph letter books.

CARACAS LIBRARIES

Academia Nacional de la Historia. Biblioteca.
Academia Nacional de la Historia. Hemeroteca.
Biblioteca Arcaya.
Biblioteca de la Sociedad Bolivariana de Venezuela.
Biblioteca del Congreso Nacional.
Biblioteca del Teniente Coronel Pérez Tenreiro.
Biblioteca de Pedro Grases.

Biblioteca Nacional.
Fundación John Boulton. Biblioteca.

NEWSPAPERS

El Agricultor. Caracas. 1844–1845, 1855.
El Alerta. Caracas. 1849–1850.
Alerta. Cumaná. 1825–1826
El Amigo del Pueblo. Caracas. 1846.

El Anglo-Colombiano. Caracas. 1822.

El Argos. Caracas. 1825.

Asmodeito. Caracas. 1855.

Asmodeo. Caracas. 1850.

La Aurora. Barcelona. 1835.

La Aurora. Caracas. 1855.

Las Avispas. Caracas. 1846.

Los Ayes del Pueblo. Caracas. 1844–1845.

El Bachaquero. Caracas. 1853.

La Bandera Nacional. Caracas. 1837–1839.

El Barinés. Barinas. 1845–1846.

Boletín. Caracas. 1832.

El Caduceo. Angostura. 1845.

El Carabobeño Libre. Valencia. 1852.

El Caraqueño. Caracas. 1850–1851.

El Censor. Caracas. 1836.

El Centinela de la Patria. Caracas. 1846–1847.

Cicerón a Catilina. Caracas. 1845.

El Clamor Público. Caracas. 1850.

El Colombiano. Caracas. 1823–1826.

El Cometa. Caracas. 1852.

El Conciso. Caracas. 1832, 1834–1835, 1837–1838.

El Constitucional. Caracas. 1834.

El Constitucional Caraqueño. Caracas. 1824–1825.

El Constitucional de Maracaibo. Maracaibo. 1836–1838.

La Corneta del Juicio Universal. Caracas. 1853.

Correo de Caracas. Caracas. 1839–1841.

Correo de Caracas. Caracas. 1851–1854.

Correo de la Ciudad de Bogotá. Bogotá. 1822–1823.

Correo del Orinoco. Angostura. 1818–1821. Caracas: Academia Nacional de la Historia, 1939.

El Correo Nacional. Maracaibo. 1821.

El Correo de Occidente. Barquisimeto. 1849–1850.

La Democracia. Caracas. 1852–1853.

La Democracia. Valencia. 1852–1853.

El Demócrata. Valencia. 1846.

El Diablo Asmodeo. Caracas. 1850.

El Diamante. Caracas. 1850.

Diario de Avisos y Semanario de las Provincias. Caracas. 1850–1855.

Diario de Debates. Caracas. 1849, 1852–1855.

Diario de Debates del Congreso Constituyente de Venezuela del año de 1830. Valencia. 27–29 May 1830.

Diario de la Diputación Provincial de Carabobo. Valencia. 1848–1849.

Diario de la Tarde. Caracas. 1846.

El Eco de los Andes. Caracas. 1855.

El Eco del Pueblo. Valencia. 1844.

El Eco de Venezuela. Caracas. 1846–1847.

El Eco Popular. Caracas. 1840.

El Economista. Caracas. 1855.

El Eden. La Victoria. 1849.

Elecciones Libres. Valencia. 1853–1854.

Epistolas Catilinarias Sobre el 8 de Julio. Caracas. 1835.

La Epoca. Caracas. 1846.

El Estandarte Nacional. Caracas. 1842.

Este es el Hombre. Caracas. 1851.

El Fanal. Caracas. 1829–1831.

El Faro. Caracas. 1848–1849.

Gaceta Constitucional de Caracas. Caracas. 1831–1832.

Gaceta de Carabobo. Valencia. 1849, 1852, 1854, 1855.

Gaceta de la Sociedad Republicana. Caracas. 1830.

La Gaceta de Venezuela. Caracas. 1831–1844, 1846–1855.

El Horizonte. Puerto Cabello. 1855.

La Iberia. Caracas. 1851–1852.

La Ilustración. Caracas. 1854.

El Independiente. Barquisimeto. 1843–1844.

El Independiente. Caracas. 1845–1846.

Indicador del Orinoco. Cumaná. 1825.

El Iris. Caracas. 1849.

El Laberinto. Caracas. 1845.

La Libertad. Caracas. 1850–1851.

El Liberal. Caracas. 1837–1848.

La Lira. Caracas. 1827.

La Mañana. Caracas. 1841.

El Manzanares. Cumaná. 1843.

El Mara. Maracaibo. 1854–1856.

La Mariposa. Maracaibo. 1840–1842.

El Mensajero. Guanare. 1844.

La Mercurial. Valencia. 1831.

Mercurio de Caracas. Caracas. 1844.

Mercurio Venezolano. Caracas. 1811. (Sesquicentenario de la Independencia, No. 25.) Caracas: Academia Nacional de la Historia, 1960.

Un Militar Retirado. Caracas. 1833.

La Nación. Caracas. 1850.

El Nacional. Caracas. 1848.

El Noticioso de Caracas. Caracas. 1849.

El Observador. Coro. 1843–1845.

El Observador Caraqueño. Caracas. 1824–1825.

La Opinión. Caracas. 1854.

El Patriota Venezolano. Caracas. 1832–1833.

Pláticas del Diablo Asmodeo. Caracas. 1850.

La Prensa Ministerial. Caracas. 1855.

El Promotor. Caracas. 1843–1844.

El Publicista de Venezuela. Caracas. (Sesquicentenario de la Independencia, No. 8.) Caracas: Academia Nacional de la Historia, 1959.

Rabo del Diablo Asmodeo. Caracas. 1850.
La Razón. Caracas. 1846.
El Republicano. Caracas. 1834.
Semanario de Caracas. Caracas. (Sesquicentenario de la Independencia, No. 9.) Caracas: Academia Nacional de la Historia, 1959.
El Sin Camisa. Caracas. 1844.
El Sol de la Justicia. Valencia. 1855.

El Sol de Oriente. Barcelona. 1850.
La Tarde. Caracas. 1837–1838.
El Trabuco. Caracas. 1844–1845.
El Vehículo. Valencia. 1835–1836.
El Venezolano. Caracas. 1822–1824, 1840–1846.
Los Venezolanos. Caracas. 1832.
La Verdad. Caracas. 1839.
El Vigia. La Guaira. 1845.

BOOKS AND ARTICLES

Acosta Saignes, Miguel. "Culturas negras en Venezuela," X Aniversario de la Fundación de la Escuela de Sociología y Antropología. (Mesa Redonda No. III.) Caracas: 11–16 February 1963.

———. "Los negros cimarrones de Venezuela," El movimiento emancipador de Hispanoamérica. Actas y ponencias. Vol. III (Mesa Redonda de la Comisión de Historia del Instituto Panamericano de Geografía e Historia.) Caracas: Academia Nacional de la Historia, 1961.

———. La trata de esclavos en Venezuela. Caracas: Centro de Estudios Históricos, Revista de Historia, 1961.

———. Vida de los esclavos negros en Venezuela. Caracas: Hesperides, 1967.

Acotaciones Bolivarianas. Decretos marginales del Libertador (1813–1830). Caracas: Fundación John Boulton, 1960.

Anales. 11 vols. Caracas: Academia Nacional de la Historia, 1889–1892.

Arcaya, Pedro M. Insurrección de los negros de la serranía de Coro. (Publicación No. 7, Instituto Panamericano de Geografía e Historia.) Caracas, 1949.

Archivo del General Miranda. Vol. XXIV. Havana: Editorial Lex, 1950.

Arcila Farías, Eduardo, et al. La obra pía de Chuao, 1568–1825. Caracas: Universidad Central de Venezuela, 1968.

Arellano Moreno, Antonio. *Orígenes de la economía venezolana.* 2d ed. Caracas: Ediciones Edime, 1960.

Aurrecoechea, José María. *Memoria geográfico-económico-política del departamento de Venezuela, publicada en 1814 por el intendente de ejército D. . . . quien la reimprime con varias notas aclaratorias y un apéndice.* Madrid: D. Manuel G. Ural, 1845.

Austria, José de. *Bosquejo de la historia militar de Venezuela.* 2 vols. (Sesquicentenario de la Independencia, Nos. 29 and 30.) Caracas: Academia Nacional de la Historia, 1960.

Badillo, V. M. and C. Bonfanti. *Indice bibliográfico agrícola de Venezuela.* Vol. I; Caracas: Fundación Eugenio Mendoza, 1957. Vol. II; Maracay: Fundación Eugenio Mendoza, 1962.

Bierck, Harold A., Jr. "The Struggle for Abolition in Gran Colombia," *Hispanic American Historical Review,* XXXIII (August 1953), 365–386.

Blanco, José Félix and Ramón Azpurúa. *Documentos para la historia de la vida pública del Libertador de Colombia, Peru, y Bolivia.* 14 vols. Caracas, 1875–1877.

Blanco-Fombona, Rufino. *Bolívar y la guerra a muerte. Epoca de Boves, 1813–1814.* Caracas: Impresores Unidos, 1942.

Bolívar y Santander: Correspondencia, 1819–1820. Bogota: Estado Mayor General, Ministerio de Guerra, 1940.

Brazil. Instituto Brasileiro de Geografia e Estatística, Conselho Nacional de Estatística, *Anuario estatístico do Brasil. Ano V, 1939–1940.* Rio de Janeiro, [1940?].

Briceño Perozo, Mario. *El Archivo General de la Nación.* Caracas: Biblioteca Venezolana de Historia, 1964.

Brito Figueroa, Federico. *Ensayos de historia social venezolana.* Caracas: Universidad Central de Venezuela, 1960.

————. *La Estructura económica de Venezuela colonial.* Caracas: Universidad Central de Venezuela, 1963.

————. *Las insurrecciones de los esclavos negros en la sociedad colonial venezolana.* Caracas, 1961.

————. *La liberación de los esclavos.* Caracas, 1951.

Bushnell, David. *The Santander Regime in Gran Colombia.* Newark, Delaware: University of Delaware Press, 1954.

Cajigal, Juan Manual. *Memorias del Mariscal de Campo Don . . . sobre la revolución de Venezuela.* Caracas: Ministerio de Justicia, Junta Superior de Archivos, 1960.

Carrera Damas, Germán. *Crítica Histórica: artículos y ensayos.* Caracas, Universidad Central de Venezuela, 1960.

————. *Cuestiones de historiografía venezolana.* Caracas: Universidad Central de Venezuela, 1964.

————. "Cuestiones económico-sociales de la emancipación," *Crítica Contemporanea,* X (March–April 1963), Caracas.

————. *Historia de la historiografía venezolana (textos para su estudio).* Caracas: Universidad Central de Venezuela, 1961.

————. *Historiografía marxista venezolana y otros temas.* Caracas: Universidad Central de Venezuela, 1967.

————. "Intervención," *X Aniversario de la Fundación de la Escuela de Sociología y Antropología.* (Mesa Redonda No. III.) Caracas: 11–16 February 1963.

————. *Sobre el significado socio-económico de la acción histórica de Boves.* Caracas: Universidad Central de Venezuela, 1964.

————. *Tres temas de historia.* Caracas: Universidad Central de Venezuela, 1961.

————, et al. *El concepto de la historia en Caracciolo Parra Pérez.* Caracas: Universidad Central de Venezuela, 1962.

————, et al. *El concepto de la historia en José Gil Fortoul.* Caracas: Universidad Central de Venezuela, 1961.

————, et al. *El concepto de la historia en Laureano Vallenilla Lanz.* Caracas: Universidad Central de Venezuela, 1966.

Cartas del Libertador. 3 vols. 2d ed. Caracas: Fundación Vicente Lecuna, Banco de Venezuela, 1964; and Vols. V–VI, 1st ed. Caracas, Litografía y Tipografía del Comercio, 1929.

Catálogo. Donación Villanueva a la Academia Nacional de la Historia. Caracas, 1965.

Causas de infidencia. 2 vols. (Sesquicentenario de la Independencia, Nos. 31 and 32.) Caracas: Academia Nacional de la Historia, 1960.

Censo del Café. Caracas: Ministerio de Agricultura y Cría, 1943.

Codazzi, Agustín. *Obras escogidas.* 2 vols. Caracas: Ediciones del Ministerio de Educación, 1960.

Coll y Prat, Narciso. *Memoriales sobre la independencia de Venezuela.* (Sesquicentenario de la Independencia, No. 23.) Caracas: Academia Nacional de la Historia, 1960.

Conservadores y Liberales. Los grandes temas políticos. (Pensamiento político venezolano del siglo XIX, Vol. XII.) Caracas: Publicaciones de la Presidencia de la República, 1961.

Cortázar, Roberto and Luis Augusto Cuervo, eds. Congreso de Angostura. Libro de Actas. Bogota, 1921.

————. Congreso de 1824. Cámara de Representantes. Actas. (Biblioteca de Historia Nacional, Vol. LXV.) Bogota: Editorial Librería Voluntad, 1942.

Costeloe, Michael P. Church Wealth in Mexico: A Study of the "Juzgado de Capellanías" in the Archbishopric of Mexico, 1800–1856. Cambridge: Cambridge University Press, 1967.

Cuerpo de leyes de la república de Colombia. Caracas: Universidad Central de Venezuela, 1961.

Curtin, Philip D. The Atlantic Slave Trade. A Census. Madison: University of Wisconsin Press, 1969.

Dávila, Vicente. Investigaciones históricas. 2 vols. Quito: Colegio "Don Bosco," 1955.

Davis, David Brion. The Problem of Slavery in Western Culture. Ithaca, New York: Cornell University Press, 1966.

Decretos del Libertador. 3 vols. Caracas: Publicaciones de la Sociedad Bolivariana de Venezuela, 1961.

Depons, Francisco. Viaje a la parte oriental de Tierra Firme en la América meridional. 2 vols. trans. Enrique Planchart. Caracas: Banco Central de Venezuela, 1960.

Díaz Sánchez, Ramón. "Los factores sociales en la independencia de Venezuela," Cultura Universitaria, XC (January–March, 1966), 142–158.

————. Guzmán. Elipse de una ambición de poder. Caracas: Ediciones del Ministerio de Educación Nacional, 1950.

Egaña, Miguel R. Labores fiscales y económicos de nuestros primeros congresos. Caracas: Tipografía La Nación, 1950.

Elkins, Stanley M. Slavery. A Problem in American Institutional and Intellectual Life. Chicago: University of Chicago Press, 1959.

Feliú Cruz, Guillermo. La abolición de la esclavitud en Chile: estudio histórico y social. Santiago: Universidad de Chile, 1942.

Las fuerzas armadas de Venezuela en el siglo XIX. 8 vols. Caracas: Publicaciones de la Presidencia de la República, 1963–1965.

Genovese, Eugene D. and Laura Foner. Slavery in the New World: A Reader in Comparative History. Englewood Cliffs, N.J.: Prentice-Hall, 1969.

Gil Fortoul, José. Historia constitucional de Venezuela. 3 vols. 4th ed. Caracas: Ministerio de Educación, 1953–1954.

Gilmore, Robert L. *Caudillism and Militarism in Venezuela, 1810–1910*. Athens, Ohio: Ohio University Press, 1964.

Gómez Canedo, Lino. *Los archivos históricos de Venezuela*. Maracaibo: Universidad del Zulia, 1966.

González, Juan Vicente. *La doctrina conservadora*. 2 vols. (*Pensamiento político venezolano del siglo XIX*, Vols. II and III.) Caracas: Publicaciones de la Presidencia de la República, 1961.

González Guinán, Francisco. *Historia contemporánea de Venezuela*. 15 vols. Caracas: Ediciones de la Presidencia de la República de Venezuela, 1954.

Grases, Pedro. *Estudios bibliográficos*. Caracas: Imprenta Nacional, 1961.

————. "Introducción a la guía de fuentes bibliográficos relativos a Venezuela." Reprint from the *Boletín de la Biblioteca General*, VI (January–June, 1964).

————. *Materiales para la historia del periodismo en Venezuela durante el siglo XIX*. Caracas: Universidad Central de Venezuela, 1951.

————. *Nuevos temas de bibliografía y cultura venezolanas*. Maracaibo, 1960.

———— and Manuel Pérez Vila. "Gran Colombia. Referencias relativas a la bibliografía sobre el período emancipador en los países grancolombianos (desde 1949)," *Anuario de Estudios Americanos*, XXI (1964), 151–195.

Great Britain. Foreign Office. *Correspondence on the Slave Trade with Foreign Powers, Parties to Treaties and Conventions, under which Captured Vessels are to be Tried by Tribunals of the Nation to which they Belong, from January 1 to December 31, 1843, Inclusive. Presented to Both Houses of Parliament by Command of Her Majesty, 1844*. London: William Clowes and Sons, for Her Majesty's Stationery Office, 1844.

Griffin, Charles C. *Los temas sociales y económicos en la época de la independencia*. Caracas: Fundación John Boulton and Fundación Eugenio Mendoza, 1962.

Guzmán, Antonio Leocadio. *La doctrina liberal*. 2 vols. (*Pensamiento político venezolano del siglo XIX*, Vols. V and VI.) Caracas: Publicaciones de la Presidencia de la República, 1961.

Harris, Marvin. *Patterns of Race in the Americas*. New York: Walker and Company, 1964.

Humboldt, Alexander von. *Viaje a las regiones equinocciales del nuevo continente hecho en 1799, 1800, 1801, 1802, 1803 y 1804 por . . . y A. Bonpland.* 5 vols. trans. Lisandro Alvarado, 2d ed. Caracas: Ediciones del Ministerio de Educación, 1956.

Hussey, Roland D. *La compañía de Caracas, 1728–1784.* Caracas: Banco Central de Venezuela, 1962.

Indice de la Revista de la Sociedad Bolivariana de Venezuela: 1939–1955. Caracas: Sociedad Bolivariana de Venezuela, 1959.

"Indice General de las hojas sueltas del Archivo Aristides Rojas: años 1807–1895. Indice de las hojas sueltas adicionales del Archivo Aristides Rojas." 2d Section, Carpetas Nos. 31–47. Typescript in the Academia Nacional de la Historia, Caracas.

Indices y guía de la colección. (Pensamiento político venezolano del siglo XIX, Vol. XV.) Caracas: Publicaciones de la Presidencia de la República, 1962.

Irrazábal, Carlos. *Venezuela esclava y feudal.* Caracas: Pensamiento Vivo, 1964.

King, James F. "The Latin American Republics and the Suppression of the Slave Trade," *Hispanic American Historical Review,* XXIV (August 1944), 387–411.

———. "A Royalist View of the Colonial Castes in the Venezuelan War of Independence," *Hispanic American Historical Review,* XXXIII (November 1953), 526–537.

Klein, Herbert S. *Slavery in the Americas. A Comparative Study of Virginia and Cuba.* Chicago: University of Chicago Press, 1967.

Konetzke, Richard. *Colección de documentos para la historia de la formación social de Hispanoamérica, 1493–1810.* 3 vols. Madrid: Consejo Superior de Investigaciones Científicas, 1953.

Landaeta Rosales, Manuel. *La libertad de los esclavos en Venezuela.* Caracas, 1895.

Lander, Tomás. *La doctrina liberal. (Pensamiento político venezolano del siglo XIX,* Vol. IV.) Caracas: Publicaciones de la Presidencia de la República, 1961.

Lecuna, Vicente. *Crónica razonada de las guerras de Bolívar.* 2 vols. 2d ed. New York: Ediciones de la Fundación Vicente Lecuna, 1960.

Lecuna, Vicente, ed. *Proclamas y discursos del Libertador.* Caracas, 1939.

Level de Goda, Andrés. "Antapodosis. Memorias de . . . 1808–1831." Manuscript, Academia Nacional de la Historia, Caracas.

Liberales y Conservadores: Textos doctrinales. 2 vols. (*Pensamiento político venezolano del siglo XIX,* Vol. X and XI.) Caracas: Publicaciones de la Presidencia de la República, 1961.

La Libertad de los esclavos en Venezuela. Caracas, 1895.

Libro de actas del supremo congreso de Venezuela, 1811–1812. 2 vols. (Sesquicentenario de la Independencia, Nos. 3 and 4.) Caracas: Academia Nacional de la Historia, 1959.

Lisboa, Consejero. *Relación de un viaje a Venezuela, Nueva Granada y Ecuador.* Caracas: Publicaciones de la Presidencia de la República, 1954.

Lombardi, John V. "Los esclavos en la legislación republicana de Venezuela," *Boletín Histórico,* XIII (January 1967), 43–67.

————. "Los esclavos negros en las guerras venezolanas de la independencia," *Cultura Universitaria,* XCIII (October–December 1966), 153–168.

————. "Manumission, *Manumisos,* and *Aprendizaje* in Republican Venezuela," *Hispanic American Historical Review,* XLIX (November 1969), 656–678.

————. "Sociedad y esclavos en Venezuela. La era republicana. 1821–1854," *Boletín* (Academia Nacional de la Historia), LII (July–September 1969), 515–527.

————, and James A. Hanson. "The First Venezuelan Coffee Cycle, 1820–1854." *Agricultural History* (November 1970).

Masur, Gerhard. *Simón Bolívar.* Albuquerque, New Mexico: University of New Mexico Press, 1948.

Materiales para el estudio de la cuestión agraria en Venezuela (1800–1830). Vol. I. Caracas: Universidad Central de Venezuela, 1964.

Mellafe, Rolando. *La esclavitud en Hispanoamérica.* Buenos Aires: Eudeba, 1964.

Millares Carlo, Agustín. *Archivo del Registro Principal de Maracaibo. Protocolos de los antiguos escribanos (1790–1836). Indice y extractos.* Maracaibo: Centro Histórico del Zulia, 1964.

————. *Los archivos municipales de Latinoamérica. Libros de actas y colecciones documentales. Apuntes bibliográficos.* Maracaibo: Universidad del Zulia, 1961.

————. *Notas para una bibliografía de la imprenta y el periodismo en Venezuela.* Maracaibo: Editorial Universitaria LUZ, 1965.

Miranda, Francisco. *Textos sobre la independencia.* (Sesquicentenario de la Independencia, No. 13.) Caracas: Academia Nacional de la Historia, 1959.

Monsalve, J. D. *Actas de la diputación permanente del Conrgeso de Angostura*. (Biblioteca de Historia Nacional, Vol. XL.) Bogota: Imprenta Nacional, 1927.

Montenegro y Colón, Feliciano. *Historia de Venezuela*. 2 vols. (Sesquicentenario de la Independencia, Nos. 26 and 27.) Caracas: Academia Nacional de la Historia, 1960.

Morales Padrón, Francisco. "La vida cotidiana en una hacienda de esclavos," *Revista del Instituto de Cultura Puertoriqueña*, IV, No. 10 (January–March, 1961), 23–33.

El movimiento emancipador de Hispanoamérica. 4 vols. (Mesa Redonda de la Comisión de Historia del Instituto Panamericano de Geografía e Historia. Actas y ponencias.) Caracas: Academia Nacional de la Historia, 1961.

Núñez Ponte, José Manuel. *Estudio histórico acerca de la esclavitud y de su abolición en Venezuela*. Caracas: El Cojo, 1911.

La Obra Pía de Chuao, 1568–1825. Intros. Eduardo Arcila Farías, et al. Caracas: Universidad Central de Venezuela, 1968.

Olavarría, Domingo Antonio. *Historia patria, décimo estudio histórico-político. Refutación al "Manifiesto Liberal" de 1893*. 2d ed. Valencia: Tipografía Artística Mijares, 1895.

Páez, José Antonio. *Autobiografía del General. . . .* 2 vols. New York: Hallet y Breen, 1867.

Parra Aranguren, Fernando Ignacio. *Antecedentes del derecho del trabajo en Venezuela, 1830–1928*. Maracaibo: Universidad del Zulia, 1965.

Parra Márquez, Héctor. *Centenario de la abolición de la esclavitud en Venezuela*. San Juan de los Moros, 1954.

———. *Presidentes de Venezuela. El Dr. Francisco Espejo: ensayo biográfico*. Caracas: Editorial Cecilio Acosta, 1944.

Parra Pérez, Caracciolo. *Historia de la Primera República de Venezuela*. 2 vols. (Sesquicentenario de la Independencia, Nos. 19 and 20.) Caracas: Academia Nacional de la Historia, 1959.

———. *Mariño y la independencia de Venezuela*. 5 vols. Madrid: Ediciones Cultura Hispánica, 1954–1957.

Pensamiento político venezolano del siglo XIX. Textos para su estudio. 15 vols. Caracas: Publicaciones de la Presidencia de la República, 1960–1962.

Pérez Vila, Manuel. *Indice de los documentos contenidos en las Memorias del general Daniel Florencio O'Leary*. 2 vols. Caracas: Sociedad Bolivariana de Venezuela, 1956–1957.

————. *Vida de Daniel Florencio O'Leary. Primer edecán del Libertador.* Caracas: Sociedad Bolivariana de Venezuela, 1957.

Polanco Martínez, Tomás. *Esbozo sobre historia económica venezolana. Primera etapa. La colonia, 1498–1810.* 2 vols. 2d ed. Madrid: Ediciones Guadarrama, 1960.

Porter, Robert Ker. *Sir Robert Ker Porter's Caracas Diary, 1825–1842: A British Diplomat in a Newborn Nation.* ed. Walter Dupouy. Caracas: Instituto Otto y Magdalena Blohm, 1966.

Posada, Eduardo and Carlos Restrepo Canal, ed. *La esclavitud en Colombia: Leyes de manumisión.* 2 vols. Bogota: Imprenta Nacional, 1933–1938.

Revenga, José Rafael. *La hacienda pública de Venezuela en 1828–1830. Misión de . . . como ministro de Hacienda.* Caracas: Banco Central de Venezuela, 1953.

Robertson, William Spence. *La vida de Miranda.* Caracas: Banco Industrial de Venezuela, 1967.

Rojas, Pedro José. *La doctrina conservadora.* 2 vols. (Pensamiento político venezolano del siglo XIX, Vols. VII and VIII.) Caracas: Publicaciones de la Presidencia de la República, 1961.

Rondón Márquez, R. A. *La esclavitud en Venezuela.* Caracas: Tipografía Garrido, 1954.

Segundo Sánchez, Manuel. *Obras.* 2 vols. Caracas: Banco Central de Venezuela, 1964.

Santana, Arturo. *La campaña de Carabobo (1821). Relación histórica militar.* Caracas: Litografía del Comercio, 1921.

Sección venezolana del Archivo de la Gran Colombia. *Indice sucinto.* Caracas: Fundación John Boulton, 1960.

Siso, Carlos. *La formación del pueblo venezolano. Estudios sociológicos.* 2 vols. Madrid: Editorial García Enciso, 1953.

Snodgrass, Donald. *Ceylon: An Export Economy in Transition.* Homewood, Ill.: Irwin, 1966.

Sociedad Económica de Amigos del País. *Memorias y estudios, 1829–1839.* 2 vols. Caracas: Banco Central de Venezuela, 1958.

Suriá Vendrell, Jaime. *Catálogo general del Archivo Arquidiocesano de Caracas.* Madrid: Escuelas Profesionales "Sagrado Corazón de Jesús," 1964.

Tannenbaum, Frank. *Slave and Citizen, the Negro in the Americas.* New York: Knopf, 1946.

Testimonios de la época emancipadora. (Sesquicentenario de la

Independencia, No. 37.) Caracas: Academia Nacional de la Historia, 1961.

Toro, Fermín. *La doctrina conservadora.* (*Pensamiento político venezolano del siglo XIX,* Vol. I.) Caracas: Publicaciones de la Presidencia de la República, 1960.

Vallenilla Lanz, Laureano. *Cesarismo democrático: estudios sobre las bases sociológicas de la constitución efectiva de Venezuela.* 4th ed. Caracas: Tipografía Garrido, 1961.

Veloz, Ramón. *Economía y finanzas de Venezuela desde 1830 hasta 1944.* Caracas: Impresores Unidos, 1945.

Verlinden, Charles. "Esclavage Médiéval en Europe et Esclavage Colonial en Amérique," *Six Etudes Historiques* (*de la découverte de la veille de l'indépendance*), (Paris, n.d.), 29–45.

Verna, Paul. *Robert Sutherland, un amigo de Bolívar en Haiti.* Caracas: Fundación John Boulton, 1966.

Vila, Pablo; Federico Brito Figueroa, A. L. Cárdenas, et al. *Geografía de Venezuela.* 2 vols. Caracas: Ministerio de Educación, 1960–1965.

Williamson, John G. A. *Caracas Diary, 1835–1840. The Journal of . . ., First Diplomatic Representative of the United States to Venezuela,* ed. Jane Lucas de Grummond. Baton Rouge, La.: Camellia, 1954.

Yanes, Francisco Javier. *Relación documentada de los principales sucesos ocurridos en Venezuela desde que se declaró estado independiente hasta el año de 1821.* 2 vols. Caracas: Academia Nacional de la Historia, 1943.

PAMPHLETS AND BROADSIDES

Agostini, Rafael. . . . *a sus conciudadanos.* Caracas: Imprenta Boliviana por Domingo Salazar, 1845.

Los amigos de la justicia. Caracas: Tomás Antero, 1834.

Colección completa de las leyes, decretos y resoluciones vijentes sobre manumisión, expedidas por el Congreso constituyente de la República y gobierno supremo de Venezuela, desde 1830 hasta 1846. Caracas: Reimpreso en "La Nueva Imprenta," por Elías León, 1846.

Cuervos, Juan. *La verdad ante la justicia.* Caracas: Tomás Antero, 1834.

Decreto sobre manumisión de esclavos, 18 agosto 1823. AGN, Gran Colombia–Intendencia de Venezuela, CXLIX (1823), 15.

Estadística general de la provincia de Caracas, en 1855. Caracas: Salvador Larrazábel, 1856.

Hablen los hechos. Caracas: George Corser, 1846.

Horrendo atentado contra el cual reclama la justicia y la humanidad. Caracas: Tomás Antero, 1834.

Ideas patrióticas. Caracas: Tomás Antero, 1830.

Instituto de crédito territorial. Caracas: George Corser, 1845.

Instituto llamado de "crédito territorial." Caracas: Valentín Espinal, 1845.

Junta de tenedores de vales de abolición. Caracas, 1855.

La ley de 10 de abril y el comercio de Venezuela. Valencia: Bartolomé Valdés, 1838.

Memoria de los abonos, cultivos y beneficios que necesitan los diversos valles de la provincia de Caracas para la plantación de café. Presentada al Real Consulado por un patriota que se interesa en la prosperidad de la agricultura, en 26 de octubre de 1809. Adicionada por un amigo de la agricultura con una instrucción para el gobierno de las haciendas de cacao. Caracas: Tomás Antero, 1833. A typescript copy in the possession of Don Pedro Grases, Caracas.

Mosquera, Joaquin. *Memoria sobre la necesidad de reformar la ley del Congreso constituyente de Colombia, de 21 de julio, de 1821, que sanciona la libertad de los partos, manumisión, y abolición del tráfico de esclavos y bases que podrían adoptarse para la reforma.* Caracas: Tomás Antero, 1829.

————. *Memoria sobre la necesidad de reformar la ley del Congreso constituyente de Colombia, de 21 de julio de 1821, que sancionó la libertad de partos, manumisión, y abolición del tráfico de esclavos y bases que podrían adoptarse para la reforma.* Bogota: F. M. Stokes, 1825.

Muchos comerciantes. Al público. Caracas: Simón Camacho, 1847.

Nemesis. [Caracas]: Tomás Antero, 1843.

Obregón, Pedro. *El jueves santo.* Caracas: Tomás Antero, 1853.

Un observador. Las fortunas: fortunas coloniales y fortunas republicanas. Caracas: George Corser, 1843.

Padrón, J. *Quejas de un patriota contra los procedimientos de la junta calificadora del impréstito agrícola.* Caracas: José Núñez de Cáceres, 1825.

Los propietarios de la provincia de Guayana a los propietarios y hombres imparciales del mundo. Caracas: Tomás Antero, 1838.

Protesta razonada. Caracas: Valentín Espinal, 1845.

Al público. Caracas: George Corser, 1845.

Al público. Caracas: Tomás Antero, 1846.

Reforma de la ley de 10 de abril de 1834. Caracas: Fortunato Corvaïa, 1848.

Representación al Congreso pidiendo la reforma de la lei de espera. Caracas: George Corser, 1850.

Rojas, Alberto. *Influencia de la ley de 10 de abril de 1834 sobre la propiedad territorial en Venezuela.* Caracas: Imprenta Boliviana por Domingo Salazar, 1844.

Sanavria, Tomás José Hernández de. *Fomento de la agricultura. Discurso canónico-legal sobre la necesidad de una ley que reduzca los censos en Venezuela.* Caracas: Domingo Navas Spínola, 1823.

A los señores agricultores de la provincia. Caracas: Imprenta de "El Venezolano," 1843.

La servidumbre convertida en libertad por la beneficencia de una ley. Caracas: Fermín Romero, 1838.

La Sombra de Fermín. Caracas: Tomás Antero, 1846.

Tabla de derechos que se cobran en la república. [Caracas]: Fermín Romero, 1838.

POLICIA

Carabobo. 1838. *Ordenanza de policía, expedida por la Diputación Provincial de Carabobo, en el año de 1837.* Valencia: Juan P. Gil, 1838.

———. 1850. *Ordenanzas y resoluciones expedidas por la Diputación Provincial de Carabobo en sus sesiones de 1849.* Valencia: Juan de Sola por Luis Pérez, 1850.

———. 1852. *Ordenanzas, resoluciones y acuerdos de la h. Diputación Provincial de Carabobo.* Caracas: Narciso Carrasquero, 1852.

———. 1855. *Ordenanzas y resoluciones expedidas por la h. Diputación Provincial de Carabobo, en sus sesiones de 1854.* Valencia: Juan de Sola, 1855.

Caracas. 1824. *Bando de policía formado por la muy ilustre municipalidad de Caracas.* Caracas: Valentín Espinal, 1824.

————. 1827. *Bando de policía formado por la m. i. municipalidad de esta capital.* Caracas: Valentín Espinal, 1827.

————. 1832. *Proyecto de reglamento general de policía.* Caracas: Valentín Espinal, 1832.

————. 1834. *Ordenanzas, resoluciones y acuerdos de la Diputación Provincial de Caracas: que se hallan vigentes el dia 10 de diciembre de 1834, impreso por acuerdo especial de la Diputación.* Caracas: A. Damirón, 1834.

————. 1835. *Ordenanzas, resoluciones y acuerdos de la Diputación Provincial de Caracas en su reunión constitucional de 1835. Impreso por acuerdo especial de la Diputación.* Caracas: Valentín Espinal, 1835.

————. 1837. *Ordenanzas, resoluciones y acuerdos de la Diputación Provincial de Caracas en su reunión constitucional de 1836. Impreso por acuerdo especial de la Diputación.* Caracas: Valentín Espinal, 1837.

————. 1838. *Ordenanzas, resoluciones y acuerdos de la Diputación Provincial de Caracas que se hallan vigentes el dia 9 de diciembre de 1837. Impreso por acuerdo especial de la Diputación.* Caracas: Valentín Espinal, 1838.

————. 1839. *Ordenanzas, resoluciones y acuerdos de la Diputación Provincial de Caracas en sus reuniones ordinarias de 1838 y 1839. Edición oficial.* Caracas: George Corser, 1839.

————. 1841. *Ordenanzas, resoluciones y acuerdos de la Diputación Provincial de Caracas en su reunión ordinaria de 1840. Impreso por acuerdo especial de la Diputación.* Caracas: Francisco de P. Núñez, 1841.

————. 1841. *Ordenanzas, resoluciones y acuerdos espedidos por la h. Diputación Provincial de Caracas en 1841.* Caracas: George Corser, [1841].

————. 1843. *Ordenanzas, resoluciones y acuerdos espedidos por la h. Diputación Provincial de Caracas en 1842.* Caracas: George Corser, 1843.

————. 1843. *Ordenanzas, resoluciones y acuerdos espedidos por la h. Diputación Provincial de Caracas en 1843.* Caracas: George Corser, 1843.

————. 1844. *Ordenanzas, resoluciones y acuerdos de la h. Diputación Provincial de Caracas, espedidos en 1844.* Caracas: George Corser, 1844.

————. 1845. Reglamento de policía para la provincia de Caracas, decretada por la Diputación Provincial en 1834. Caracas: Imprenta Boliviana por Domingo Salazar, 1845.

————. 1845. Ordenanza de la h. Diputación Provincial de Caracas, espedida en 1844 sobre las funciones de los comisarios de policía. Caracas: Imprenta Boliviana por Domingo Salazar, 1845.

————. 1845. Ordenanzas y resoluciones espedidas por la h. Diputación Provincial de la provincia de Caracas, en 1845. Caracas: George Corser, 1845.

————. 1845. Ordenanzas de policía espedidas por la h. Diputación Provincial de la provincia de Caracas, en 1845. Caracas: George Corser, [1845].

————. 1847. Ordenanza de 3 de diciembre de 1844, designando las funciones de los comisarios de policía [Caracas]: Domingo Salazar, 1847.

————. 1847. Ordenanzas, resoluciones y acuerdos de la honorable Diputación Provincial de Caracas. Vigentes el dia 10 de diciembre de 1846. Caracas: George Corser, 1847.

————. 1847. Ordenanzas, resoluciones y acuerdos de la h. Diputación Provincial de Caracas, espedidas en 1847. Caracas: Simón Camacho, 1847.

————. 1848. Ordenanza de 10 de diciembre de 1847, que reforma la 3 de diciembre de 1844, designando las funciones de los comisarios de policía. Caracas: Imprenta Boliviana por Domingo Salazar, 1848.

————. 1848. Ordenanzas, resoluciones y acuerdos de la h. Diputación Provincial de Caracas, expedidos en 1848. Caracas: José de Jesús Castro, 1848.

————. 1849. Ordenanzas, resoluciones y acuerdos de la honorable Diputación Provincial de Caracas espedidos en 1849. Caracas: Andrés A. Figueira, 1849.

————. 1851. Ordenanzas, resoluciones y acuerdos de la h. Diputación Provincial de Caracas, expedidos en 1850. Caracas: Mariano de Briceño, 1851.

————. 1851. Ordenanzas, resoluciones y acuerdos de la h. D. Provincial de Caracas aprobados en 1851. Caracas: Ramón Alcalde Piña, 1851.

————. 1852. Ordenanzas, resoluciones y acuerdos de la honorable

Diputación Provincial de Caracas en 1852. Caracas: Briceño y Campbell, 1852.

——. 1853. *Ordenanzas, resoluciones y acuerdos de la h. Diputación Provincial de Caracas en 1853.* Caracas: Jesús María Soriano, 1853.

——. 1854. *Ordenanzas, resoluciones y acuerdos de la h. Diputación Provincial de Caracas, vigentes el dia 10 de diciembre de 1853.* Caracas: Tomás Antero, 1854.

——. 1854. *Ordenanzas, resoluciones y acuerdos de la h. Diputación Provincial de Caracas en 1854.* Caracas: Ramón Alcalde Piña, 1854.

——. 1856. *Ordenanzas, resoluciones y acuerdos de la h. Diputación Provincial de Caracas en 1855.* Caracas: Jesús María Soriaño y Compañía, 1856.

Coro. 1852. *Reglamento de policía expedido por la h. D. Provincial de Coro. Año de 1852.* Coro: [A. W. Neuman], 1852.

——. 1853. *Reglamento de policía expedido por la h. D. Provincial de Coro. Año de 1853.* Coro: A. W. Neuman, [1853].

Cumaná. 1831. "Ordenanzas de Policía," AGN, Interior y Justicia, XXXIX (1831), 120–149.

——. 1834. *Ordenanzas de policía.* Cumaná: Pedro Cova, 1834.

——. 1837. *Ordenanza de la Diputación Provincial. O reglamento general de policía. Sancionado en 8 de diciembre de 1836, año 7° de la ley, y 26° de la independencia.* Cumaná: Pedro Cova, 1837.

——. 1845. *Reglamento de policía. Sancionado por la h. Diputación Provincial de Cumaná en 1844.* Cumaná: Pedro Cova, 1845.

——. 1848. *Ordenanza que designa funciones a los comisarios de policía, sancionada por la honorable Diputación Provincial de Cumaná en 1848.* Cumaná: Antonio M. Martínez, 1848.

Guayana. 1854. *Actos sancionados por la h. Diputación Provincial de Guayana, en sus sesiones ordinarias de 1854. Código de policía.* Ciudad Bolívar: Imprenta Municipal, Sandalio Alcalá, 1854.

Maracaibo. 1832. "Reglamento de policía," AGN, Interior y Justicia, LXXVIII (1832), 18–35.

——. 1834. "Reglamento de policía," AGN, Interior y Justicia, XCIX (1834), 262–290.

——. 1838. *Reglamento de policía, expedido por la Diputación*

Provincial de Maracaibo, en su reunión constitucional de 1837. Maracaibo: Miguel A. Baralt, 1838.

Margarita. 1834. "Reglamento de policía," AGN, Interior y Justicia, XCIX (1834), 363–381.

Trujillo, 1844. Código de policía, expedido por la honorable Diputación Provincial de Trujillo en sus sesiones de 1843. Maracaibo: Miguel A. Baralt dirijida por Juan Carmen Martel, 1844.

Venezuela. 1817. Disposiciones gubernamentales circulares a todos los tenientes justicias mayores de la provincia de Venezuela que manda publicar, cumplir y puntualmente egecutar el Sr. Capitán general de ella, a consequencia de lo dispuesto por el Escmo. Sr. D. Pablo Morillo en su cuartel general de Maracay a 3 de los corrientes. Caracas: 1817.

———. 1827. Proyecto de decreto sobre policía general que somete al exámen público El Libertador. Caracas: Valentín Espinal, 1827.

OFFICIAL GOVERNMENT PUBLICATIONS

Apure. 1838. "Memoria del gobernador de Apure," AGN, Interior y Justicia, CLXXX (1838), 101–112.

Barcelona. 1839. "Memoria del gobernador de la provincia de Barcelona a la honorable Diputación Provincial en su reunión constitucional de 1839," AGN, Interior y Justicia, CXCV (1839), 44–51.

———. 1850. "Memoria del gobernador de Barcelona," AGN, Interior y Justicia, CDXXXV (1850), 437–458.

Barquisimeto. 1834. Memoria que el gobernador de Barquisimeto presenta a la honorable Diputación Provincial de 1834. Barquisimeto: Pablo M. de Unda, 1834.

Carabobo. 1844. Exposición que dirige a la honorable Diputación de la provincia de Carabobo sobre los diversos ramos de la administración municipal, el gobernador. Valencia: Juan de Sola, 1844.

———. 1845. Exposición que dirige a la honorable Diputación de la provincia de Carabobo, sobre varios ramos de la administración municipal, el gobernador en 1845. Valencia: Juan de Sola, [1845].

———. 1847. Exposición que dirige a la honorable Diputación de la provincia de Carabobo, sobre los diversos ramos de la administración municipal, el gobernador. Valencia: Juan de Sola, 1847.

――――. 1849. Exposición que dirije el gobernador de Carabobo a la h. Diputación Provincial sobre varios ramos de la administración municipal, en 1849. Valencia: Juan de Sola, 1849.

――――. 1852. Memoria que a la h. Diputación Provincial de Carabobo, en su reunión de 1852, le presenta el gobernador Miguel Martínez. Valencia: Imprenta del Teatro de Legislación a cargo de Narciso Carrasquero, 1852.

――――. 1854. El gobernador de Carabobo, a la h. Diputación Provincial en sus sesiones ordinarias de 1854. Valencia: Juan de Sola, 1854.

――――. 1855. El gobernador de Carabobo, a la h. Diputación Provincial en sus sesiones ordinarias de 1855. Valencia: Juan de Sola por J. M. Villalobos, 1855.

Caracas. 1833. Memoria que presenta el gobernador de la provincia de Caracas a la honorable Diputación de la misma reunida en sus sesiones ordinarias de 1833. Caracas: Damirón y Dupuy, 1833.

――――. 1834. La Diputación Provincial de Caracas a los ciudanos de la provincia. Caracas, 1834.

――――. 1834. Memoria que el Concejo Municipal del canton de Caracas presenta a la h. Diputación Provincial en su reunión ordinaria de 1834. Caracas: Valentín Espinal, 1834.

――――. 1837. Memoria del gobernador de la provincia de Caracas a la honorable Diputación Provincial en 1837. Caracas: Valentín Espinal, 1837.

――――. 1840. Memoria que presenta el Concejo Municipal de Caracas a la h. Diputación Provincial en su reunión de 1840. Caracas: Valentín Espinal por C. Machado, 1840.

――――. 1841. Esposición que dirige a la h. Diputación Provincial en 1841 el Concejo Municipal de Caracas. Caracas: George Corser, [1841].

――――. 1845. El Consejo Municipal del canton Caracas. Caracas, 1845.

――――. 1848. Memoria que dirige a la h. Diputación Provincial en su décima octava reunión constitucional el gobernador de la Provincia de Caracas en 1848. Caracas: Fortunato Corvaïa, 1848.

――――. 1849. Informe de la comisión de mejoras dirigido a la honorable Diputación de Caracas en su décima nova reunión.

Caracas: Imprenta de "El Patriota," por Andrés A. Figueira, 1849.

———. 1854. *Exposición que dirige a la h. D. Provincial de 1854 el gobernador de Caracas.* n.p., n.d.

———. 1855. *Memoria que dirige a la h. Diputación Provincial el gobernador interino de la provincia de Caracas en 1855.* Caracas: Vicente Manzo, 1855.

Guaira. 1848. *Memoria del Concejo Municipal del canton Guaira, 1848.* Caracas: Imprenta de "El Patriota," por J. J. Castro, 1848.

Margarita. 1838. "Memoria del gobernador de Margarita," AGN, Interior y Justicia, CLXXX (1838), 84–92.

Trujillo. 1853. "Memoria del gobernador de Trujillo," AGN, Interior y Justicia, DVII (1853), 69–73.

Valencia. 1854. *Exposición que dirije el Concejo Municipal del canton Valencia a la h. Diputación Provincial en su reunión de 1854.* Valencia: Juan de Sola, 1854.

Venezuela. Hacienda. 1832. *Exposición que dirige al Congreso de Venezuela en 1832, el secretario de Hacienda sobre los negocios de su cargo.* Caracas: Valentín Espinal, [1832].

———. ———. 1833. *Exposición que dirige al Congreso de Venezuela en 1833 el secretario de Hacienda sobre los negocios de su cargo.* Caracas: Valentín Espinal, 1833.

———. ———. 1834. *Exposición que dirige al Congreso de Venezuela en 1834 el secretario interino de Hacienda.* Caracas: Valentín Espinal, 1834.

———. ———. 1835. *Exposición que dirige al Congreso de Venezuela en 1835 el secretario de Hacienda.* Caracas: Valentín Espinal, 1835.

———. ———. 1836. *Exposición que dirige al Congreso de Venezuela en 1836 el secretario de Hacienda.* Caracas: Valentín Espinal, 1836.

———. ———. 1837. *Exposición que dirige al Congreso de Venezuela en 1837 el secretario de Hacienda.* Caracas: Valentín Espinal, 1837.

———. ———. 1838. *Exposición que dirige al Congreso de Venezuela en 1838 el secretario de Hacienda.* Caracas: Valentín Espinal, 1838.

———. ———. 1839. *Exposición que dirige al Congreso de Venezuela en 1839, el secretario de Hacienda.* Caracas: Valentín Espinal, 1839.

————. ————. 1840. *Exposición que dirige al Congreso de Venezuela en 1840 el secretario de Hacienda.* Caracas: Valentín Espinal, 1840.

————. ————. 1841. *Exposición que dirige al Congreso de Venezuela en 1841 el secretario de Hacienda.* Caracas: Valentín Espinal, 1841.

————. ————. 1842. *Exposición que dirige al Congreso de Venezuela en 1842, el secretario de Hacienda.* Caracas: Valentín Espinal, 1842.

————. ————. 1843. *Exposición que dirige al Congreso de Venezuela en 1843, el secretario de Hacienda.* Caracas: Valentín Espinal, 1843.

————. ————. 1844. *Exposición que dirige al Congreso de Venezuela en 1844, el secretario de Hacienda.* Caracas: Valentín Espinal, 1844.

————. ————. 1845. *Exposición que dirige al Congreso de Venezuela en 1845, el secretario de Hacienda.* Caracas: Valentín Espinal, 1845.

————. ————. 1846. *Exposición que dirige al Congreso de Venezuela en 1846, el secretario de Hacienda.* Caracas: Domingo Salazar, 1846.

————. ————. 1847. *Exposición que dirige al Congreso de Venezuela en 1847, el secretario de Hacienda.* Caracas: Domingo Salazar, 1847.

————. ————. 1848. *Exposición que dirije al Congreso de Venezuela en 1848, el secretario de Hacienda.* Caracas: Fortunato Corvaïa, 1848.

————. ————. 1849. *Exposición que dirije al Congreso de Venezuela en 1849, el secretario de Hacienda.* Caracas: Fortunato Corvaïa, 1849.

————. ————. 1850. *Exposición que dirige al Congreso de Venezuela en 1850, el secretario de Hacienda.* Caracas: Andrés A. Figueira, 1850.

————. ————. 1851. *Exposición que dirige al Congreso de Venezuela en 1851, el secretario de Hacienda.* Caracas: F. Antonio Alvarez, 1851.

————. ————. 1852. *Exposición que dirije al Congreso de Venezuela en 1852, el secretario de Hacienda.* Caracas: Briceño y Campbell, 1852.

————. ————. 1853. *Exposición que dirige al Congreso de Vene-*

zuela en 1853 el secretario de Hacienda. Caracas: Briceño y Campbell, 1853.

————. ————. 1854. *Exposición que dirige al Congreso de Venezuela en 1855 el secretario de Hacienda.* Caracas: Oficina del Teatro de Legislación, 1854.

————. ————. 1855. *Exposición que dirige al Congreso de Venezuela en 1855, el secretario de Hacienda.* Caracas: Oficina del Teatro de Legislación, [1855].

————. ————. 1856. *Exposición que dirije al Congreso de Venezuela en 1857, el secretario de Hacienda.* Caracas: Jesús María Soriano y Compañía, 1856.

————. ————. 1857. *Exposición que dirije al Congreso de Venezuela en 1857, el secretario de Hacienda.* Caracas: Jesús María Soriano, 1857.

————. ————. 1858. *Exposición que dirige a la convención nacional de Venezuela en 1858, el secretario de Hacienda.* Valencia: M. M. Zarzamendi, 1858.

————. Interior y Justicia. 1826. *Esposición que el secretario de estado del despacho del Interior de la república de Colombia hace al Congreso de 1826 sobre los negocios de su departamento.* Bogota: Manuel M. Viller-Calderón, 1826.

————. ————. 1831. *Memoria sobre los negocios correspondientes a los despachos del Interior y Justicia del gobierno de Venezuela, que presenta el encargado a ellos al Congreso constitucional del año de 1831.* Valencia, 1831.

————. ————. 1832. *Memoria que presenta el secretario del Interior de los negocios de su departamento al Congreso de 1832.* Caracas: G. F. Devisme, [1832].

————. ————. 1833. *Memoria que presenta el secretario del Interior de los negocios de su departamento al Congreso de 1833.* Caracas: G. F. Devisme, [1833].

————. ————. 1834. *Memoria que presenta el secretario del Interior de los negocios de su departamento al Congreso de 1834.* Caracas: Damirón y Dupuy, [1834].

————. ————. 1835. *Memoria que presenta el secretario del Interior al Congreso de 1835.* Caracas: A. Damirón, [1835].

————. ————. 1836. *Exposición que dirige al Congreso de Venezuela en 1836 el secretario del Interior y Justicia.* Caracas: A. Damirón, [1836].

————. ————. 1837. *Exposición que dirige al Congreso de Venezuela en 1837 el secretario del Interior y Justicia*. Caracas: A. Damirón, 1837.

————. ————. 1838. *Exposición que dirige al Congreso de Venezuela en 1838 el secretario del Interior y Justicia*. Caracas: A. Damirón, 1838.

————. ————. 1839. *Exposición que dirige al Congreso de Venezuela en 1839 el secretario del Interior y Justicia*. Caracas: A. Damirón, 1839.

————. ————. 1840. *Exposición que dirige al Congreso de Venezuela en 1840 el secretario del Interior y Justicia*. Caracas: George Corser, 1840.

————. ————. 1841. *Exposición que dirige al Congreso de Venezuela en 1841 el secretario de lo Interior y Justicia*. Caracas: Valentín Espinal, 1841.

————. ————. 1842. *Exposición que dirige al Congreso de Venezuela en 1842 el secretario de lo Interior y Justicia*. Caracas: Valentín Espinal, 1842.

————. ————. 1843. *Exposición que dirige al Congreso de Venezuela en 1843 el secretario de lo Interior y Justicia*. Caracas: Valentín Espinal, 1843.

————. ————. 1844. *Exposición que dirige al Congreso de Venezuela en 1844 el secretario de lo Interior y Justicia*. Caracas: Valentín Espinal, 1844.

————. ————. 1845. *Exposición que dirige al Congreso de Venezuela en 1845 el secretario de lo Interior y Justicia*. [Caracas]: Imprenta Boliviana por Domingo Salazar, 1845.

————. ————. 1846. *Exposición que dirige al Congreso de Venezuela en 1846 el secretario de lo Interior y Justicia*. Caracas: Valentín Espinal, 1846.

————. ————. 1847. *Exposición que dirije al Congreso de Venezuela en 1847 el secretario del Interior y Justicia*. Caracas: Fortunato Corvaïa, 1847.

————. ————. 1849. *Exposición que dirije al Congreso de Venezuela en 1849 el secretario del Interior y Justicia*. Caracas: Fortunato Corvaïa, 1849.

————. ————. 1850. *Exposición que dirije al Congreso de Venezuela en 1850 el secretario del Interior y Justicia*. Caracas: Fortunato Corvaïa, 1850.

————. ————. 1851. *Exposición que dirige al Congreso de Venezuela en 1851 el secretario del Interior y Justicia*. Caracas: Diego Campbell, 1851.

————. ————. 1852. *Exposición que dirige al Congreso de Venezuela en 1852, El secretario del Interior y Justicia*. Caracas: Franco y Figueira, 1852.

————. ————. 1853. *Exposición que dirige al Congreso de Venezuela en 1853, El secretario del Interior y Justicia*. Caracas: Felix E. Bigotte, 1853.

————. ————. 1854. *Exposición que dirige al Congreso de Venezuela en 1854 el secretario del Interior y Justicia*. Caracas: Imprenta Republicana de Eduardo Ortiz a cargo de Federico Madriz, 1854.

————. ————. 1855. *Exposición que dirige al Congreso de Venezuela en 1855 el secretario del Interior y Justicia*. Caracas: Carreño Hermanos, 1855.

————. ————. 1856. *Exposición que dirige al Congreso de Venezuela en 1856 el secretario del Interior y Justicia*. Caracas: Imprenta y Litografía Republicana de Federico Madriz, 1856.

————. ————. 1857. *Exposición que dirije al Congreso de Venezuela en 1857. El secretario del Interior y Justicia*. Caracas: Jesús María Soriano, 1857.

————. ————. 1858. *Informe al Congreso de 1858 sobre el estado del departamento del Interior y Justicia por el secretario de estos ramos*. Caracas: Jesús María Soriano, 1858.

————. ————. 1860. *Exposición que dirige al Congreso de Venezuela en 1860 el secretario de estado de los despachos de lo Interior y Justicia*. Caracas: Imprenta al Vapor de M. M. Zarzamendi, 1860.

————. ————. 1861. *Exposición que dirige al Congreso de Venezuela en 1861 el secretario de estado en los despachos del Interior y Justicia*. Caracas: Imprenta de "El Heraldo," 1861.

————. ————. 1863. *Memoria que el secretario de estado en los despachos de lo Interior y Justicia dirije a la Asamblea constituyente de la Federación Venezolana*. [Caracas]: Jesús María Soriano, 1863.

————. ————. 1865. *Exposición que dirije a la Legislatura Nacional en 1865. El ministro de lo Interior y Justicia*. Caracas: Melquiades Soriano, 1865.

NOTES

1. Historiography is a much neglected science among Venezuelanists. The best efforts along these lines have come from Germán Carrera Damas whose collection *Historia de la historiografía venezolana* (*textos para su estudio*) (Caracas: Universidad Central de Venezuela, 1961) with its provocative introduction is a good beginning. The same author's *Historiografía marxista venezolana y otros temas* (Caracas: Universidad Central de Venezuela, 1967) contains four excellent essays on historiographical subjects. Also worthy of inclusion here are the collections of papers prepared on three prominent Venezuelan historians by students in Carrera Damas's advanced seminar on Venezuelan historiography: *El concepto de la historia en José Gil Fortoul* (Caracas: Universidad Central de Venezuela, 1961); *El concepto de la historia en Caracciolo Parra Pérez* (Caracas: Universidad Central de Venezuela, 1962); *El concepto de la historia en Laureano Vallenilla Lanz* (Caracas: Universidad Central de Venezuela, 1966). These essays, although of uneven quality, are an encouraging sign of the increasing interest in Venezuelan history and historians.

2. A detailed analysis of the major failings of Venezuelan historiography is in Carrera Damas, *Historia de la historiografía*, pp. xxii–lx and the same author's essay "Los estudios históricos en Venezuela," *Cuestiones de historiografía*, pp. 15–62.

3. This somewhat arbitrary division of Venezuela's historians is open to considerable controversy. Few Venezuelan historians would accept such categories without objections. But since this bibliographical essay refers only to the short period from 1830 to 1854, the validity of these categories becomes more apparent. For a contrary view of Venezuelan historical development see, for example, Mario Briceño-Iragorry, "Nuestros estudios históricos," in Carrera Damas, *Historia de la historiografía*, pp. 65–71; Diego Carbonell, "Escuelas de historia en América," ibid., pp. 80–134; Ramón Díaz Sánchez, "Evolución de la historiografía venezolana," ibid., pp. 163–172.

4. Although Díaz Sánchez is singled out for special comment, it should not be assumed that his work is unreliable. Quite the opposite is true, but the accuracy of Díaz Sánchez's observations must be verified by extra research in the same way González Guinán's facts must be checked. Thus, Díaz Sánchez is classified as an elaborator because of methodological failings rather than because of questionable interpretations or lack of new information.

5. Since most revisionists claim some kind of kinship to Marxist ideology, the best way to appreciate their achievements and failings is through the

excellent study by Carrera Damas, "Sobre la historiografía marxista venezolana," *Historiografía marxista*, pp. 101–156.

6. Although most writers on the 1820 to 1854 period can be put into one of the two categories discussed above, some mention must be made of the mavericks. There are a few elaborators whose work rises far above the average. Parra Pérez is one, particularly because of his use of scholarly apparatus. Also included here is Vallenilla Lanz, whose provocative essays bring him close to the revisionist ideal of fresh, new ideas but whose political philosophy places him irrevocably with the elaborators.

7. Ramón Veloz, *Economía y finanzas de Venezuela desde 1830 hasta 1844* (Caracas: Impresores Unidos, 1945).

8. This is so in spite of such works as Carlos Siso, *La formación del pueblo venezolano. Estudios sociológicos*, 2 vols. (Madrid: Editorial García Enciso, 1953) where there is much interpretation and little documentation.

9. See the useful guide to the archive by Mario Briceño Perozo, *El Archivo General de la Nación* (Caracas: Biblioteca Venezolana de Historia, 1964).

10. Jaime Suriá Vendrell, *Catálogo general del Archivo Arquidiocesano de Caracas* (Madrid: Escuelas Profesionales "Sagrado Corazón de Jesús," 1964).

11. For a detailed survey of the archival resources see Lino Gómez Canedo, *Los archivos históricos de Venezuela* (Maracaibo: Universidad del Zulia, 1966).

12. Special mention must be made of the outstanding documentary collection compiled by Pedro Grases and Manuel Pérez Vila, *Pensamiento político*. In fifteen volumes these indefatigable scholars have brought together an amazingly representative collection of the polemical literature of the nineteenth century. For some studies of the history of journalism in Venezuela see Pedro Grases, ed., *Materiales para la historia del periodismo en Venezuela durante el siglo XIX* (Caracas: Universidad Central de Venezuela, 1951) and Agustín Millares Carlo, *Notas para una bibliografía de la imprenta y el periodismo en Venezuela* (Maracaibo: Editorial Universitaria LUZ, 1965).

Index

209

The Decline and Abolition of
Negro Slavery in Venezuela, 1820–1854
was composed in Linotype Electra with
Deepdene display type by The Book Press,
Brattleboro, Vermont. The entire book
was printed by offset
lithography.